Best Career Transition
Resumes for $100,000+ Jobs

By Wendy S. Enelow

Best Career Transition Resumes for $100,000+ Jobs

Wendy S. Enelow, CCM, MRW, JCTC, CPRW

IMPACT PUBLICATIONS
Manassas Park, VA

Best Career Transition Resumes for $100,000+ Jobs

ISBN: 1-57023-237-7

Library of Congress: 20055925114

Publisher: For information on Impact Publications, including current and forthcoming publications, authors, press kits, online bookstore, and submission requirements, visit our website: www.impactpublications.com

Sales/Distribution: All bookstore sales are handled through Impact's trade distributor: National Book Network, 15200 NBN Way, Blue Ridge Summit, PA 17214, Tel. 1-800-462-6420. All other sales and distribution inquiries should be directed to the publisher: Sales Department, IMPACT PUBLICATIONS, 9104 Manassas Drive, Suite N, Manassas Park, VA 20111-5211, Tel. 703-361-7300, Fax 703-335-9486, or email: info@impactpub lications.com.

The Author: Wendy S. Enelow is a recognized leader in the executive job search, career coaching, and resume writing industries. For more than 20 years she has assisted thousands of job search candidates through successful career transitions. She is the founder and past president of the Career Masters Institute, an exclusive training and development association for career professionals worldwide. Author of nearly two dozen career books focusing on resumes, letters, interviews, and the career transition process, she has earned several distinguished professional credentials – Master Resume Writer (MRW), Credentialed Career Master (CCM), Job and Career Transition Coach (JCTC), and Certified Professional Resume Writer (CPRW). Wendy can be contacted at wendy@wendyenelow.com.

Contents

Are You In Career Transition?

Are you …

- Transitioning from one job to another?
- Transitioning from one profession to another?
- Transitioning from one industry to another?
- Transitioning from an entrepreneurial or consulting career to a corporate career?
- Transitioning from a corporate career to an entrepreneurial or consulting career?
- Transitioning from a military career to a civilian career?
- Transitioning from a specialized job function to a general management career?
- Transitioning from a management position to a C-level position?

If you answered yes to any of the above questions, then this book is your key to writing and designing a best-in-class career transition resume … a resume that highlights the skills, experience, knowledge, qualifications, and achievements which you have acquired that are transferable to your new career. With a powerful career transition resume in hand, you'll be poised for remarkable career performance and success.

> **TRANSFERABILITY** of skills, experience, knowledge, qualifications, and achievements is the foundation for every successful career transition resume.

CHAPTER 1

The Essentials of Resume Writing

Do You Recognize Yourself?

Meet Edward Anders, a 51-year-old manufacturing manager who has spent the past 28 years working in the textile industry. Edward has had a wonderful career with many notable achievements, ranging from multi-million dollar reductions in plant operating costs to double-digit gains in bottom-line profitability. He's secure and relatively happy in his current job, but has decided to leave the textile industry to move into an industry where there are more career opportunities – namely, computer and/or telecommunications hardware manufacturing. Edward's challenge, therefore, is to craft a resume that depicts himself not only as a qualified manufacturing manager, but as a qualified manufacturing manager with some degree of technology expertise.

The single most important strategy underlying Edward's career transition resume is to connect himself to his target industry by highlighting his qualifications, experience, achievements, skills, knowledge and more that relate directly to technology. In addition to all of his other manufacturing management responsibilities and financial achievements, Edward coordinated the company's introduction of e-commerce technology, led the consulting team that installed a global network and Intranet, and spearheaded the acquisition and implementation of several manufacturing technologies to accelerate production and improve product quality.

Although these activities may only have been a minor part of his most recent experience, they are the things that Edward wants to focus his resume on, bringing those items to the forefront, highlighting them in bold, and drawing as much attention to them as possible. Edward wants a prospective employer to pick up his resume and say, "This candidate really does have some great technology experience for someone who has never worked directly in our industry. I think we should interview him." If Edward can accomplish that, he will have taken huge strides in facilitating his transition from textiles to technology. He'll no longer be an outsider. Rather, he'll be perceived as an insider who already has experience within the technology sector and, therefore, is a well-qualified candidate.

> **RESULT:**
> With the combination of a powerful career transition resume and a strong interviewing style, Edward landed a position as the Director of Manufacturing Operations with a multinational telecommunications technology company.

Now, let's meet Melanie Cooke, a 35-year-old registered nurse with 20 years of experience in patient care. Like many nursing care professionals today, Melanie has decided to leave the field of nursing to pursue a career in sales where she believes there are better opportunities for greater compensation and advancement. She knows many other nurses who have successfully made the transition from a nursing career into a sales career with major pharmaceutical and medical equipment companies, and she's now ready to do the same.

When Melanie writes her career transition resume, she does not want to create a resume that communicates, "I'm a nurse." That will be obvious to anyone reading her resume. Rather, Melanie wants to connect herself to her new career by highlighting her related non-nursing responsibilities. Over the years, she has participated in clinical trials of new pharmaceuticals, met with medical equipment vendors to evaluate new product lines, and led in-house training sessions for nurses and technicians on the use and maintenance of medical instrumentation. Although these were not her daily responsibilities, they are the experiences and skills that she must highlight in her resume in order to position herself as a qualified sales candidate . . . someone who understands how to sell to, and communicate with, doctors, nurses, health care administrators, and others involved in product selection, evaluation, and purchase. Her hands-on nursing background is, of course, important to her new career track, but it's the "extras" that distinguish her as a well-qualified candidate worthy of serious consideration for a top-paying sales position within the pharmaceutical and/or medical equipment industries.

RESULT:
The combination of Melanie's new career transition resume, her excellent interviewing and communication skills, and her knowledge of the health care marketplace positioned her for a great opportunity with a large pharmaceutical company, where she was able to triple her annual salary within the first year.

Edward's and Melanie's stories are representative of two of the largest categories of people in career transition – individuals transitioning into new industries (Edward) and into new jobs/careers (Melanie). As we progress through each chapter of this book, you'll be introduced to scores of resumes for job seekers, all of whom were actively engaged in a career transition, and all of whom, with the help of professional resume writers, were able to effectively highlight their transferable skills, experience, and qualifications, and position themselves for successful career transitions. And now, at this point, let's consider what resumes are and how to write them.

A Resume Is . . .

Before we delve any further into the specifics of writing career transition resumes, it's best to begin with a discussion of precisely what a resume is and what it is not.

A resume is a:

- Sales and marketing document written to sell you – the job seeker – into your next position or launch you into your next career.
- Dynamic text that effectively communicates your professional skills, qualifications, knowledge, experience and achievements as they relate to your current career objectives. (This is particularly important to job seekers in career transition!)
- Distinctive communication that presents a clear and concise picture of who you are (as it relates to your current career objectives) and the value you bring to an organization.
- Powerful tool designed to sell the high points of your professional career.
- Visually attractive document that communicates a sharp, executive image.

A resume is not a:

- Biography of your entire life, every job you've ever had, every course you've ever taken, and every activity you've ever participated in.
- Dense document containing lengthy job descriptions and long lists of duties and responsibilities that may or may not be relevant to your current career objectives.
- Passive, low-energy and narrative summary of your working life.

With that definition in mind, consider the one and only true purpose of a resume – **to help you get an interview**. That's it. Your resume will NOT get you a job. Your only expectation should be that it will generate enough interest for a prospective employer to call and offer you the opportunity for an interview. Remember, a resume is a sales and marketing document designed to make you – the product – attractive to your buying audience.

Consider this. You're in a bookstore and a really attractive book cover catches your attention. What do you do? You pick up the book. Maybe you're shopping in a department store one day and see a beautifully designed gift box that you just have to pick up and look inside. Or, perhaps at your last visit to an electronics store, you couldn't resist the well-designed new flat-screen monitors on display. Retailers work hard to make you notice their merchandise and, in turn, purchase their products.

It is your challenge to do the same with your resume by integrating appropriate merchandising strategies and techniques that will get your resume noticed and not passed over! If you make your resume attractive, interesting, dynamic, and success-oriented, employers will want to know more about the product and, in turn, will call you for an interview. It's referred to as career merchandising or talent merchandising – the ability to write and design a resume that represents the job seeker as a well-qualified, competent, and success-bound candidate who would be a "wonderful buy" for an prospective purchaser (company).

To further explain, resume writing (in particular) and job search (in general) are both about communicating your success and achievements - what you have accomplished thus far in your career (either through your work experience and/or academic training) and how that indicates what you might accomplish in the future. Said another way, past performance is the best predictor of future performance, so be sure you include your past successes and track record of performance so prospective employers will appreciate what you've accomplished thus far in your career.

That concept – **past performance is the best predictor of future performance** – is the foundation for the latest trend in job interviewing. Known as behavioral (or situational) interviewing, companies and recruiters now use this strategy to get a better understanding of what candidates have done in the past and how they would react to future situations. If you're not familiar with behavioral or situational interviewing, do an online search and spend some time reading about it. Readers who want more information can check the order form at the back of this book or Impact Publications's website, www.impactpublications.com.

Now, back to our discussion about using your resume to communicate your success and achievements. Today's difficult economic market has forced companies to look carefully at each new hire to evaluate whether or not that individual can bring value to their organization – value that can be measured in increased revenues, improved profits, cost savings, productivity improvements, efficiency gains, and more. No longer do companies hire "just to hire." Rather, they hire to fill a need and they demand measurable results. If an employee cannot add value – monetarily, intellectually, operationally, or organizationally – then there is no reason for the company to hire or retain that employee.

Therefore, your challenge is to write a resume that showcases your unique talents, skills, and qualifications, and how they will benefit the hiring company. It's the same challenge every job seeker faces, whether a recent college graduate, a highly skilled engineer, or a CEO. Your resume must, within the first few words, grab your reader and hold his attention by clearly articulating what you know, what you've done, and what you can do for that organization. If you are able to do that, you will have won the first half of the job search battle – you'll have gotten yourself in the door for an interview!

For the individual in career transition, the concept of showcasing your unique talents, skills, and qualifications in your resume becomes even more critical. Not only must you highlight your successes and your value to make yourself attractive to a hiring company, you must highlight them in such a way that they support your current objectives – a new type of job, a new industry, a transition from a military to a corporate career or a corporate to consulting career, a promotion to a management-level position, or a rise to a C-level opportunity.

Resume Format Style: Making the Best Choices

Before you can even begin to write your resume, you must decide which of the three basic resume styles you are going to use. The style that you select will be dictated by your specific work history and your current career objectives. If you want to focus on your strong track record of employment experience, you'll most likely want to use a Chronological Resume. If, on the other hand, you want a heavy focus on your skills, qualifications, and achievements (more emphasis than on your work history), the Functional Resume will be your best choice. And finally, if you want to integrate your strong work history with a heavy emphasis on your skills and qualifications, you may consider using a Combination Resume. The latter offers the "best of both worlds" as you will note from many of the samples in this book, allowing you to start your resume with a strong summary of skills and then follow up with powerful highlights of your work experience.

Exploring the pluses and minuses of each of the three resume formats will help you determine which is right for you.

THE CHRONOLOGICAL RESUME

Chronological resumes provide a step-by-step path through your career. Starting with your current or most recent position, chronological resumes are written backwards, allowing you to put the most emphasis on your current and most recent experiences. As you progress further back in your career, job descriptions are shorter with an emphasis on achievements and notable projects, and often little mention of day-to-day job responsibilities.

Chronological resumes are the resume style preferred by the vast majority of employers and recruiters. They are easy to read and understand, clearly communicating where you have worked and what you have done. Unless your particular situation is unusual, a chronological resume is generally your best career marketing tool.

THE FUNCTIONAL RESUME

Functional resumes focus on the skills and qualifications you offer to a prospective employer. It is this type of information that is brought to the forefront and highlighted, while your employment experience is briefly mentioned at the end. Individuals who might consider a functional resume are career changers, professionals returning to work after an extended absence, individuals who have been in the job market for a lengthy period of time, or candidates who are 55+ years of age. If you fall into one of these categories or any other related category, you will want to focus your resume on your specific expertise, qualifications, and competencies, and not the specific chronology of your employment experience.

Functional resumes are much less frequently used. Many corporate human resource professionals and recruiters look at these resumes with less interest, believing that the candidate is hiding something or attempting to "change reality." Be extremely careful if you decide this is the right style for you (which it might very well be), and be sure to include your job history at the end of your resume, complete with employee names, job titles, and dates.

THE COMBINATION-STYLE RESUME

The most recent trend in resume writing is to combine the structure of the chronological resume with the skills focus of the functional resume. By starting your resume with a Career Summary, you can begin with a heavy focus on the qualifications and value you offer (functional approach), and then substantiate it with solid, well-written, and accomplishment-oriented position descriptions (chronological approach). Many of the resumes in this book reflect this new Combination Style Resume, which is well-received by both recruiters and corporate human resource professionals.

Combination Style Resumes give you the "best of both worlds" – an intense focus on your qualifications combined with the strength of a solid employment history. Theses resumes are powerful career marketing tools.

Resume Presentation Style: Making the Best Choices

Just as with the resume format style, you also need to give careful consideration to the resume presentation style (or styles) that will be right for you and your job search based on how you plan to "use" your resume. Chances are you will be sending just as many resumes via email (electronic resume) as you will on paper (printed resume), if not more. Therefore, it is critical to understand the similarities and the differences in the visual presentation of the two. What's more, over the past several years, the Web resume has appeared – a Web-based resume presentation that offers tremendous flexibility in how you present your qualifications, and combines the aesthetic qualities of the printed resume with the ease in transmission of the electronic resume.

THE TRADITIONAL PRINTED RESUME

The single most important thing to remember when you are preparing a printed resume is that you are writing a sales document. You have a product to sell – yourself – and it must be attractively packaged and presented. To compete against hundreds, if not thousands, of other qualified candidates, your resume must be sharp, distinctive, and dynamic in both its wording and its visual presentation.

Your resume should have an up-to-date style that is bold and attracts attention. This doesn't mean using an italic typeface, cute logos, or an outrageous paper color. Instead, be conservatively distinctive. Choose a sharp-looking typeface such as Tahoma, Bookman, Georgia, Krone, Garamond, or Fritz, or if your font selection is limited, the more common Times Roman, CG Omega, or Arial typefaces. The samples in this book will further demonstrate how to create documents that are sharp and upscale while still remaining conservative and "to the point."

Paper color should be conservative, preferably white, ivory, or light gray. You can even consider a bordered paper (e.g., light gray paper with a narrow white border around the perimeter.) Only for "creative" professions (e.g., graphic arts, theater, media) can colored papers be appropriate and an important part of the packaging. For these individuals, the visual presentation of their resume package is additionally important to communicate their creative talents.

If possible, adhere to these formatting guidelines when preparing your printed resume:

- Do not expect readers to struggle through 10-15 line paragraphs. Substitute 2-3 shorter paragraphs or use bullets to offset new sentences and sections.

- Do not overdo bold and italics type. Excessive use of either defeats the purpose of these enhancements. If half of the type on the page is bold, nothing will stand out.

- Use nothing smaller than 10-point type. If you want employers to read your resume, make sure they don't need a magnifying glass!

- Don't clutter your resume. Everything you have heard about "white space" is true. Let your document "breathe" so readers do not have to struggle through it.

- Use an excellent printer. Smudged, faint, heavy or otherwise poor quality print will discourage red-eyed readers.

THE ELECTRONIC RESUME

When discussing electronic resumes, take everything that is really important about preparing a visually pleasing printed resume and forget it! Electronic resumes are an entirely different creature with their own set of rules. They are "plain-Jane" resumes stripped to the bone to allow for ease in file transfer, email, and other technical applications. Professional resume writers, who work so hard to make each resume look distinctive and attractive, cringe, while engineers love how neat and clean these resumes are!

If possible, adhere to these formatting guidelines when preparing your electronic resume:

- Avoid bold print, underlining, italics, and other type enhancements. If you want to draw attention to a specific word, heading, or title, use CAPITALIZATION to make it stand out.

- Type all information starting on the left-hand side of the page. Do not center or justify any of the text, for it generally does not translate well electronically.

- Leave lots of white space just as you would with a printed resume. Ease in readability is a key factor in any type of communication.

- Length is not as critical a consideration with electronic resumes as it is with printed resumes. Therefore, instead of typing all your technical skills in a paragraph form, type them in a long list. Instead of putting your keywords in a double-column format, type them in a list. It is a much easier read for the human eye!

NOTE: Your electronic resume will automatically be presented in Courier typestyle (default font).

THE EMERGING WEB RESUME

Coming into the mainstream, a new type of resume – the Web resume – allows you to merge the visual distinction of the printed resume with the ease of the electronic resume. The Web resume is hosted on your own website where you can refer recruiters, colleagues, potential employers, and others. Rather than pasting your plain-looking electronic resume into an email message, include a link in your email to your URL. With just one click, your printed resume instantly appears. It is easy and efficient, the visual presentation is sharp and classy, and resume writers around the world are breathing much easier!

With a Web resume, you have the opportunity to include more information than you would with the traditional printed resume that is mailed or given to the employer. You can have separate sections (separate Web pages) for achievements, project highlights, management competencies, technology skills, and more. Everything you want to convey can be accessed by just a click.

For those of you in technology industries, you can even go one step further and create a multimedia presentation of your Web-based resume. Never before have you been able to create a resume that actually demonstrates your technical expertise. Just think of the competitive advantage a Web resume can give your job search.

One final note about presentation style . . . it is quite likely that you will have at least two versions of your resume – the printed version and the electronic version. In today's employment market, chances are that you will need both, allowing you to send your resume in the manner that is preferred by a particular company or recruiter. With that said, career professionals recommend that you prepare both versions at the same time so you will have them available as necessary.

Web resumes are not yet the norm so you may not need one today. However, they are increasingly being accepted and used, so don't be surprised if the opportunity for you to use a Web-based resume appears over the next year or two.

The 10 Critical Rules of Resume Writing

Resume writing is part art and part science, and perhaps that's what can make the process seem so difficult. In order to overcome some of the obstacles that many people face when writing their resumes, carefully review the 10 critical rules of resume writing outlined below. If you follow these resume instructions, you'll find that the writing process moves along much more smoothly and more quickly, and that your new career transition resume is a powerful marketing tool.

10 CRITICAL RULES OF RESUME WRITING

Rule #1	There are no rules in resume writing!
Rule #2	Sell it to me, don't tell it to me!
Rule #3	Use the "big" and save the "little."
Rule #4	Choose the "right" words, language, and tone.
Rule #5	Write in the first person.
Rule #6	Use the right keywords.
Rule #7	Remain in the realm of reality.
Rule #8	One size does not fit all.
Rule #9	No need to tell your whole life story!
Rule #10	100% perfection is the standard.

Now, let's explore each of these rules in greater detail.

Rule #1: There are no rules in resume writing! One of the greatest challenges of resume writing is that there are no specific rules about what to write, how to write it, and how to visually present it. There are certain guidelines, of course, such as including your work experience and education credentials. Beyond that, however, there are no formal rules or standards for how to write a resume, and this can make the process seem difficult and frustrating.

Don't be alarmed! As you read through this book and review all of the sample resumes, you'll be able to determine what type of resume is right for you, how to write it, how to format it, and how to prepare a powerful visual presentation that will showcase your skills, qualifications, and experience. Use these examples to provide you with the direction and insights you need in order to build your own powerful resume.

Rule #2: Sell it to me, don't tell it to me! Earlier in this chapter, I discussed the concept that your resume is really a sales and marketing document. It is your calling card, your promotional copy, your personal advertisement. But, it's not enough just to say that. Rather, your resume must be written in such a fashion that it does indeed sell, market, and promote your skills, qualifications, and experience.

The most effective way to achieve that is by using the "sell it to me, don't tell it to me" writing strategy. More simply put, you don't just want your resume to TELL your reader what you have done. Instead, you want your resume to SELL what you have accomplished and the VALUE you bring to a hiring organization.

So, how do you do that? The answer is simple. You write powerful sentences that highlight your capabilities, skills, qualifications, and achievements. Here are a few examples of how effective this strategy can be:

Telling It: Managed a field sales force of 45.

Selling It: Led a 45-person field sales team to record revenue performance in both 2003 and 2004. Increased annual key account sales 32% despite emerging competition, reduced field sales costs 12% by introducing new technologies, and improved bottom-line profits by 24%.

Here's another example:

Telling It: Selected to manage corporate-wide product development task force.

Selling It: Hand-selected by CEO to plan and lead a team of 14 managers and executives guiding the company's worldwide product R&D programs. Over three years, introduced two new product families that delivered $4.8 million in sales.

You can see for yourself what a significant difference in impact there are between each of the two sets of statements. Be sure that you SELL yourself when writing your resume and don't simply TELL the facts. Remember that each and every word in your resume should be written to communicate skill, knowledge, success, and achievement. If you can accomplish this, you will have created your own winning resume that is bound to open doors, generate interviews, and help you land a great professional opportunity in your career of choice.

Rule #3: Use the "big" and save the "little." When you actually sit down and begin to write, remind yourself that your resume should be written as a "teaser," with just enough information to entice someone to offer you an interview. If you don't hold back some information about yourself, there won't be anything left that's different, unique, and interesting to share during your job interviews.

To achieve this, the best strategy is the "big-to-little" technique where you share the BIG things in your resume to communicate the overall message of who you are and then save the LITTLE things (the specific projects, activities, achievements, etc.) for the interview. So, what does that mean? Here's a great example:

The BIG (for your resume) - Honored as the "Top Business Unit Manager of the Year" with a 12% gain in net profits.

The LITTLE (for your interview) - I was selected as the "Top Business Unit Manager of the Year" based on the combination of my performance in team building, team leadership, customer relationship management and bottom-line profit performance. In fact, we closed 2004 with a 12% gain in net profits in my business unit, the only business unit in the company to show positive growth. In addition, we brought in six new key accounts, restructured our product warehousing system to better control inventory, eliminated three unnecessary support positions, and are just launching a massive capital technology project."

Here's another example:

The BIG –   Led the development of a new series of children's books, now a key revenue center for the publisher and one of only three categories that are currently under expansion.

The LITTLE – In 1998, I was selected to lead the development of an entirely new series of children's books targeted specifically for the bibliotherapeutic marketplace. With a team of only four, we sourced new authors, acquired several exceptional titles, and managed the entire book editing, publishing, production, and marketing cycle. To date, we've published six titles and sold more than 200,000 books in both retail and specialty markets.

You can see how effective this strategy can be in accomplishing two distinct benefits for you: First, it will help you craft a powerful resume. Second, your resume will become an effective tool for guiding the interview precisely where you want it to go so that you can share the highlights of your career as they relate directly to your current career objectives.

Rule #4: Write with the "right" words, language, and tone. The words that you include in your resume will set the tone and energy of the entire document. If you use words such as "responsible for" or "duties included," your resume becomes passive, repetitive, and not very exciting. But, when you use action verbs such as "designed," "developed," "facilitated," and "led," your resume comes to life and communicates energy, drive, enthusiasm, results, and success. Compare these two sentences:

Without the "right" words: Responsible for daily accounts payable and accounts receivable functions for the company.

With the "right" words: Planned, staffed, and directed daily accounts payable and accounts receivable for a $2 million company with 145 corporate customers and hundreds of vendors nationwide.

You can easily see and feel the difference in tone. Sentence #1 simply states the facts of the job while sentence #2 much more effectively communicates the scope of the position and the magnitude of responsibility.

Rule #5: Write in the first person. Always write in the first person (dropping the "I's"); never in the third person. What does this mean? Here's an example:

First Person – (I) Orchestrated the start-up of the company's first on-site fundraising campaign following the Asian tsunami crisis in 2004/5.

Third Person - Jerry Dibbs orchestrated the start-up of the company's first on-site fundraising campaign following the Asian tsunami crisis in 2004/5.

Can you see the difference? The first example communicates, "I did this." The second example communicates, "Jerry Dibbs, some other guy, did that" and moves ownership away from you. Your resume must be a part of who you are and not a distant third-party voice. Writing in the first person will accomplish this.

Rule #6: Use the "right" keywords. It is essential that you use keywords specific to your professional goals and aspirations. If you're looking for a job in sales, write about your skills in customer service, public relations, communications, and product merchandising. If you're interested in a position in product engineering management, be sure to highlight keywords specific to both engineering (e.g., product design, manufacturability, failure analysis) and management (e.g., training, team building, budgeting). If your goal is a C-level position, focus on your successes in strategic planning, profit management, organizational leadership, marketing positioning, company vision, and more.

Not only are keywords critical in communicating that you have the "right stuff" for the job, they are also the foundation for technology-based resume scanning. Right or wrong (we won't have a philosophical discussion here!), chances are that when you submit your resume, a computer may view it before human eyes ever see it. When the computer is scanning your resume, it's looking for specific words and phrases that the company has identified as key to the position (thus, keywords). If those words are in your resume, you'll get passed along to the next step: hopefully, a real person. If those words are not in your resume, that's it. The computer is not going to read between the lines and assume that, because you did one thing, you also have experience with the other thing. Thus, using keywords specific to the job you are pursuing is critical in order to get you and your resume noticed.

Rule #7: Remain in the realm of reality. Most everyone you know pushes the envelope just a bit when writing their resume. Remember, your resume is a sales and marketing document. In fact, most employers will know that you've pushed your experience to the edge, so to speak, in order to make yourself appear as an extremely well-qualified candidate. And you know what? That's okay . . . okay as long as you remain in the realm of reality! Resume writing is a self-promoting activity and, as such, it is expected that you work hard to sell yourself. However, always remember that every single thing you write on your resume must be 100% accurate, truthful, and verifiable. Only push so far. If you go beyond reality, you will lose the opportunity and your credibility.

Rule #8: One size does NOT fit all! Ever looked at someone else's resume and thought it was great? The wording was right on target and the visual presentation was really sharp. "Okay," you thought to yourself, "I'll just copy this resume when I write mine." Wouldn't that be so easy?

Unfortunately, resume writing is not that standardized and it is often difficult to take one resume sample and simply plug in your information and have it "work" for you. Resume writing is a much more customized process than that, where your goal is to highlight YOUR specific skills, qualifications, and achievements, which, in most instances, will be quite different from those of your friends and colleagues. You can certainly use resume samples (like the ones in this book and those of your friends, associates, mentors and others), but you will have to individualize the document to ensure that it is selling you and your specific talents.

Rule #9: No need to tell your whole life story! It is important to remember that resume writing is not the same as writing an autobiography. You want to consider EVERYTHING about yourself – all of your work experience and all of the experiences and knowledge that you've gained, educational credentials, training programs, technology skills, honors and awards, professional memberships, volunteer work, and more. Then, critically evaluate each of those items to determine which are relevant to your current career transition goals and which are not. It's that simple . . . only include what matters. Obviously, you must include your work experience and educational credentials, but how you include them and what specifics you highlight will depend entirely on where you are currently headed in your work life.

Rule #10: 100% perfection is the standard. Forbidden: Typographical, spelling, punctuation, and grammatical errors. Your resume reflects of the quality of work that you will produce on a company's behalf, so be sure that it's perfect. Nothing less is acceptable!

Top 20 Resume Writing Mistakes to Avoid

In the preceding pages, I've outlined the 10 critical rules for resume writing that every job seeker should live by. Now, we're going to switch gears and focus on the top 20 resume writing mistakes that you must avoid.

All too often job seekers submit resumes with serious writing errors, errors that I can almost guarantee will put you out of the running for a position. A prospective employer will think to himself, "If this is the quality of work that this individual produces, I certainly don't want them in my organization. I can't have the company sending out correspondence that is confusing and disorganized, and fraught with typographical, grammatical, and wording errors. My customers would be appalled!"

To be sure that this doesn't happen to you, avoid the following common errors:

1. Resume is unrelated to the position being filled. If you're in a career transition mode, be sure that your resume highlights the skills, qualifications, experience, and more that you have as they directly relate to the new position. If you just focus on your past experiences (and not your current objectives), you will probably be passed over.

2. Resume is too long or too short.

3. Resume is unattractive with a poorly designed format, small typestyle, and little "white space," making it extremely difficult to read.

4. Resume is sloppy with handwritten corrections.

5. Resume has misspellings and poor grammar, is wordy and repetitive.

6. Resume has obvious punctuation errors.

7. Resume appearance is amateurish, gimmicky, or too slick; in other words, it's over-produced.

8. Resume is too boastful, aggressive, and egocentric.

9. Resume repeatedly uses the word "I," making the job seeker appear overly self-centered.

10. Resume includes information that seems "questionable" and untruthful.

11. Resume lacks credibility and content and includes lots of fluff and canned language.

12. Resume is missing major categories such as Education or Experience.

13. Resume is difficult to interpret because of poor organization or lack of focus and, therefore, it is difficult to determine what the job seeker has done and wants to do now.

14. Resume has no evidence of past accomplishments or a pattern of strong performance from which a prospective employer can predict future performance

15. Resume uses jargon and abbreviations unknown to the reader.

16. Resume states a strange, unclear, or vague objective.

17. Resume includes distracting personal information that does not enhance the resume nor the individual's candidacy for the position.

18. Resume fails to include critical contact information (e.g., telephone number, email address, mailing address).

19. Resume does not clearly communicate, "This is the value I bring to your organization."

20. Resume looks and reads the same as everyone else's resume, giving you no edge over your competition.

Top 15 Resume Production and Distribution Mistakes to Avoid

After you have written your resume and carefully reviewed it to be sure that you haven't committed any of the 20 critical resume writing mistakes, it's time to move on to the actual production and distribution of your resume. This process is also often fraught with very common errors that you can easily avoid if you pay close attention to detail. Here's what you should avoid:

1. Resume is poorly typed and poorly reproduced, making it difficult to read.

2. Resume is printed on odd-sized, poor-quality, or extremely thin or thick paper.

3. Resume is soiled with coffee stains, fingerprints, or ink marks.

4. Resume is sent to the wrong person or department.

5. Resume is mailed, faxed, or emailed to "To Whom It May Concern" or "Dear Sir." (Be smart . . . call and get a name whenever possible!)

6. Resume is emailed, but the attachment (or pasted-in copy of the resume) is missing.

7. Resume is mailed in a tiny envelope that requires the resume to be unfolded and flattened several times.

8. Resume is mailed in an envelope that is double-sealed with tape and virtually impossible to open.

9. Back of envelope includes a handwritten note stating that something is missing on the resume, that the phone number has changed or some other important message.

10. Resume is accompanied by extraneous enclosures (e.g., recommendations, transcripts, samples of work) which were not requested.

11. Resume arrives without proper postage and the company has to pay!

12. Resume arrives too late for consideration.

13. Resume arrives without a cover letter.

14. Cover letter repeats exactly what's on the resume, does not command attention and, therefore, does not entice the reader to action (calling you for an interview).

15. Cover letter is filled with typographical, grammatical, wording, and/or punctuation errors.

Expert Resources

In order to give yourself a competitive job search advantage and be sure that you adhere to the 10 critical resume writing rules and avoid all of the mistakes outlined on the preceding pages, it is often wise to consult a resume, career, or job search expert. These individuals can provide you with insights and expert guidance as you plan and manage your job search – today and in the many years to come. You have your choice of working with a professional resume writer, career coach, career counselor, outplacement consultant, recruiter, or others who deliver job search services and support to candidates just like yourself.

What's more, there are companies that will post your resume online, other companies that post position announcements online, and still others that produce targeted email and print campaigns to send your resume to prospective employers whom you select. There are reference-checking companies, coaches who specialize in interview training, and publications galore on resume writing, job search, and career marketing.

The list of potential resources is virtually endless, from the resume writer down the street to the global outplacement consulting firm with offices on six out of seven continents. The emergence of all these firms has created a wealth of resources for job seekers, but it has also made the process much more difficult with so many choices. How do you determine exactly what help you need and from whom? And how do you find the right person?

That's easy! The 19 professionals who contributed their resumes to this book are all expert resume writers who work with job seekers worldwide to help them plan and manage successful search campaigns. What's more, each and every one of these writers, in addition to other career-related credentials they may have, has also attained one of the following five prestigious resume writing certifications:

- **MRW - Master Resume Writer** (awarded by the Career Masters Institute – www.cminstitute.com)

- **CPRW - Certified Professional Resume Writer** (awarded by the Professional Association of Resume Writers – www.parw.com)

- **NCRW - Nationally Certified Resume Writer** (awarded by the National Resume Writers' Association – www.nrwaweb.com)

- **CFRWC - Certified Federal Resume Writer & Coach** (awarded by The Resume Place – www.resume-place.com)

- **CRW - Certified Resume Writer** (awarded by the Professional Resume Writing & Research Association – www.prwra.com)

In addition, many of these experts also offer additional services such as career coaching, career counseling, Internet resume postings, direct mail campaigns, and more. You'll find complete contact information for each of the contributors in the Appendix. Feel free to contact them for information about their services, pricing, and specific experience. They can be a wonderful addition to your job search toolkit for career transition success.

CHAPTER 2

Dissecting Career Transition Resumes

Everything in life has a pattern, a process, a system, or a strategy – from how you tie your shoes to how mortgage and interest rates are set – and resume writing is no different. There is a definite process and strategy for how to write powerful and effective career transition resumes that will get you noticed and not passed over.

In Chapter 1, we discussed the different types of resume format and presentation styles, the rules of resume writing, and the critical mistakes to avoid. When you get to Chapter 3, you'll find an in-depth discussion of how to write each section of your resume, along with a variety of examples that you can copy, edit, and use in your resume.

However, before we move on to Chapter 3, it's important to discuss the elements that are common to all career transition resumes. Once you understand these common strategies and techniques, you'll understand the most critical concepts for writing your best-in-class career transition resume. What's more, these work for every career transition – from minor "adjustments" in career focus (e.g., public relations to public affairs) to major changes in career direction (e.g., finance to human resources).

To best demonstrate those concepts, five sample resumes are showcased, each with a solid description of the unique resume writing strategies used to achieve the desired result in each job seeker's particular situation:

- Edward Anders (manufacturing industry executive transitioning into a career in the technology industry)
- Joseph Quinby (state government employee transitioning back into the private sector in a senior management role)
- Laura Wyman (consultant seeking to transition into a corporate position)
- Craig Bount (retiring military officer seeking to transition into a civilian career)
- Lucy Kerns (academic seeking to transition into the corporate marketplace)

As you review these resumes, pay close attention to how each is written and formatted, and how the different resume sections are pulled together to create a single whole, a new perception of that job seeker, which matches his or her current career transition goals. You will also notice some of the many "tricks" of the resume writing trade, techniques professional resume writers use all of the time and which can have a remarkable impact on how you position yourself and your resume.

EDWARD ANDERS

Career Objective: To transition from a senior-level management position in the plastics manufacturing industry into a similar top-level position in the technology manufacturing industry.

Resume Writing Strategy: Bring any and all technology-related experience to the forefront of his resume to (1) demonstrate that he has a strong background in technology, (2) document that he has worked with leading-edge technologies, and (3) position him as a "technology industry insider."

Writing Tips and Techniques:

1. Note the placement of Edward's email address at the very top of his resume, right under his name. By doing this, the moment that someone picks up his resume, they see he's tech-savvy. Not only that, because it is more prominently displayed than his phone number, it also indicates that this is his preferred method of communication . . . just like any other technology industry executive!

2. The headline format at the top of Edward's career profile section instantly accomplishes three things:

   - Line one immediately communicates "who" he is – a "Manufacturing Industry Executive."
   - Line two clearly identifies the "level" of position he is seeking – "Vice President/ Chief Operating Officer/General Manager."
   - Line three immediately and effectively positions him for his industry transition by highlighting one unique area of his expertise – "Incorporating Advanced Information & Manufacturing Technologies To Optimize Productivity."

3. Continuing on in the career summary section of Edward's resume, you'll note 10 areas of expertise that were identified, highlighting a broad cross-section of skills across diverse VP/COO-level functions. In particular, this section demonstrated his expertise in manufacturing (Multi-Site Operations Management . . . Process Redesign & Performance Optimization), finance (Multi-Site P&L Management . . . Budgeting, Finance, & Cost Reduction), business development (Global Sales & Marketing Leadership . . . Opportunity Development & Profitability), **AND** technology (Robotics & Automated Process. . . Product R&D & Commercialization).

4. Next, look at Edward's current position with Premier Plastics and notice that the line immediately under the company name describes Premier as a "$40 million manufacturer with a state-of-the-art technology center," the perfect descriptor to support Edward's career transition. No need to mention that they manufacture plastics products. It's obvious and it's unrelated.

5. Notice the format of the job description under Premier. It begins with a short paragraph which clearly positions Edward as a top-level executive within the manufacturing industry (e.g., "Recruited as #2 executive in a small, growth-driven, global manufacturer . . . Joint P&L responsibility with company president." In addition, this short paragraph details Edward's most significant management responsibilities (including "introducing advanced technologies to improve productivity and profitability").

6. The functional format (focus on skills) that follows was done to draw immediate visual attention to words and phrases that were important to support Edward's transition. The first section – "Revenue & Profit Growth" – is the most critical for any senior executive and, therefore, always should be positioned as the #1 area of experience. The second and third sections – "E-Commerce" and "Technology Advances" – were prominently highlighted to immediately make the connection that Edward has strong technology expertise. It is important to note that although these two items were at the top of the list, they were NOT his primary, day-to-day responsibilities. Rather, they were special projects that he had managed. However, they were critically important to facilitating his shift into the technology industry and, as such, were given such prominent "play." The remaining three sections – "Sales & Marketing Leadership," "International Business Development," and "Manufacturing Operations" – were included to round out the presentation of Edward's experience and achievements as a qualified manufacturing industry executive.

7. On the second page of Edward's resume, you'll note that the other two positions are presented in the same functional format as used on page one – a short paragraph (emphasizing general management plus technology expertise), followed by "Revenue & Profit Growth" achievements (always first!) and then technology achievements ("Information Technology" and "Technology Development"). The message this communicates is that Edward has always been in the manufacturing industry, has always excelled and delivered strong results, and has always been on the forefront of technology. A perfect presentation to facilitate his successful career transition!

EDWARD R. ANDERS
anders444@inmind.com

1 Mission Circle • Miami, Florida 33389 • 612-315-3334

SENIOR MANUFACTURING INDUSTRY EXECUTIVE
Vice President / Chief Operating Officer / General Manager
Incorporating Advanced Information & Manufacturing Technologies To Optimize Profitability

- Multi-Site Operations Management
- Global Sales & Marketing Leadership
- Key Account Relationship Management
- Process Redesign & Performance Optimization
- Opportunity Development & Profitability

- Multi-Site P&L Management
- Budgeting, Finance, & Cost Reduction
- Joint Ventures & Acquisitions
- Product R&D & Commercialization
- Robotics & Automated Processes

Entrepreneurial spirit and drive with outstanding strategic planning, problem solving, decision making, and negotiating skills. Creative, with strong communication, team building, and leadership skills. **Executive MBA.**

PROFESSIONAL EXPERIENCE:

Vice President & General Manager   1998 to Present
PREMIER PLASTICS CORPORATION, Reading, PA
($40 million manufacturer with state-of-the-art technology center)

Recruited as #2 executive in a small, growth-driven, global manufacturer. Given full responsibility for recreating the entire business infrastructure, introducing advanced technologies to improve productivity and profitability, redesigning worldwide sales and market development programs, realigning engineering and manufacturing operations and eliminating excessive costs. Joint P&L responsibility with company president.

- **Revenue & Profit Growth.** Reduced break-even by $1.5 million within first nine months. Currently projecting 30% revenue growth and 400% income growth in 2000.

- **E-Commerce.** Established the corporation's first website to launch massive E-commerce initiative currently on track to generate $2.5 million in first-year sales.

- **Technology Advances.** Directed technology team responsible for software development, customization, and implementation of advanced EDI system. Spearheaded acquisition of $200,000 in automated manufacturing technologies, systems, and processes.

- **Sales & Marketing Leadership.** Created a best-in-class global sales organization that captured three multi-million dollar, exclusive customer accounts with Flint Ink, PPG Industries, and Sherwin Williams. Currently negotiating final agreement with DuPont. Total value of $5-10 million in revenue.

- **International Business Development.** Built and led a completely new European sales organization projected to deliver $8 million in sales in 1999 and $15 million in 2000.

- **Manufacturing Operations.** Spearheaded cost reduction, quality improvement, and productivity improvement programs projected to reduce annual expenses by 12% while enhancing product quality and customer satisfaction/retention. Currently finalizing ISO 9001 for certification in 2000.

21

Vice President & Chief Operating Officer   1996 to 1998
NEUMANN, INC., Gladstone, PA
($20 million US division of $300 million world-class manufacturer)

Recruited to US division of German-based manufacturer supplying major corporations worldwide (e.g., BASF, DuPont, Hershey, Sun Chemical) to revitalize lackluster operations and reposition for long-term growth and profitability. Full operating, manufacturing, technology, engineering, R&D, sales, marketing, HR, and P&L responsibility for US operations supplying customers throughout North America.

- **Revenue & Profit Growth**. Delivered first-year revenue growth of 50.3% and profit growth of 544.6%, achieving 10% EBIT in a traditionally low-margin market. Sustained performance results through year two and positioned for continued accelerated growth.

- **Information Technology**. Led team of consultants facilitating the implementation and transition from UNIX-based to PC-based technology infrastructure. Resulted in double-digit gains in productivity for several key operating departments.

- **Sales & Marketing Leadership**. Transitioned sales into a value-added partner to the manufacturing organization. Recruited direct sales force, introduced incentive program, developed website and product catalog, expanded product line offerings, and created a targeted sales/market penetration program.

General Manager & Chief Operating Officer   1987 to 1996
TECHFORM CORPORATION, Valley Forge, NJ
($35 million international division of $350 million manufacturer)

Recruited to plan and orchestrate an aggressive reengineering and turnaround of this specialty manufacturer faced with tremendous competition, cost overruns, poor market penetration and faltering sales performance. Held full planning, operating, marketing, HR, technology, and P&L responsibility for the entire international division, including 14 manufacturing locations, two company presidents, and a 200-person staff. Challenged to drive earnings growth and ROA while repositioning and stabilizing the organization.

- **Revenue & Profit Growth**. Drove revenues from $18 million to $35 million over seven years with a better than 18% increase in bottom-line profitability. Credited with creating the business and marketing plans that successfully revitalized and repositioned the organization.

- **Technology Development**. Led project team in the design, development, prototyping, and full-scale manufacturing of several new product technologies to advance market positioning.

- **Cost Reduction & Performance Improvement**. Launched a massive cost reduction initiative, introduced automated production techniques, lowered headcount, and reduced production costs by 30-70% over two years. Added $500,000+ to profits.

- **Operating Turnaround**. Reversed $250,000/month negative cash flow in Latin American division and restored to positive cash position. Increased revenues and net income year-over-year in Mexico and Brazil during periods of hyperinflation (2000%) resulting from economic and political turmoil.

Previous Professional Experience: Fast-track promotion through a series of increasingly responsible engineering and manufacturing management positions with Delco (1978 to 1987).

EDUCATION: **Executive MBA** – New York University - 1999
                        BS – Industrial Engineering – Newark College of Engineering – 1978

JOSEPH QUINBY

Career Objective: To transition from an executive management position in the public sector back into a senior management position in the private sector where he began his career.

Resume Writing Strategy: Bring his older career experience to the forefront of his resume to instantly communicate that he **IS** an experienced President/CEO of a private sector company while simultaneously downplaying his most recent experience as a "state government employee" which would not necessarily favorably position him for a corporate C-level opportunity.

Writing Tips and Techniques:

1. In order to understand how Joseph's resume was prepared, it is important to look at his professional experience section on page two. A quick review (starting from the bottom of page two) will tell you that he began his career as an Entrepreneur/President/CEO of a small electronics distribution company that grew phenomenally over the years into a $100+ million corporation. He then followed that as President of a successful consulting firm, and now holds a unique Executive Management Liaison position with the state of Vermont. Most critical to his successful transition from government back into the corporate world is his ability to present himself as a qualified corporate executive and **NOT** a "state government employee" who does not understand how the corporate world works.

2. To facilitate this successful industry transition, a unique format was used on page one in order to bring Joseph's earlier career experience to the forefront. The information on page one is not a chronological listing of his work history but, rather, highlights of his prominent positions, job titles, and achievements. In essence, it's a functional, achievement-based resume format that provides the opportunity to highlight older experience more prominently than it would appear in a more traditional, chronological resume format. When you review this resume, it instantly communicates that Joseph is an experienced "President & CEO of a $100 Million, Multi-State Corporation," which is 100% factual.

3. The achievements highlighted in each section on page one were selected to represent Joseph's diverse and cross-functional expertise, from his success in revenue/profit performance and cost reduction to his ability to negotiate and close multi-million dollar deals. Quantifiable numbers were used whenever possible to validate his capabilities.

4. The remaining section on page 1 of Joseph's resume – "Core Executive Qualifications" – was included for two very precise reasons:

- To communicate a broad cross-section of executive skills and qualifications.
- To fill page one with "corporate executive" information and be sure that Joseph's current position with the state of Vermont did not appear until the reader turned to page two.

5. Page two of Joseph's resume is what you might consider a "standard" chronological format of his professional work experience. Beginning with his most recent position and working backwards, each of his job descriptions focuses on the challenge or opportunity of that particular assignment and his most notable responsibilities, activities, and achievements (being careful **NOT** to repeat specific achievements already noted on page one).

6. Pay special attention to the wording under Joseph's current position with the state of Vermont and you will note that it is very corporate in its content. It doesn't address such topics as this governmental program or that fiscal agency. Rather, it focuses on such items as introducing "corporate business processes, infrastructure, and operations" and providing "strategic, operating, and financial expertise," making it clear to the reader that Joseph's value to this government organization is his corporate experience and the reason he was recruited for the position.

JOSEPH QUINBY

Justin Square Circle
Burlington, Vermont 05402

(802) 254-1254

quinjos@aol.com

PRESIDENT & CEO - $100 Million, Multi-State Corporation

- Built emerging electronics, telecommunications, video, and appliance distribution company from **$300,000 to $100 million in annual sales**.

- Directed purchase and resale of **$1+ billion in merchandise** over 15 years.

- Achieved and maintained **profitability for 15 consecutive years**.

- Negotiated multi-million dollar partnerships with **Sony, Sanyo, Panasonic, Tappan, Litton, BASF**, and other major US and international manufacturers.

- Created a **state-of-the-art distributed PC network** to automate and inventory all core business functions.

PRESIDENT & CEO — Executive Consulting & Management Advisory Firm

- Negotiated $500+ million in financing, lending, and credit transactions. Prepared sophisticated financial documentation for M&A, IPO, franchise, and lease transactions.

- Acquired substantive industry experience in consumer goods manufacturing, retail sales, wholesale distribution, commercial real estate, industrial products manufacturing, and automotive. Client engagements included **North American Phillips, Polaroid, Bendix/Fram, Mazda, Chrysler,** and **Bridgestone**.

- Partnered with **Prudential, John Hancock,** and **Metropolitan Life** to market their commercial real estate portfolio. Negotiated a total of $250 million in transactions.

EXECUTIVE MANAGEMENT LIAISON - $3 Billion Organization

- **Delivered $3-$5 million in annual operating cost reductions** through redesign of core purchasing and supply chain management processes/systems.

- Partnered with EDS Technology to develop and implement a master health care program that **saved $5+ million** annually.

- Conceived and currently implementing migration from checks to electronic processing with projections to **save $5 million annually**. Introduced technologies forecasted to **improve cash flow $10+ million annually**.

CORE EXECUTIVE QUALIFICATIONS

- Full P&L Responsibility
- Multi-Site Operations
- Sales & Marketing Leadership
- Productivity & Performance
- Strategic Planning
- Product Management
- Corporate Legal Affairs
- Government Relations
- Corporate & Investment Finance
- Domestic & Foreign Business
- Distribution & Warehousing
- Logistics & Supply Chain Management

Outstanding organizational, communications, negotiation and leadership skills. Extensive M&A, IPO, franchising, alliance, and partnership development/transactions experience. Top-flight personnel training/management skills.

PROFESSIONAL EXPERIENCE:

Executive Management Liaison   2002 to Present
STATE OF VERMONT, Burlington, Vermont

Recruited by senior executive staff to introduce "corporate" business processes, infrastructure, and operations into a heavily regulated government organization. Challenged to drive major cost savings while optimizing productivity, performance, and efficiency. On-site at headquarters providing strategic, operating, and financial expertise to all 17 operating departments (budgets of $500 million to $1 billion each).

Reinvented virtually all major operating processes to eliminate redundancy, optimize staff performance, improve the allocation of state and federal funds, and build a best-practices organization. Created strategic plans to drive future operations, growth, and transformation.

President & Chief Executive Officer   1995 to 2002
JQ ENTERPRISES / LIK ASSOCIATES, Providence, RI & Boston, MA

Launched private consulting firm offering management advisory, leadership training, strategic planning, negotiating, and operating management services to emerging, turnaround and high-growth organizations. Consulted with presidents, CEOs, CFOs, and other senior executives to resolve core operating issues, implement growth plans, and drive bottom-line revenue and profit growth. Established an extensive network of contacts with bankers, attorneys, accountants, and other professional providers to the corporate community. Leveraged relationships to expand client base.

Engagements involved a broad range of functions with particular emphasis on P&L, strategic and marketing plans, cash flow, financial analysis, organizational needs assessment, purchasing, product management, sales, contracts, legal affairs, banking and lending, letters of credit, and surplus inventory liquidations.

President & Chief Executive Officer   1980 to 1995
MOORE DISTRIBUTORS, INC., Hartford, CT & Providence, RI

Acquired small entrepreneurial electronics, appliance, telecommunications, and video products wholesaler generating $300,000 in annual sales revenues. Built to $100+ million in annual sales. Challenged to drive profitable growth through an aggressive product and market expansion initiative. Held full strategic, operating, and P&L responsibility. Negotiated/managed banking, lending, and credit relationships. Orchestrated several acquisitions.

Scope of responsibility included all core executive leadership, operating management, sales, marketing, human resources, purchasing, finance, accounting, supply chain management, warehousing, transportation, distribution, technology, customer service, and administrative functions. Led a team of up to 200 employees at two large warehouse/showroom/service centers (approx. 300,000 sq. ft.) and four satellite distribution centers throughout the northeastern US. Managed over 5,000 product lines and SKUs.

Captured key customer accounts in the retail chain, independent store, department store, catalog, and fulfillment markets. Maintained long-term account relationships averaging 10+ years. Created high-performance sales team. Introduced innovative customer service, support, and loyalty programs.

EDUCATION: **BS – Business Administration** – BOSTON UNIVERSITY – 1983
                        Graduate of 100's of hours of continuing management and leadership training.

LAURA WYMAN

Career Objective: To transition from an extensive consulting career back into the corporate arena while continuing to leverage her expertise in sales process, productivity, and performance improvement.

Resume Writing Strategy: Position Laura as an expert in the design, development, and delivery of sales process, productivity, and performance improvement programs, and portray her as a "corporate insider" and not "just" a consultant by leveraging the significant name value of the corporations for which she has worked/consulted.

Writing Tips and Techniques:

1. Note the headline format used at the beginning of Laura's resume. With just three short lines at the top of the resume, three critical items are communicated: (1) her expertise is in sales process, productivity, and process improvement; (2) she has "worked" with/ for major U.S. corporations (Armour, Chevron, Citibank, and others); and (3) she has worked in both U.S. and international business markets. This information gives the reader an immediate perception of "who" Laura is and the value she brings to their organization.

2. It is particularly important to play attention to line two of the headline on Laura's resume where an interesting strategy has been used. In order to get the most leverage out of the company names, line two includes a combination of firms that she has either consulted with (currently) and/or been employed with (in the past). In the style in which this information is presented, Laura is immediately perceived as someone who has worked "inside" these companies, a great selling strategy for an individual seeking to transition back into the corporate arena. And, in fact, don't many consultants really work "inside" the companies they are consulting with?

3. The remaining text included in Laura's career summary focuses on her core skills and achievements (e.g., sales, sales management, organizational leadership) and the scope of that which she has managed (e.g., "organizations with up to 30,000 sales personnel worldwide). Note that nowhere in the summary does she include the word "consultant."

4. Move on to Laura's current job description – the remainder of page one – and you will notice that the names of her key accounts were put in bold print and, as such, jump off the page. In glancing at that job description, you instantly see names such as Coors, Nabisco, General Mills, and more, again positioning Laura as someone who understands the inner workings of these major companies, a great selling point to facilitate her career transition.

5. Another important consideration in reviewing Laura's current job description is how each of the bulleted items begin. The first bullet – "Partnered with newly appointed UK

Sales Director of Walkers Snack Foods"– clearly communicates that she worked "inside" the company. The second bullet – "Currently leading Nabisco's Frontline Sales Team" – demonstrates that not only is she working inside the company, she is actually leading their field sales organization. And, finally, the third bullet – "Currently engaged with General Mills to recreate the sales and distribution processes" – again reiterates the fact that she is intimately involved with the operations of the company. A smaller type size was used for the actual achievements listed in each bullet in order to be able to include as much information as possible. Pay attention to the fact that although the type size is smaller, it is still easy and quick to read, a great strategy which allows you to include a bit more information than would normally fit on a page.

6. Turning our attention to page two of Laura's resume, you will instantly note the same style and format were used for the job description under Dynamic Systems; again, notable client names were put in bold print to draw attention to them. So, although we may see another consulting position, what we really see is someone who knows the inner workings of all of these companies.

7. The final two employers listed – Frito-Lay and Armour – are presented in a more traditional format since Laura was actually working as an employee for these two notable corporations. The messages that these two job descriptions convey are (1) rapid promotion and (2) notable and quantifiable achievements. They create a picture of a well-qualified individual who worked her way up the corporate ladder and delivered measurable value to each organization, the exact message she wants to communicate to successfully position herself for a new corporate position.

LAURA WYMAN

48 Emerson Place
Boston, Massachusetts 02114

Home: 617-215-7845
Office: 617-986-3628

Email: laura@mwaii.com
Website: www.mwaii.com

SALES PROCESS, PRODUCTIVITY, & PERFORMANCE IMPROVEMENT EXPERT
Armour, Chevron, Citibank, Coors, Dataserve, Frito-Lay, Nabisco, PepsiCo, Wells Fargo
US & Global Customer Markets

Inventive and results-driven Executive credited with creating sales, sales management, and organizational leadership processes that have enabled companies to work smarter and at less cost for dramatic revenue, market share, and profit growth.

- Pioneered innovative and successful sales processes, feedback systems, team building processes, standards, growth mapping processes, consultative selling systems, and sales management processes for organizations with up to 30,000 sales personnel worldwide.
- Architected and introduced integrated sales processes for all sales distribution channels (e.g., direct, distributor, retail outlet, wholesale outlet, contract business).
- Created more than 300 client-specific sales training and process improvement templates, customized to the specific operations of each sales and distribution channel.

PROFESSIONAL EXPERIENCE:

LAURA WYMAN & ASSOCIATES INT'L, INC., Boston, Massachusetts   1989 to Present

President – Founded one of the most respected sales training, productivity improvement, and performance management organizations in the US. Specialize in the creative, strategic, and tactical design/implementation of sales processes to enhance productivity, improve customer service, and drive strong revenue, market share, and profit growth.

Over the past nine years, completed 50+ engagements with major consumer products companies worldwide. Key clients have included **American Olean Tile** (division of **Armstrong World Industries**), **Coors**, **Frito-Lay**, **Nabisco International**, and **PepsiCo Foods International**. Retained for all engagements through direct client referrals.

- Partnered with newly appointed UK Sales Director of **Walkers Snack Foods** to redefine and reenergize field sales organization through process development/implementation.
  - Led one of the company's most successful sales team turnarounds, positioning Walkers as the #1 profit-producing unit in all of **PepsiCo Foods International**.
  - Sales processes were implemented worldwide, contributing to PFI's position as the #1 PepsiCo division.

- Currently leading **Nabisco's Frontline Sales Team**, a task force organized to study and enhance frontline sales processes of 17,000-person organization. Initiated pilot study in 450-person sales region to create prototype for subsequent deployment worldwide.
  - Developed and introduced new hire, new account planning and new frontline sales management processes to strengthen sales growth, productivity, and customer service performance.
  - Currently leading efforts to bring $10+ million project on line throughout 17,000-person sales organization.

- Currently engaged with **General Mills International** to recreate the sales and distribution processes of $50 million Caribbean business.
  - Restructured sales organization and sales territories, developed improved customer database, revised sales compensation, and initiated a series of customer service improvement and retention programs.
  - Currently leading implementation of growth mapping, gaining commitment, and distributor database management processes.

Home: 617-215-7845
Office: 617-986-3628

Email: laura@mwaii.com
Website: www.mwaii.com

DYNAMIC SYSTEMS, INC., Springfield, Massachusetts   1981 to 1989

Senior Vice President (1985 to 1989)
Vice President (1981 to 1985)

Instrumental in transitioning regional management consulting firm into an international firm with offices in NY, LA, Chicago, Atlanta, Dallas, and Toronto, and serving 450+ clients in 30 countries. Major clients included **Chevron**, **Frito-Lay**, **PepsiCo**, **Swift**, **Square D**, and major banking institutions in the US and Canada. Appointed to Executive Committee in 1984.

Principal responsibility for design/delivery of customer consulting and training programs across a broad range of industries,. Equally strong contributions in new venture development, new product development, business planning, and business systems automation (resulting in dramatic cost reduction, significant gain in productivity, and critical competitive advantage).

- Contributed to the highest gross margins and profit in the company's history with revenue growth from $1.2 million in 1982 to $7.8 million in 1989 (compounded rate of 38%).
- Orchestrated the development and marketing of five sales training systems for bank calling officers at **Barclays**, **California Federal S&L**, **Citibank**, **Security Pacific**, **The Royal Bank of Canada,** and **Wells Fargo**. Created a strong and steady new revenue stream.

FRITO-LAY, INC., Dallas, Texas   1978 to 1981

Senior Vice President (1979 to 1981)
National Sales Training Coordinator (1978 to 1979)

Dual responsibility for the conceptualization, design, development, implementation, and leadership of internal sales, operations, and manufacturing training programs for Frito-Lay facilities and sales organizations nationwide. Identified and leveraged core competencies to drive productivity, quality, and revenue/profit growth within an intensely competitive industry.

- Created, documented, and led basic selling and route sales training programs for the company's 8,000 route sales associates. Trained over 2,000 individuals annually.
- Redesigned and shortened new-hire sales training program.
- Designed and taught manufacturing training in 40 locations throughout the US, involving nearly 10,000 personnel in established and start-up production facilities. Established new standards for manufacturing training and developed internal trainer certification program.

ARMOUR FOODS COMPANY, Phoenix, Arizona   1971 to 1978

Manager of Sales Training (1976 to 1978)
District Sales Manager (1975 to 1976)
Product Department Manager (1973 to 1975)
Sales Representative (1971 to 1973)

- As Manager of Sales Training, designed, led sales training for 1,000+ reps and managers.
- As District Sales Manager, led $50 million sales region to record revenue performance.
- As Department Manager, grew volume 20% and delivered $1.4 million net profit.
- As Sales Representative, increased sales revenue 500%. Won numerous sales awards.

EDUCATION: **BS – Mathematics** – Boston University - 1971

CRAIG BOUNT

Career Objective: To transition from a distinguished military career into a senior-level management or executive position within the corporate arena.

Resume Writing Strategy: Position Craig as an experienced "general manager" and "operations manager," while downplaying the fact that all of his experience was acquired with the U.S. Navy. With no previous corporate employment experience, it is critical to create the perception that Craig has the skills, knowledge, qualifications, and track record of performance similar to those of experienced corporate managers and executives.

Writing Tips and Techniques:

1. Begin reviewing Craig's resume by reading his Career Profile. In just four short sentences, he clearly positions himself as a well-qualified "Management Executive," with no mention at all of his 20+ year military career. Using such phrases as "building and leading top-performing, efficient, and cost-effective operations for a global organization . . ." and "management qualifications in strategic planning, reengineering, process redesign . . . ," Craig creates an immediate picture that he is a top-level management candidate — which is 100% factual. Remember, the only information you want to highlight when writing your career summary is information relevant to your current career transition objectives. For Craig, it is **NOT** relevant to mention at this point in his resume that all of his expertise was acquired through military service. Readers will immediately see this as they move down the first page of his resume.

2. Pay close attention to the format used to present Craig's "job title" and "employer" immediately under the heading of Professional Experience. Rather than listing each of his assignments, he summarized all of his experience under an appropriate job title – "Management Executive" – which encapsulates all of the different positions he has held during his military career. This is what is referred to as an "umbrella" job title, one that summarizes all of the specific titles, positions, and work assignments. By using an umbrella job title, Craig is able to further solidify the fact that he is an experienced executive. Just as important to note is how briefly his employer – the United States Navy – is mentioned. With just one quick line, it is presented with no additional information about whether or not Craig was enlisted, an officer, or a civilian employee of the Navy. This is precisely the vague picture that he wanted to create on page one of his resume. And, in fact, you will notice that there is nowhere else on page one that the Navy is even mentioned.

3. The introductory paragraph listed under the U.S. Navy focuses on Craig's rapid promotion and his depth of experience across a wide range of executive management disciplines (e.g., operating, resource management, finance, human resources). Most important in this section is the sentence that reads, "Acted in the capacity of Chief Operating Officer, General Manager, and Management Executive." This resume does not misrepresent Craig and state that he actually held these titles. Rather, it clearly commu-

nicates the scope of his assignments and their "equivalent" corporate functions. This is an extremely effective strategy for use on a military-to-civilian career transition resume.

4. In an effort to further advance the perception that Craig is a general management executive, the information under his job description is presented in a functional (skills-based) format. Beginning with the heading of "General Management/Operations Management," the resume lists all of his notable responsibilities, deliverables, and achievements as they pertain to a general management role (business plans, strategic plans, organizational goals, budgeting, quality, and more). These are precisely the skills that a general manager in a corporation would have and the functions for which he may be responsible. Again, it's a perfect match to facilitate Craig's transition.

5. On page two of Craig's resume, you will note that a similar functional format was continued to highlight his experience in "Human Resource Leadership," "Information & Telecommunications Technology," and "Asset Management." These three additional sections were included based on a combination of where Craig was most interested in pursuing corporate opportunities and where he had the most notable experience.

6. The next section that follows is a brief "career path" of Craig's actual positions, all of which have been converted from "military lingo" to "corporate" lingo. Nowhere are his various ranks mentioned or his military occupational specialties. This information has no real value to a corporation. Rather, they want to understand "who" Craig is and "what" he has done as it relates to their corporate needs. And, in fact, from looking at Craig's career path, it is still difficult to discern if he was enlisted, an officer, or a civilian employee. Fine! This is information he can share during an interview — the ultimate goal of the resume.

7. The final section included under Professional Experience was a brief summary of the many military honors and awards that Craig has earned. Rather than listing things such as "Meritorious Service Medal," this information was briefly summarized to communicate that he has received numerous awards for his performance in leadership management, quality, productivity, and cost reduction. Again, the perfect mixture of qualifications for a corporate management executive, and a great tool to help facilitate Craig's successful career transition.

CRAIG BOUNT
432 Colonel Marshall Way
Lovingston AFB, Colorado 38837

Phone: (876) 352-4726
Fax: (876) 354-3827

Voice Mail: (876) 352-3827
Email: commander@aol.com

CAREER PROFILE:

High-caliber Management Executive with over 15 years' experience building and leading top-performing, efficient, and cost-effective operations for a global organization. Strong general management qualifications in strategic planning, reengineering, process redesign, quality and productivity improvement. Excellent experience in personnel training, development, and leadership. Skilled public speaker and executive liaison.

PROFESSIONAL EXPERIENCE:

MANAGEMENT EXECUTIVE   1982 to Present
UNITED STATES NAVY – U.S. & WORLDWIDE ASSIGNMENTS

Fast-track promotion through a series of increasingly responsible management positions directing large-scale operating, resource management, finance, and human resource organizations. Acted in the capacity of Chief Operating Officer, General Manager, and Management Executive developing and leading high-profile business units supporting global operations. Expertise includes:

General Management/Operations Management

- Planned, staffed, and directed business affairs for organizations with up to 4,200 personnel assigned to over 15 different sites worldwide. Held full decision-making responsibility for developing annual business plans and long-range strategic plans, evaluating human resource and training requirements, and implementing advanced information technologies.

- Consulted with senior executive management team to evaluate long-term organizational goals and design supporting business and financial systems to control operations.

- Managed over $300 million in annual budget funds allocated for operations, research and development, and general expenses. Slashed 22% from the budget through reallocation of resources, personnel, and technologies.

- Conducted ongoing analyses to evaluate the efficiency, quality, and productivity of diverse operations (e.g., administrative, equipment, maintenance, transportation, human resources, inventory control). Streamlined operations and reduced staffing requirements by 18%.

- Negotiated and administered multi-million dollar vendor contracts supporting over $80 million in field construction and renovation projects. Delivered all projects on time and within budget.

- Appointed to several headquarters committees working to professionalize the global organization, introduce proven business management strategies, and enhance internal accountabilities.

Human Resource Leadership

- Directed staffs of up to 100+ technical, professional, and support personnel. Fully accountable for personnel scheduling, job assignments, performance reviews, merit promotions, and daily supervision. Coordinated manpower planning to meet operational requirements and realigned workflow to optimize productivity.

- Designed and led hundreds of personnel training and professional skills development programs throughout career. Topics included budgeting/finance, leadership, team building, information technology, communications, reporting, and diversity.

- Introduced innovative training technologies (e.g., remote, video, telecommunications).

Information & Telecommunications Technology

- Spearheaded the selection, acquisition, and implementation of over $45 million in technologies over the past 10 years (e.g., Internet and Intranet, data mining, data warehousing, CADCAM, Microsoft Office, GIS).

Asset Management

- Controlled over $175 million in capital equipment, materials, and supplies. Redesigned logistics support programs and reduced inventory costs by $3 million annually.

Career Path:

Commanding Officer (2002 to Present)
Resource Management Director (1997 to 2002)
Executive Officer (1995 to 1997)
Business/Finance Manager (1992 to 1994)
Operations Officer (1986 to 1992)
Administrator/Program Coordinator/Educational Officer (1982 to 1986)

Received several distinguished awards and commendations for outstanding leadership qualifications, management expertise, quality/productivity improvements, and cost reductions.

EDUCATION:

MS – Executive Management – Naval Postgraduate School – 1988

BS – Management – U.S. Naval Academy – 1982

Graduate – 500+ hours of leadership and executive management training

LUCY KERNS

Career Objective: To transition from a technology leadership position within academia into a technology leadership position in the corporate sector.

Resume Writing Strategy: Highlight the wealth of Lucy's technology experience which transcends all major systems and applications, with particular attention to the joint ventures and alliances where she has partnered with major U.S. corporations. The latter was utilized to create the perception that Lucy is a corporate "insider" and **NOT** an academic.

Writing Tips and Techniques:

1. The first thing you will notice about this resume is the unique structure and style of Lucy's career summary. It was important to present her as a skilled "Information Technology Executive" by demonstrating her expertise across two major functions: (1) her "leadership, management, and business expertise," required of any executive within the technology industry and (2) her actual "technology expertise," which spans a wide range of systems, applications, and solutions. Each of those subsections, although brief, is extremely comprehensive in highlighting Lucy's core skills and knowledge as they are most important to a for-profit technology corporation. A smaller type size was used for the actual items listed in each subsection in order to be able to include everything. Pay attention to the fact that, although the type size is smaller, it is still quick and easy to read.

2. The second and only other section on page one of Lucy's resume is titled "Technology and Leadership Achievements." This was the perfect strategy to allow Lucy to highlight her most prominent projects and "business partners" (BankOne, Microsoft, Ericsson, Bell Atlantic, Corning, Eastman Kodak, and others). As you may be aware, a great deal of initial technology development comes out of partnerships between universities and private corporations, and this has been where Lucy has spent much of her career. Rather than listing all of this information under her current employer (Arizona State University) and positioning her as an academic, by highlighting these achievements in a separate section, she was able to disentangle her "corporate" work from the university and position herself much more effectively for her career transition. In fact, you will notice that nowhere on page one do you even see any mention of Arizona State.

3. Turn your attention to the top of page two of Lucy's resume and look at how her current employer is presented. Instead of Arizona State University having top billing, the Technology Research and Development Center is what you see first, with just a brief mention of the university following. Again, this proactively positions Lucy as a Technology Executive and not an academic.

4. All of the information included in Lucy's job description under the Technology R&D Center focused on her leadership/management responsibilities and technological achievements. Nowhere do you see information about university committees, deans,

education administration, and the like. What you do see is a picture of a talented executive who has pioneered innovative technologies, turned around non-performing technology operations, recruited talented technologists to the team, and more – the ideal skills any corporation would seek in their top technology executives.

5. Lucy's consulting experience was presented as a separate position to accomplish two important things: (1) communicate the fact that she has already "worked" for corporations and is, therefore, not a corporate outsider; and (2) highlight leading-edge technologies in which she has been involved in development and evolution.

6. An important note about Lucy's Education section and, in particular, her Ph.D. degree. This is a notable achievement in and of itself and is critically important to include in that section. However, it was just as critical that she NOT include her Ph.D. next to her name at the top of pages one and two of her resume. If you put "Lucy Kerns, Ph.D." at the top of the resume, she is instantly positioned as an academic, totally changing the perception of what she was attempting to create with her career transition resume.

7. The final section of Lucy's resume – Personal Profile – includes a brief mention of her publishing and public speaking experience. If she had intended to use this resume in an academic environment, each and every one of her publishing and public speaking engagements would be listed. However, since her objective is a successful transition to corporate employment, it was only necessary to include highlights of this information to further solidify her credibility within the industry and strengthen her position as a valuable asset to any corporation's senior technology team.

LUCY KERNS

One Greenley Circle
Puma, Arizona 89876
ccc@arizonanet.net

Phone: (815) 987-3728

Office: (815) 362-8746

INFORMATION TECHNOLOGY EXECUTIVE
Advanced Information, Voice, Data, & Telecommunications Technologies

IT Executive successful in gaining competitive market advantages through technology innovation and leadership. Expert technical qualifications with strong performance in strategic planning, corporate partnering, budgeting, technical staffing, technology development, and product commercialization. Personally credited with driving the development of technologies that currently generate over $8 billion annually in business and consumer sales.

Leadership, management, and business expertise includes:

- Strategic Alliances, Joint Ventures, & Corporate Partnerships
- New Product Design, Engineering, Funding, & Commercialization
- Financial Planning/Analysis, Financial Modeling, Budgeting, & Cost Management
- Quality, Reliability, Performance, & Productivity Improvement
- Training, Team Building, & Competitive Benchmarking

Technology expertise includes:

- UNIX & PC Hardware, Software, & Peripheral Devices
- Artificial Intelligence, Expert Systems, & Relational Databases
- Wireless & Wired Voice & Data Communications
- Mobile Data Application Architectures & Deployment
- Multimedia, Video Conferencing, Voice Mail, & Speech Synthesis
- Internet & Intranet Solutions

TECHNOLOGY & LEADERSHIP ACHIEVEMENTS:

- Technology Director for more than 100 technology development and commercialization projects with total investment of over $500 million:
  - $45-million artificial intelligence system for **BankOne** (*generated $1.2 million in first-year savings*)
  - $18-million relational database design with **Microsoft** (*generated $4 million in first-year sales*)
  - $89-million telecommunications system for **Ericsson** (*generated $50 million in sales in three years*)

- Personally negotiated over $85 million in partnership agreements, strategic alliances, and joint ventures with leading corporations worldwide to drive cooperative technology development programs. Partners included **Bell Atlantic, Corning, Dow Chemical, Dupont, Eastman Kodak, Mitsui (Japan), Merck Pharmaceutical, Nokia (Sweden), Westinghouse,** and **Weyerhaeuser.**

- Restored failing technology development project jointly funded by Arizona State University and the Department of Defense. Redefined project objectives, restaffed key technology positions, accelerated product development cycle, and eliminated cost overrides. Delivered project on time and within budget.

- Partnered with **IBM, HP, Data General,** and **Microsoft** to fund over $8 million in joint software development and commercialization projects.

37

PROFESSIONAL EXPERIENCE:

TECHNOLOGY RESEARCH & DEVELOPMENT CENTER   1985 to Present
Arizona State University, Puma, Arizona

Executive Director – Technology R&D (1995 to Present)
Assistant Director – Technology R&D (1992 to 1995)
Project Manager/Systems Engineer – Systems Development (1985 to 1992)

Promoted through a series of increasingly responsible technology leadership positions to current assignment as the most senior executive leading a 44-person technology development team. Challenged to identify and capture opportunities for the development of advanced information and telecommunications technologies in cooperation with corporate and government partners. Manage $50+ million annual operating budget.

- Revitalized Technology R&D Center and built a technologically sophisticated infrastructure with large-scale IBM and DEC mainframes, UNIX and Windows operating systems, voice and data communications, 6 videoconferencing sites, T1 backbone, and a centralized client/server LAN.
- Led project teams in the development of 100+ new technologies that have been successfully commercialized and currently generate over $8 billion in annual sales revenues worldwide.
- Recruited top technologists from corporations and universities nationwide to build a best-in-class R&D team successful in meeting aggressive technology development and commercialization goals.
- Created Technology Leadership Forum, Technology Quality Council, and IS Executive Task Force.

TECHNOLOGY CONSULTANT   1994 to 1998

Corning, Inc. – Systems Development Group
Merck Pharmaceuticals – Worldwide Technology Development Team
NASA/Goddard Space Flight Center – Laboratory for Terrestrial Physics

- Senior Advisor, Consultant, and Project Director to Arizona State University's business partners for joint technology development projects. Led onsite project teams of up to 20 technical and professional staff. Managed project budgets from $2 million to $120 million.
- Led development of advanced technologies for commercial applications (e.g., artificial intelligence, expert systems, relational databases, bio-geophysical systems, satellite imagery, acoustics).

EDUCATION:

Ph.D., Information Technology, Arizona State University, 1989
M.S., Information Architecture, Arizona State University, 1987
B.S., Management Information Systems, Ball State University, 1985

PERSONAL PROFILE:

Publications: Author of 50+ magazine and journal articles on emerging information systems, technologies, and applications. Publications include *Computing Monthly, IT Quality Council, Journal of Technical Computing, Forbes,* and *The Wall Street Journal.*

Public Speaking: Presented over 200 lectures, symposia, and technical conferences on emerging industry trends. Keynote Speaker – 2004 IT Conference and 2002 DPMA Conference.

CHAPTER 3

Building Your "Best" Career Transition Resume

Step-by-Step Process

Writing your best career transition resume would be an easy task if there were a single outline or template you could use. All you would need to do is answer the questions and fill in the blanks, and your resume would be ready. Not much time, not much serious thought, and no tremendous effort.

Unfortunately, as we all know, this is not the case. Each resume must be custom-written to sell each candidate's individual talents, skills, qualifications, experience, educational credentials, professional activities, technical proficiency, and more. Resumes are **NOT** standardized, they are **NOT** prescribed, and there is **NO** specific formula. On the one hand, this gives you tremendous flexibility and the opportunity to be creative and unique in the presentation of your skills. On the other hand, it makes resume writing a much more difficult task, for there is no single road map to follow.

Combine that with the fact that your resume is a document designed to sell you into your next position, not to simply reiterate where you have worked, what you did, and what you accomplished. Rather, you are taking all of your past experiences and then "re-weighting" them to support your current objectives. This further confounds the process and requires that you give tremendous thought to what you will include in your resume, how, and where. It is not a 30-minute task. Most likely, it will take days and days of thought, writing, editing, and hard work to create your own best career transition resume.

Although resumes do vary dramatically in their structure, format, tone, and presentation, they do share certain common features. Specifically, most resumes will include Experience and Education sections. In addition, there are many other categories that you may include if they are relevant to your career, background, and current objectives. They include Objective, Career Summary, Technology Qualifications, Professional Affiliations, Civic Affiliations, Honors and Awards, Publications, Public Speaking, Teaching Experience, International Experience, and Personal Information. Some will be appropriate for you; others will not.

To help you better understand the structure and function of these sections, a short but thorough discussion of each follows, along with specific examples. Use the information below to help you determine (1) if you need to include a particular section in your resume, and (2) what style and format to use for that section. Remember, the two key sections are Experience and Education, with the other categories surrounding them to strengthen the presentation of your qualifications and sell you into your next job.

Career Objective

One of the greatest controversies in resume writing focuses on the use or omission of an Objective. There are three questions to ask yourself that will help you decide whether or not you need an Objective on your resume.

1. *Do you have a specific Objective in mind?* A specific position? A specific industry? If so, you can include a focused Objective statement such as: "Seeking an upper-level management position in the Pharmaceutical R&D industry" or "President/ CEO of an emerging telecommunications company." As you can see, each of these Objective statements clearly indicates the type of position the candidate is seeking.

2. *Is your Objective constant?* Will your Objective stay the same for virtually all positions you apply for and all the resumes you submit? If so, include a focused Objective such as that outlined in #1 above. If not, do not include an Objective. You do not want to have to edit your resume each and every time you send it. It's a time-consuming process and stalls the flow of resumes out your door.

3. *Is your Objective unclear?* Are you considering a number of opportunities? Are you interested in a number of different industries? If your answer is YES, do not include an Objective statement, for it will be unfocused and communicate little of value. Consider an Objective such as: "Seeking a senior management position where I can lead a company to improved revenues and profits." Doesn't everyone want to help a company make money? These are useless words and add no value to your resume. They do not tell your reader "who" you are or "what" you are pursuing.

Remember, every time you forward a resume you will also be sending a cover letter. If you do not include an Objective statement on your resume, let your cover letter be the tool that communicates your Objective in that specific situation to that specific employer or recruiter.

Following are three sample Objective formats you can choose from, if you determine that an Objective is right for you and your career transition resume.

PROFESSIONAL OBJECTIVE:

Challenging Sales Management Position in the Utilities Industry.

EXECUTIVE CAREER GOAL:

C-Level Executive Management position in International Commerce where I can apply my 15 years' experience in Investment Finance, International Banking and International Trade.

CAREER OBJECTIVE: SUPPLY CHAIN MANAGEMENT – TEXTILE INDUSTRY

Career Summary/Career Profile

Consider this. When you write an Objective, you are telling your reader what you want **FROM** them. When you start your resume with a Career Summary or Career Profile, you are telling your reader what you can do **FOR** them, what value you bring to their organization, what expertise you have, and how well you have performed in the past. In both, you are writing about the same concepts, the same professions, or the same industries. However, the Career Profile is a much more upscale, more executive, and more hard-hitting strategy for catching your reader's attention and making an immediate connection. And isn't that the point of your resume? Your goal is to intrigue a prospective employer to (1) read your resume, (2) invite you for an interview, and (3) offer you a position.

To simplify this concept, compare the two examples below:

Example #1:
PROFESSIONAL OBJECTIVE: Senior-Level Corporate Financial Management
                                                                Position

Example #2:
CAREER PROFILE:

Top-flight financial management career with Dow Chemical, American Express, and Microsoft. Expert in mergers, acquisitions, joint ventures, and international corporate development. Personally transacted over $200 million in new enterprises, slashed $14 million from bottom-line operating costs, and contributed to a 33% increase in corporate valuation. Astute planner and negotiator. PC and Internet proficient.

In both of these examples, is it clear that the individual is seeking a senior-level financial management position? Yes, they are both communicating the same overall message – that the candidate is a qualified finance executive.

Now, ask yourself which is a stronger presentation. Obviously, the Career Profile is stronger. It is more dynamic, more substantive, and clearly communicates the success of the candidate. Finally, ask yourself if you started your resume with a Career Profile as presented above, would you need an Objective that stated your goals? Probably not. The Career Profile paints a clear and concise picture of "who" you are. It is not necessary to include a statement above the Career Profile that states, "I want a job as a such-and-such."

Career Profiles are particularly powerful tools for job seekers in career transition. As you'll recall from our discussion in Chapter 1, it is imperative that individuals in transition use their resume to highlight the skills, qualifications, experience, knowledge, and more that are transferable into their new position or new industry. The Career Profile is the perfect vehicle for showcasing those attributes and talents, allowing you to bring all of that pertinent information to the forefront of your resume and immediately capture your reader's attention. Except for particularly rare situations, it is strongly recommended that each career transition resume begin with a Career Profile.

Following are five sample Career Profile formats that you might consider for your career transition resume:

Headline Format:

MANUFACTURING MANAGER/PRODUCTION MANAGER
Production Planning / Logistics / Multi-Site Operations
MBA – Executive Management
MS – Manufacturing Systems & Technologies

Paragraph Format:

CAREER SUMMARY

INTERNATIONAL FINANCE EXECUTIVE with 15 years' experience in domestic and global financial accounting, reporting, and controls. Strengths in process improvement, audit, strategic planning and forecasting, business/financial analysis, and compliance. Substantial experience implementing GAAP and Sarbanes-Oxley controls and standards. Effective team leadership across functional, cultural, geographic, and linguistic boundaries. International experience throughout continental Europe. MBA; CPA.

Core Competencies Summary Format:

Business Development & Relationship Management Executive

Outsourcing/Offshore Strategies & Solutions

Strategic and growth-oriented leader with broad expertise in business development, marketing, operations, and consultative solution-selling. Twelve-year track record of identifying and capturing new business opportunities, developing and maintaining marquee client relationships, and aligning products/services with strategic markets.

_____Core Competencies_____

- Strategic Planning & Tactical Execution
- P&L Management

- Mergers & Acquisitions
- Strategic Alliance & Channel Development
- Business & Technology Liaison
- Rainmaker Marketing

- Customer Acquisition, Retention, & Extension
- Customer, Vendor, & Partner Relationship Management
- Deal Structuring & Contract Negotiation
- Cross-Functional Team Leadership
- Strategic Account Management
- Quantitative & Business Analysis

Category Format:

PROFESSIONAL CAREER HIGHLIGHTS

Experience: 12 years as a Maintenance Director & Manager for Dow Corning and its subsidiaries

Education: **Graduate Certificate in Facilities Maintenance & Engineering**—University of Idaho
BS—Operations Management—University of Oregon

Publications: "Improving Workforce Productivity Through Maintenance Systems Design & Optimization," *American Manufacturing Association,* 2001
"Redesigning Maintenance Processes To Enhance Productivity," *National Facilities Maintenance Association,* 1999

Awards: Employee of the Year, Dow Corning, 2003
Employee of the Year, Bell Laboratories, 1998

Career Highlights Format:

Executive Summary

Senior Operations Executive with a track record of building successful businesses, delivering rapid revenue growth, and creating world-class operational structures to sustain growth and profitability. Experience as President, COO, VP/General Manager, and Board of Directors member for public and private companies, start-ups, and international expansions. Talent for communicating vision and aligning team and individual efforts toward common goals.

Career Highlights

- Built the most successful business unit at Rapido, Inc.—$150MM revenue within 3.5 years, with the highest profit margins and greatest level of client satisfaction in the company.
- Transformed R&D innovation and $10MM investment into multiple revenue streams, a unique international manufacturing model and a $400MM valuation in less than 2 years. (Stanford Company)

■ Fused decentralized distribution operation into a tight-knit team that achieved operating efficiencies of the parent company 5 times its size. (International Beverage)

Writing Your Career Summary Section: Strategies For Success

1. Resume writing is a consolidation process. In theory, you are taking your entire career and consolidating it onto one, two, or maybe three pages. Then, take those pages and consolidate them into one or two inches at the top of your resume. You will then have your Career Profile.

2. Write your Career Profile LAST! How can you write the Profile if you haven't yet written the text and determined what information you want to include in your Profile, how and where to support your new career transition objectives? You can't. Write all of the other sections in your resume first; save the Profile for last. If you employ this strategy, you will find that the words will come much more easily and tie directly into the text of your resume.

3. If you would rather use a heading other than Career Summary or Career Profile, consider the following: Executive Profile, Management Profile, Senior Management Summary, Career Accomplishments, Professional Profile, Career Overview, Executive Qualifications, Performance Summary, Professional Credentials, or Qualifications Summary. In essence, each of these headings communicates the same overall message, so use whichever you're most comfortable with. Bear in mind, however, that headings that use words such as "executive" and "senior management" communicate a higher-level message than words such as "overview" and "summary."

Professional Experience

This will generally be the single most important section in your resume. It is your opportunity to highlight your professional experiences, qualifications, and achievements as they relate to your current career objectives. It is your chance to "toot your own horn," for no one else will. It is the time to sell everything that is great about you. It's why you are the best! Give careful thought and consideration to what information you include for each position, working to highlight all of your skills, experiences, special assignments, project highlights, achievements, and more that are transferable into your new career. EVERY WORD COUNTS!

When you are writing your Professional Experience, your challenge is to briefly, yet strongly, describe your employment history with an emphasis on four important issues as they relate to your career transition. Depending on your particular situation – changing industries or changing jobs/careers – some of these items may be important to you and others may not.

- *The company*. Is it a manufacturer, distributor, worldwide technology leader, or multi-site service organization? What are the company's annual revenues? How many locations? How many employees? Give a brief summary of the company and its operations, customers, products, markets, or technologies as they relate to your current objectives and ONLY as they relate. If your current employer is a technology company and you are looking to remain in the technology industry, briefly highlight the company and what it does, as it is relevant to your current career objectives. If, however, you currently work for a pet products manufacturer and your goal is a position with a consumer products manufacturing company, do not mention your current employer's particular product lines and markets. Rather, refer to them as a $29 million, state-of-the-art manufacturing organization.

- *The challenge*. Is the company a start-up venture, turnaround, or high-growth multinational? Were you hired to lead an international expansion initiative? Were the company's costs out of control? Were there organizational weaknesses? If there were any particular challenges associated with the company and/or your position, be sure to clearly state them. Prospective employers will put tremendous value on your ability to produce and deliver results in a challenging organization. A great introduction to a job description could be, "Recruited by CEO to plan and orchestrate a complete turnaround and revitalization of the company's nationwide field sales organization. Challenged to reduce costs, recruit and retain top talent...."

- *Your accountability*. Include your major areas of responsibility (e.g., functions, departments, organizations, personnel, budgets, revenue and profit objectives, facilities, operations). In just a few sentences you want to communicate the depth and range of your overall responsibilities. For example, "Senior Management Executive with full P&L responsibility for a 42-person nationwide call center servicing more than 3 million customers annually."

- *Your achievements*. Herein lies the heart and soul of your resume. Not only do you want to **TELL** your reader what you were responsible for, you want to **SELL** how well you have performed and what value you delivered. Did you contribute to revenue or profit improvements? Reduce costs? Design new products? Implement new technologies? Better train your staff? Improve efficiencies and productivity? Reduce liability and risk exposure? Penetrate new markets? Streamline operations? Eliminate redundant operations? Negotiate big deals? Raise money? The list of potential achievements goes on and on. Be sure that you include all of your achievements – big and small – particularly those that demonstrate the skills and experiences you will need as you transition your career.

Follow the same format all the way through your resume, becoming briefer and briefer as you get further back in time. Do not focus on the day-to-day responsibilities of your older positions, unless they were particularly unusual. Rather, focus on your achievements, notable company names (employers and/or clients), emerging products and technologies, international experience, or anything else distinguishing about that particular position.

Following are seven sample Professional Experience formats that you can use as examples to help you write your job descriptions.

Achievement Format:

(Emphasizes each position, overall scope of responsibility, and resulting achievements.)

TECHNOLOGY INNOVATORS, INC., Stamford, CT   **2004–Present**
Vice President

Turned around a sinking business…drove operational improvements, cemented client relationships, improved customer satisfaction, and firmly positioned company to reach strategic goal of 100% revenue growth. One of 3-member senior management team developing strategy, objectives, tactics, and operational measurements for $15MM software development and services company. Manage P&L for Services & Support division representing 60% of company revenue.

- **Grew Services & Support revenue 44%** in one year.
- **Boosted programmer productivity 27%** through process and operational improvements as well as organizational refocusing.
- **Maintained 100% client retention** for follow-on projects.
- **Drove client satisfaction improvements that built retention and led to prestigious "Premier Partner" status with IBM.**
  - Improved IBM-rated client-satisfaction score from 76% to 83% and earned elevation to Premier Partner.
  - Earned 95% "satisfied/would rehire" rating in post-project client surveys.
- **Brought on board new strategic partners and managed all alliance relationships** (IBM, Global Software, Now Generation). Built service capabilities, developed co-marketing opportunities, and generated new revenue (e.g., $80K in first-year revenue through Now Generation, $3MM projected by year-end 2005).

Challenge, Action, & Results (CAR) Format:

(Details context, stages, and results of key challenges.)

Vice President of Operations (2002 to Present)
Plant Manager (1999 to 2002)
WIP SYSTEMS INTERNATIONAL, Bulverde, Texas

Challenge: Lead turnaround and return to profitability of $42 million technology manufacturer plagued with cost overrides, poor productivity, dissatisfied customers, and massive annual losses.

Action: Rebuilt management team, introduced advanced technologies and systems to expedite production flow, retrained all employees, and implemented team-based work culture.

Results: ■ Achieved/surpassed all turnaround objectives and returned the operation to profitability in first year. Delivered strong and sustainable gains:
- **70%** improvement in operating efficiency.
- **75%** improvement in product quality ratings.
- **100%** on-time customer delivery.

■ Upgraded facility, replaced obsolete equipment with state-of-the-art systems, introduced stringent standards to achieve OSHA compliance, and established in-house day-care facility.

■ Restored credibility with one customer, now generating over $30 million a year in revenues.

Career-Track Format:
(Emphasizes fast-track promotion, overall scope of responsibility, and notable achievements.)

STEPHENS INDUSTRIES, INC., Worcester, MA

Vice President, Global Business (Worcester, 2003–Present)
Managing Director, Europe (London, 2001–2003)
Product Development Director (Worcester, 1999–2001)
Marketing Services Manager (West Hillsboro, PA, 1998–1999)
Fast-track promotion through a series of increasingly responsible positions to current role as VP of Global Business. Built a top-tier global organization; recruited and developed a talented management team that led the company from $8 million revenue (1998) to 2004 volume of $24 million.

◆ Delivered 20% annual revenue growth while increasing margins 5% despite declining industry trend.
◆ Relocated headquarters from rural Pennsylvania to campus of Worcester Technical Institute, providing a vital pool of engineering and business talent to achieve corporate vision and growth objectives.
◆ Spearheaded opening and expansion of 2 manufacturing operations in China, with resulting sales growth of 200% in Asia over a 3-year period.
◆ Negotiated acquisition of 2 US businesses ($5 million and $8 million) that generated profitable revenue streams, opened a new untapped customer base and expanded product offerings.
◆ Closed 2 facilities and secured $5 million to fund expansion and modernization of 4 other plants.

Project-Highlights Format:
(Places emphasis on specific projects, their scope, and associated achievements.)

MANAGER, INFORMATION SYSTEMS: Alpha Health Insurance, Milwaukee, WI   2002–2005

Controlled $3MM budget and led 13–25 IS professionals in supporting and improving enterprise applications for the company's life/health network and national accounts business users. Responded rapidly to shifting priorities in constantly changing business environment. Consistently delivered projects on schedule and within budget.

Project Highlights:

> **FINANCIAL SYSTEMS INTEGRATION:** Managed a technically challenging integration following merger with Midwest Health; required new interfaces and new systems across all application areas. **RESULTS: Shortened month-end close by 75% in larger, more complex organization.**

> **LEGACY SYSTEM REPLACEMENT:** Selected and installed new Oracle-based system to replace aging and inefficient Sales & Marketing system. **RESULTS: Delivered in a tight 5-month timeframe and captured $200K annual savings.**

> **CRITICAL PROBLEM SOLVING:** Led multi-department team in an intense exercise to resolve and prevent errors in monthly financial reporting. **RESULTS: Revamped the job stream and accelerated the close process from 7 days to 24 hours.**

> **COMMISSION TRACKING SYSTEM:** Refined commission system to improve accuracy of checks issued; concurrently, developed an online book of business to track current payment activity for each agent based on contract sales. **RESULTS: Achieved 100% accuracy in commission sales payments for the first time in company history.**

Table Format:

Visually emphasizes strong financial results.)

Achieved operational turnaround, revitalized financial performance, and drove steady growth:

	FY 1999	FY 2000	FY 2001	FY 2002	FY 2003
Revenue	$99MM	$150MM	$203MM	$195MM	$271MM
Earnings	$18MM	$22MM	$38MM	$43MM	$49MM
Branches	68	84	107	115	125

Functional Format:

(Emphasizes functional areas of responsibility within the job and associated achievements.)

SENIOR VICE PRESIDENT, PharmaCare, Inc., Chicago, IL, 2000–2005
Transformed region from declining performance to top national status in revenue, profitability, customer satisfaction, and cost control. Assumed leadership of Southwest region experiencing stagnant revenue, declining profits, and significant loss of its prime customer base. Drove improvement initiatives across the full scope of operations for nearly $100MM region, with full accountability for sales, finance (P&L), clinical services, and operations.

- **Turnaround Leadership/Revenue & Profit Performance:** Rebuilt the organization, strengthening management, sales and operations/administrative teams, and deeply instilling core values of customer service and efficient operations. Grew revenues 225%, profits 353%, and customer base 24% in 4 years.
- **Sales, Market Positioning, Training, & Customer Service:** Built sales focus and competency at all levels of the organization through effective training and constant communication/reinforcement.

- Reduced sales staff from 8 to 2 while more than doubling revenues.
- Drove sales growth toward high-quality customers and preferred payor mix to increase in come 2.5X with only a 24% increase in customers.
- Elevated region from last to #1 in the company in customer satisfaction.

■ **Finance, Operations, & Technology Leadership:**
- Implemented multidiscipline CRM program that provides instantly accessible information for every aspect of business performance. Successfully converted non-industry software to full functionality.
- Centralized billing operations and reduced days sales outstanding from 132 days to 51, best in the company.
- Renovated and/or relocated 5 pharmacies, creating state-of-the-art facilities.

Skills-Based Format:

(Places emphasis on the specific skills, qualifications, and expertise.)

Founder/General Manager — Law Offices of Earl W. Hadley   1998 to Present

Founded specialized legal practice providing corporate advisory services to CEOs, COOs, and other senior executives across a broad range of industries and on diverse topics/business issues. Built new venture from start-up to 3 locations and 12 employees. Achieved and maintained profitability for 6 consecutive years. Excellent reputation for ethical performance and integrity.

Serve in the capacity of a **Senior Operating Executive/General Counsel** to client companies, providing hands-on leadership in:

- Strategic Planning & Vision
- Policies & Procedures
- Growth & Expansion
- Market Analysis & Positioning
- Operations Management
- Cost Control & Avoidance
- Process Design & Analysis
- Banking & Corporate Finance
- Human Resources
- Technology
- Capital Assets
- Executive Compensation

Clients range from start-up ventures to $200 million corporations in software development, high-tech manufacturing, industrial manufacturing, consumer products, heavy equipment, transportation, automotive and marine dealerships, services, and professional trades.

Writing Your Professional Experience Section: Strategies For Success

1. Using a combination format (paragraphs plus bulleted listings of achievements or project highlights) is often the best strategy for writing job descriptions because it allows you to accomplish two things. With the introductory paragraph, you can communicate your overall responsibilities, while in the bullets you can focus on achievements, project highlights, and other successes. In theory, you're communicating to your reader, *"This is what I was responsible for and this is how well I did it."* The concept is simple; the impact, significant.

2. Focus your job descriptions on your achievements, but realize that many career achievements are **NOT** quantifiable. If you happen to be in sales and can boast that you increased regional sales revenues by 24%, that's great. However, for scores of other professions, accomplishments cannot always be so easily measured. Consider

the attorney who facilitates the implementation of a new PC-based billing system, an important achievement to include in his resume, but not one to which a number can easily be assigned. That's okay. An achievement is an achievement is an achievement, with or without a number! Be sure to include and highlight all of your achievements, successes, honors, awards, project highlights, and anything else that will distinguish you from the crowd of other candidates vying for the same positions.

3. If you would rather use a heading other than Professional Experience, consider the following: Career History, Work Experience, Employment History, Career Highlights, Executive Leadership Experience, Career Path, Performance Highlights, or Career Overview. In essence, each of these headings communicates the same overall message, so use whichever you're most comfortable with. Bear in mind, however, that headings that use words such as "executive" and "senior management" communicate a higher-level message than words such as "overview" and "summary."

Education

The Education section of your resume is generally quite easy and quick to write. Basically, you want to include your college degrees, continuing professional education, licenses, and certifications. Whether or not you include all of this information or just highlights will depend entirely on your current career goals and new career direction.

To help you get started in writing and formatting your Education, here are five sample Education sections. Select the one that most closely matches your educational credentials and then use that format for your information.

Executive Education Format:

EXECUTIVE EDUCATION

Executive Development Program	NEW YORK UNIVERSITY
Master of Business Administration (MBA)	UNIVERSITY OF PENNSYLVANIA
Bachelor of Science	UNIVERSITY OF VIRGINIA

Academic Credentials Format:

EDUCATION & PROFESSIONAL TRAINING:

M.S., Management Science, University of Colorado, 1996
B.S., Industrial Engineering, University of Nevada, 1992

Highlights of Continuing Professional Education:
- Organizational Management & Leadership, Colorado Leadership Association, 2005
- Industrial Engineering Technology, Purdue University, 2003
- SAP Implementation & Optimization, American Society for Quality Control, 1999
- Conflict Resolution & Management in the Workplace, Institute for Safety, 1998

Certifications Format:

TECHNICAL CERTIFICATIONS & DEGREES

Certified Nursing Administrator (CNA), Helen Keller School of Nursing & Health Care, 2004
Bachelor of Science in Nursing (BSN), Missouri State University at Columbia, 2002
Certificate in Advanced Cardiac Life Support (ACLS), State of Missouri, 1998
Certificate in Basic Cardiac Life Support (BCLS), State of Tennessee, 1996

Non-Degree Format:

Training & Education --

UNIVERSITY OF TOLEDO, Toledo, Ohio
BS Candidate — Management & Administration (Senior class status)

UNIVERSITY OF OHIO, Ann Arbor, Michigan
Dual Majors in Management & Human Resource Administration (2 years)

No-College Format:

PROFESSIONAL DEVELOPMENT

Management Training & Development	KELLOGG SCHOOL OF MANAGEMENT
Leadership Excellence	KELLOGG SCHOOL OF MANAGEMENT
Management Communications	PACE LEADERSHIP TRAINING

Writing Your Education Section: Strategies For Success

1. There is often much controversy about whether or not to date your education – when you studied or when you earned your degree. To clarify any confusion, if you are under 50 years of age, it is strongly recommended that you date your education. Over the past several years, job seekers have tended to exclude college graduation dates from their resumes for fear that it might date them. And, if you are over 50, this is a consideration. However, for the under-50 candidate, this is **NOT** the appropriate strategy. Include your dates and give your prospective employers a good foundation from which to track your professional career. Let them see, for example, that you graduated in 1984, went to work for Xerox, then to IBM,

and are now the president of a successful Internet venture. Paint a clear and concise picture. For the over-50 job candidate, consider how far back in your work experience you are going to go on your resume and then determine if dating your education will indeed date **you**! If so, do not include the date and only share that information once you are in the door for an interview.

2. If your list of continuing professional education is very extensive and/or unrelated to your current career objectives, it is not necessary to include it all. Just list a sampling of the programs you have attended. Refer to it as "<u>Highlights</u> of Continuing Professional Education" (as shown in the "Academic Credentials" format above), which communicates that it is not a comprehensive list.

3. If you attended several colleges prior to earning your degree, it is not necessary to include them all, unless they are notable institutions (e.g., Ivy League school, acclaimed international university such as Oxford). The only exception to this rule is for the non-degreed professional who must include colleges where he or she has studied yet not earned a degree, as demonstrated in the "No-Degree" format above.

The three sections we have just discussed – Career Summary, Professional Experience, and Education – are the foundation for virtually every career transition resume. You will find those sections on just about every resume sample in this book and on just about any resume that you see. However, in addition to those sections, there are many others that you may or may not include depending on how relevant they are to your past experience and current career objectives. Following is a discussion of each of these other resume sections, along with sample formats you can adapt for your own use.

Professional & Community Activities

Include a listing of professional and community organizations to which you belong and any specific leadership roles, committee memberships, or related accomplishments. You may also include volunteer experience if relevant to your current career objectives. However, use some discretion. If you hold three leadership positions with notable professional associations and nonprofit organizations (information that you will include in your resume), it is not necessary to include the fact that you are on the board of your local condo association! Here's an example:

PROFESSIONAL AFFILIATIONS:

Independent Manufacturers Representative Association (District President)
American Marketing Association (Professional Member & Training Committee Chair)
Sales Consultants of America (Professional Member)
Junior Achievement (Volunteer Lecturer)

Technology Qualifications

Fifteen years ago, a "Technology Qualifications" section was virtually never seen on a resume, except for people working directly in the technology industry. Today, that's changed forever! Technology is a part of every professional's life and must be addressed on your resume. You may include just a brief mention of your PC qualifications in your Career Summary, or you may have an entire section devoted to the topic, particularly if you're a programmer, hardware engineer, telecommunications engineer, technology project manager, CIO, CKO, or otherwise employed in a technology career path. You will have to determine the specific technology information and skills to include based on your current objectives. Here are two examples:

If technology is an ancillary part of your job responsibilities, include a statement in your Career Profile such as:

> Proficient with Microsoft Word, Access, and Excel, email and the Internet.

If technology is a key part of your job responsibilities, include a separate section:

TECHNOLOGY QUALIFICATIONS:

Software:	C++, C, PLSQL, COBOL, PL1, CLIST, Lotus Notes, Word, Excel, PowerPoint
Hardware:	RS6000, IBM Mainframe, Intel
Databases:	Oracle, DB2, IMS
Data Transfer:	Network Data Mover (NDM), File Transfer System (FTS)

Honors and Awards

Include your honors, awards, commendations, and other professional recognition. This information can be integrated directly into your job descriptions, included under Education (if appropriate), or compiled into a separate category at the beginning or the end of your resume (depending on its impact and relevancy). If any of your honors or awards are significant and recognizable, you might integrate them directly into your Career Profile. Here are a few examples of how and where to include your honors and awards:

In your Career Profile:
- Winner, 2000 Honors Club Award For Outstanding Sales Performance
- Winner, 1998 Presidential Award For Exemplary Service
- Winner, 1996 SuperMAX Award For New Business Development

In your job descriptions:
- Honored for outstanding revenue and profit performance with five consecutive ***"Salesman of the Year"*** awards.

In a separate section titled Honors & Awards:

HONORS & AWARDS:
- Winner, 2004 Addy Award For Creative Design & Excellence
- Winner, 2002 Clio Award For Television Set Design
- Winner, 2001 Malcolm Award For Ad Campaign Design

Publications

Publications validate your expertise and impress your reader. Many think that if you are published, then you must be an expert in your subject matter. Great! Use that to your advantage and be sure to include your book and article publications either in a separate category at the end of your resume or in your Career Profile if particularly noteworthy or relevant to your current career objectives. Include the title of the publication, name of publisher, and year of publication. Here are a few examples of how and where to include your publications:

In your Career Profile:
- Author, "Future Technology Trends," *American Computing Magazine*, 2005
- Author, "Technology Careers in 2010 and Beyond," American Management Association, 2003

In your job descriptions:
- Authored IBM's award-winning *Close To The Customer* book and accompanying multimedia presentation.

In a separate section titled Publications:

PUBLICATIONS:
- Author, "Sales Leadership 2004," *Forbes*, 2004
- Author, "Team Building & Leadership," *IMAX Magazine*, July 2003
- Author, "Winning In The Technology Wars," *Business Week*, April 2001

Public Speaking

Just as with publishing, if you have notable public speaking experience it is important to include, as it further substantiates your experience, qualifications, and marketability to a prospective employer. If this is relevant to you, be sure to include your public speaking engagements on your resume, as well as the title of presentation, audience, location, and date. If the list is extensive, include only the highlights that are most notable and/or most related to your current search objectives. Here are a few examples of how and where to include your public speaking experience:

In your Career Profile:

- Keynote Presenter, American Dental Association National Conference, Summer 2004
- Speaker, ADA Leadership Symposium, 2001

In your job descriptions:

- Spoke at the 2003 Leadership Symposium sponsored by the Wharton School of Business in cooperation with the Fortune 500 business community.

In a separate section titled Public Speaking:

PUBLIC SPEAKING:

- Keynote Presenter, American Manufacturing Association National Conference, July 2003
- Speaker, Atlanta Leadership Conference, 2003
- Panel Member, Logistics 2000 Presentation, American Quality Council Convention, 2000

Teaching & Training

If you are an educator, a corporate trainer, or otherwise employed in the field of Teaching/ Training/Education, this section will be your Professional Experience. However, if you are a business professional who has relevant teaching experience, be sure to include this information in a separate "Teaching & Training" section. Just like publications and public speaking, it immediately validates your credentials and qualifications. List the name of the course(s) that you taught, the school or organization, and the dates. Here are a few examples of how and where to include your teaching and training experience:

In your Career Profile:

- Instructor, Telecommunication Technology Trends, Dover Tech College, Spring 2005
- Instructor, Management Analysis, University of Pennsylvania, Fall 2003

In your job descriptions:

- Selected by corporate HR Director to design and deliver a corporate-wide training program on production scheduling and resource management for 2,000+ employees.

In a separate section titled Teaching Experience (or Training Experience):

TEACHING EXPERIENCE:

- Instructor, Management Philosophies, Wharton School of Business, Spring 2005
- Instructor, Statistics & Demographics, University of Pennsylvania, Fall 2003
- Corporate Trainer, IBM – International Sales Division, 1995-2001

International Experience

Today, we are a global workforce with a global economy, and the more international experience and exposure you have, the better. Be sure to include your foreign language skills and travel experience either in your Career Profile or as a separate section if the information is detailed and directly relevant. Here are a few examples of how and where to include your international experience:

In your Career Profile:
- Fluent in English, Spanish, and Portuguese.
- Lived and worked in Peru, Bolivia, and Brazil.

In your job descriptions:
- Traveled throughout Europe, Asia, and the Middle East to develop new supplier relationships and monitor supplier production controls.

In a separate section titled International Experience:
INTERNATIONAL EXPERIENCE:
- Fluent in English, French, Spanish, and Portuguese.
- Lived and worked in Belgium, France, and the UK.
- Graduate, Oxford University's Executive Leadership Course.

Personal Information

Whether or not you should include personal information on your resume has long been a point of discussion and controversy. My recommendations are straightforward and easy to apply. Do not include personal information such as birth date, marital status, health, number of children, and the like. Do not include the fact that you enjoy golfing, camping with your family, or reading. None of this is relevant to your job search, particularly early on when you are presenting a resume just to get your foot in the door.

There are certain times, however, when it is appropriate to include personal information:
- Required by the employer.
- Important to clarify your citizenship or residency status.
- Important to clarify your age.
- Unique information. I've worked with executives who were past Olympians, ascended mountains on seven continents, raced as competitive triathletes, and trekked through obscure regions worldwide. This type of information attracts others to you and can be the single reason someone calls for an interview. My motto is "Use what you have to get in the door."

If a Personal Information section is appropriate in your situation, consider the following format:

PERSONAL PROFILE:

US Citizen since 1988 (native of Switzerland)
Fluent in English, French, German, and Dutch
Competitive Triathlete and Skier

Streamlining Your Resume

A great strategy for consolidating all of the "extra" resume categories (e.g., Affiliations, Publications, Public Speaking, Foreign Languages) is to integrate them into one consolidated category called Professional Profile. You will want to consider this if you have little bits of information to include in many different categories and/or you are having trouble comfortably fitting your resume onto 1-2 pages. Here's an example of how best to consolidate:

PROFESSIONAL PROFILE:

Affiliations:	Chairman, National Industries Association
	Chairman, Industry Oversight National Association
Publications:	"Business Management," *Business World*, May 2004
	"Emerging Technologies," *Digital Design*, January 2002
	"Strategic Marketing," *Fortune*, April 2001
Languages:	Fluent in Spanish, French, and German.
PC Software:	Microsoft Word, Access, Excel, Lotus, PageMaker, WordPerfect

The Resume Writing Process

Everything in life has a process, and resume writing is no different. If you use the following structured outline, you will find that the task of writing and producing your resume is faster, easier, and more efficient than you expected. What's more, you will discover that your finished resume is a much more powerful tool that better highlights your skills, qualifications, experiences, and achievements as they directly relate to your current career objective.

1. *Open a file in your PC* and select a typestyle that (1) you like and (2) is easy to read. Type your name, address, email, and phone numbers (home, office, fax and cell). Include your office number only if you are comfortable accepting calls during the day and

can speak in confidence. NEVER include your employer's 800 number. Your current employer isn't looking for a job and should not be supporting your job search!

2. *Type in all the major headings* you will be using (e.g., Career Summary, Professional Experience, Education, Publications, Technology Qualifications).

3. *Fill in the information* for Education, Publications, Technology Qualifications, Public Speaking, Affiliations, Teaching Experience, and all the other categories EXCEPT Career Summary and Professional Experience. This information is easy to complete, requires just a bit of thought and is generally simply a listing of factual information.

4. *Type company names, job titles, dates, and locations*. Again, this information is easy to complete and will only take you a few minutes.

Now, take a look at how much of your resume you have already completed in just a few short minutes!

5. *Write your job descriptions*. Start with the very first position you ever held and work forward. The older jobs are easy to write. They are short and to the point, and include only highlights of your most significant responsibilities and achievements as they relate to your current career objectives. Then, as you work forward, each position will require a bit more text and a bit more thought. Before you know it, you will be writing your most recent (or current) job description. It will take the longest to write, but once it is finished, your resume will be 90% complete.

6. *Write your Career Summary*. This is the trickiest part of resume writing and can be the most difficult. At this point, you may want to re-read the preceding section on writing career summaries. Be sure to highlight your most notable skills, qualifications, and achievements as they relate to your current objective and create a section that prominently communicates, "This is who I am."

7. *Add bold, italics, underlining and other type enhancements* to draw the reader's attention to notable information. This should include your name at the top of the resume, major headings, job titles, and significant achievements. You may also insert lines and/ or boxes to offset key information. But be careful. Overuse of type enhancements will instantly devalue the visual presentation and cloud a prospective employer's initial reaction. If you highlight too much, the resume appears cluttered and nothing stands out, clearly defeating your purpose.

HINT: Using bold print to highlight numbers (e.g., sales growth, profit improvement) and percentages (e.g., cost savings, productivity gains) is a great strategy. Someone picks up your resume, and those numbers instantly pop out and grab their attention. You can use this same strategy to highlight other key information such as major clients, major deals and transactions, product names, honors and awards, and more.

8. *Carefully review the visual presentation.* How does it look? If your resume is two pages, does it break well between pages? Is it easy to read? Does it look professional? Even more important, does it convey a strong message to support your current career transition? At this point, you may need to adjust your spacing, change to a different typestyle or make other minor adjustments to enhance the visual presentation.

9. *Proofread your resume a minimum of THREE times.* Then have one or two other people proofread it. It MUST be perfect, for nothing less is acceptable. Remember, people are meeting a piece of paper, not you. Your resume must project professionalism, performance, and perfection.

Getting Started

You've read through all of the preceding text of this book and now it's time for you to get started writing your own winning career transition resume.

The first step in writing a powerful and effective resume that attracts prospective employers and opens new doors to new opportunities is to understand why you are the best.

1. What is it that you have accomplished, delivered, produced, created, designed, managed, revitalized, or built that demonstrates your knowledge, expertise, and excellence?

2. What have you done to positively impact financial performance of a company?

3. Have you reduced operating costs, increased revenues, and improved bottom-line profitability?

4. What have you done that is innovative and creative?

5. What have you done to improve overall performance?

6. What value do you bring to an organization?

7. Why would someone want to hire you?

8. Why are you better and more qualified than other candidates?

To help you answer those questions and more, use the worksheets on the following pages to:

1. Help you to identify your most significant skills, qualifications, and knowledge as they relate to your current career objectives.

2. Help you identify your most notable career achievements.

3. Help you clarify your career goals and objectives.

4. Help you link your skills, knowledge, and achievements with your current objectives to create a powerful and winning resume presentation.

Use the following forms to help you identify your core skills, knowledge, and achievements, and then link them to your current career objectives. This information will serve as the foundation for your entire resume presentation, what you include, where you include it, and how you include it. It will clearly outline the specific qualifications, experiences, and accomplishments that you offer to a prospective employer that tie directly into the type(s) of position you are seeking in your career transition. Just as important, these activities will help you identify information that you **DO NOT** want to include in your resume – information that is irrelevant at this point in your career and/or totally unrelated to your current career objectives. When you begin to write your resume (particularly your Career Summary and Professional Experience sections), remember that this information is what is important to highlight in order to communicate that you have the "right stuff" to support your successful career transition.

Resume Preparation Form #1
Identifying Your Skills & Knowledge

Make a complete list of the things that you do well. This list should include both professional functions (e.g., sales, product design, joint venture negotiations, technology implementation, strategic planning, budgeting) as well as more "general" skills (e.g., organization, project management, interpersonal relations, team building/leadership, oral and written communications, problem solving, decision making).

_____

_____

_____

_____

_____

_____

_____

_____

_____

_____

_____

_____

_____

_____

Resume Preparation Form #2
Identifying Your Career Achievements

Make a comprehensive list of the notable achievements, successes, project highlights, honors and awards of your career, with a focus on the past 10 years of employment. Whenever possible, use numbers or percentages to quantify results and substantiate your performance.

_____

_____

_____

_____

_____

_____

_____

_____

_____

_____

_____

_____

_____

_____

_____

_____

Resume Preparation Form #3
Identifying Your Career Objectives

List the industries and types of positions in which you are interested in career opportunities.

_____

_____

_____

_____

_____

_____

_____

_____

_____

_____

_____

_____

_____

_____

_____

_____

_____

Resume Preparation Form #4
Linking Your Skills & Achievements With Your Objectives

Using your responses to Activity #3 (Career Objectives), select skills and accomplishments from your responses to Activity #1 and Activity #2 that relate to your objectives. In doing so, you are making a connection between what you have to offer and what type of position you are interested in. For example, if your objective is a position in Technology Sales and Marketing Management, the fact that you have strong plastics products assembly skills is probably not relevant and therefore not necessary to include. However, the fact that you have excellent negotiation and account management skills is critical and should be at the forefront of your resume. The strategy is to select items from #1 and #2 that support #3.

OBJECTIVE #1: _____

RELATED SKILLS: _____

_____

_____

_____

_____

_____

RELATED ACCOMPLISHMENTS: _____

_____

_____

_____

_____

_____

_____

_____

_____

_____

_____

_____

_____

_____

_____

OBJECTIVE #2: _____

RELATED SKILLS: _____

_____

_____

_____

_____

RELATED ACCOMPLISHMENTS: _____

_____

_____

_____

_____

_____

The information above will now serve as the foundation for your resume. You have clearly outlined the specific skills, qualifications, experiences, and accomplishments that you offer which tie directly to the positions you are seeking. When you begin to write your resume (particularly your Objective, Career Summary, and Professional Experience), remember these are the most important things to highlight in order to communicate that you have the "right stuff."

CHAPTER 4

Best Resumes for Transitioning Into Sales, Marketing, and Public Relations Careers

Building the Foundation

Transferability of skills is the foundation upon which every effective career transition resume is written. Your challenge, therefore, is to identify the skills, qualifications, experiences, and competencies you have that will be of value in your new job, career, or industry. Those skills then become the key points in your resume around which everything else is written.

To help you get started with identifying your transferable skills, review the brief listing below of *some* of the skills, qualifications, and competencies that companies and recruiters look for in candidates seeking positions in sales, marketing, public relations, or related career tracks. (*Note that this is only a partial listing of the countless different skills that companies look for in qualified candidates.*)

Carefully review the keywords and keyword phrases to identify those that accurately reflect skills you possess and which are transferable into your new position. Then, be sure to incorporate those words into your resume, your cover letters, and any other career marketing documents that you create. They will capture a prospective employer's interest and open the door to interviews and opportunities.

Account Management
Brand Development & Management
Business Development
Campaign Development & Implementation
Competitive Analysis
Customer Acquisition
Customer Relationship Management
Customer Retention
Customer Service & Satisfaction
Lead Generation

Market Research & Analysis
Marketing Communications
Multimedia Marketing Campaigns
Negotiations
New Product & Service Introductions
Presentations
Press Relations
Product Pricing
Public Affairs
Sales Strategy

Sample Career Transition Resumes

Following are 11 sample resumes for individuals transitioning into sales, marketing, public relations, and related careers. Each of these resumes was written by a professional resume writer with extensive experience working with, writing for, and positioning individuals in career transition. Full contact information for each of these writers is in the Appendix. To understand why these resumes were written and designed the way that they were, it is critical that you read the following information, which explains the specific objective of each of these job seekers and the particular strategy that was used to prepare their resume.

Resume: John Lester (pages 71-72)
Writer: Roberta Gamza
Objective: To transition from owner/operator of a fencing company into a technical sales position.
Strategy: Emphasized sales skills, qualifications, and successes from his role as a small business owner and highlighted the depth of his technical knowledge acquired from several years' previous work experience to demonstrate that he could combine the two skill sets for a successful career in technical sales.

Resume: Emerson Van Rensselaer (pages 73-74)
Writer: Lorie Lebert
Objective: To transition out of the packaging industry and into another high-level sales and/or marketing management position.
Strategy: Top half of first page of resume devoted exclusively to his transferable skills, qualifications, and most notable accomplishments, with no mention of industry. Job descriptions largely focused on transferable experience with little mention of industry-specific information. Clearly positions him for top sales and marketing opportunities in a diversity of industries.

Resume: Diane Lynn West (pages 75-76)
Writer: Cindy Kraft
Objective: To transition out of academic administration and into a position in account management and/or customer relationship management.
Strategy: Highlighted her account development and management experience, people skills, business development competencies, and recruiting successes to position her as a strong candidate for an account management position. Use of an entirely functional format for page one of resume creates the perception of an experienced sales professional, not an academic.

Resume: Bruce Clayton (page 77)
Writer: Joyce Fortier
Objective: To transition out of a career in the landscaping industry and into a new career in field sales, marketing, and account management.

Strategy: Created a resume that focused primarily on his sales and marketing experience as a business owner and not on the daily operations he directed. Used a one-page, hard-hitting resume to succinctly communicate skills, talents and results.

Resume: Cheri R. Pierre (pages 78-79)
Writer: Jean Cummings
Objective: To transition out of public relations/press relations and into a unique position promoting the food and wine of France in either a sales, marketing, communications, or strategic leadership position.
Strategy: Communicated her passion, specialized knowledge, and French language fluency immediately, followed with a comprehensive listing of skills and qualifications ideal for her new position, and finished with highlights of her work experience and training in both the U.S. and France.

Resume: Rick Phillips (pages 80-81)
Writer: Annemarie Cross
Objective: To transition into a general management position directing a large sales and/or marketing organization for a major corporation.
Strategy: "Traditional" executive resume format using a headline to identify "who" he is, a strong profile to summarize his most notable qualifications and thorough job descriptions with quantifiable achievements. Clearly positions him for a one- to two-tier jump in management/leadership responsibility.

Resume: Marcia Orlando (pages 82-83)
Writer: Kirsten Dixson
Objective: To transition from journalism into a dynamic position in corporate communications/public relations.
Strategy: Original format and presentation expertly highlight her transferable skills and convey the advantages of her reporting background. Demonstrated her strongest skill (writing) in the actual text of resume to gain a truly competitive advantage over other candidates.

Resume: Jed Conley (pages 84-85)
Writer: Joyce Fortier
Objective: To transition out of the television broadcasting industry and into a public relations or marketing position in any one of a number of industries.
Strategy: Created a resume that demonstrated the transferability of this news anchor's skills into the field of public relations and marketing by using a format that draws visual attention to those skill sets and his specific experience. "Spun" the job descriptions to focus on skills that are transferable and/or of interest to his new target audience.

Resume: Mary Anne Warner (pages 86-87)
Writer: Louise Garver

Objective: To transition out of public relations/marketing/communications and into a governmental relations or public affairs position in a business/corporate setting.

Strategy: Started the resume with a headline which clearly communicates her objectives and then used a functional format to bring forward and leverage her past governmental relations experience and accomplishments on page one. Second page used solely to list employment, political activities, and education.

Resume: Carolyn M. Slater (pages 88-89)
Writer: Susan Guarneri
Objective: To transition from the nonprofit arena and into the corporate sector, in an executive-level management position directing market positioning, category management, and change management.

Strategy: Highlighted her executive management skills and revenue-producing accomplishments at the very beginning, followed up with detailed information on her core competencies as they relate to her objective. In Professional Experience section, began each bullet with a one- to three-word phrase showing her executive qualifications in that assignment.

Resume: Carl E. Hartwig (pages 90-92)
Writer: Susan Guarneri
Objective: To transition out of purchasing/finance/export and into a high-profile position in international business development.

Strategy: Introduced the resume with a two-line headline to clearly communicate his career direction and value, and followed with a powerful career summary showcasing his related skills. Job descriptions focus heavily on international experience, strategy and quantifiable results to position him for an easy career transition.

John Lester

567 Treetop Circle ▪ Arvada, CO 80007
Home: 303.528.1239 ▪ Mobile: 720.839.5632 ▪ jles@msn.net

TECHNICAL SALES

BUSINESS INTELLIGENCE ▪ ORACLE EXPERTISE

GROWING REVENUE AND PROFIT

INNOVATIVE SALES STRATEGIES FOR CLIENT ACQUISITION/RETENTION/PENETRATION

SALES AND BUSINESS STRENGTHS

- Identifying new business and market opportunities; developing niche and emerging markets.
- Reducing competitive threats and fostering loyalty by building strong customer relationships.
- Overcoming sales barriers/customer issues; achieving customer loyalty and repeat sales.
- Applying innovative marketing strategies to increase customer acquisition, retention, and penetration.
- Adapting to changing business requirements, market conditions, and emerging technologies.

SALES AND BUSINESS EXPERTISE

- Business Development
- Strategic Planning
- Tactical Implementations
- Marketing Strategies
- Lead Generation Activities
- Customer Acquisition/Retention
- Customer Service/Satisfaction
- Persuasive Communications
- Relationship Building
- Growth Strategies
- Operations/Administration
- Process Optimization
- Proposal Development
- Contract Negotiations

TECHNICAL STRENGTHS AND EXPERTISE

- Migrating data from legacy systems to optimize technology performance.
- Specifying/selecting/deploying technical solutions to complex organizational and operating needs.
- Inserting new technology into existing environments to increase market competition.
- Leveraging strategic alliances to expand market share and product penetration.
- Troubleshooting Oracle environments to enhance efficiency and productivity.

PROFESSIONAL EXPERIENCE

Lester Fencing, Inc., Arvada, CO   January 2002 – Present

General Manager. Established retail fencing business selling high-quality vinyl fencing to residential customers. Manage the daily operations, plan and implement marketing and sales activities, and perform all accounting tasks. Recruit, manage, and develop seasonal staff (up to four 2-man crews during the high season).

- ✓ Achieved profit within 12 months and more than tripled annual revenue in year two. Achieved $65K in sales in year one and $280K in year two of business while selling a high-end, high-priced product.
- ✓ Built relationships with suppliers to negotiate favorable pricing and establish credit in a cash-only industry.
- ✓ Selected from a field of 300 local fencing providers by Home Depot as 1 of only 3 installers in the Denver Metro Area. Built strong relationship with Universal Forest Products (strategic partner operating the Home Depot fencing programs) based on trust, service, and high-quality workmanship.
- ✓ Served as liaison between Universal Forest Products and Lester Fencing fostering a much needed, long-term supplier relationship for Universal Forest Products and Home Depot.

American Express, Denver, CO   March 2000 – August 2001

Database Administrator. Managed and administered the Internet site, *amex.com* and its transformation into a marketing tool for both new and existing clients. Ensured quick and easy access and navigation for visitors and clients through robust testing and performance tuning techniques.

71

John Lester

American Express Continued

- ✓ Initiated tracking and reporting capability, first with ad-hoc programs to meet the immediate needs for client data by the marketing department, and later in the selection of a robust application from outside vendors.
- ✓ Advised marketing department in the creation of a business case. Wrote justification for the need to capture client data and how it was more effective to purchase and modify off-the-shelf applications than to develop one in-house.
- ✓ Implemented and launched a major release of *amex.com* incorporating new login procedures, firewall changes, as well as separation of existing clients and visitors. Collaborated with strategic partners to allow clients access to data housed on partner's websites.

Accenture Consulting, Boston, MA   January 1998 – January 2000

Database/Data Warehouse Consultant, DRT Systems International. Member of a 55-person team providing Oracle consulting for the National Oracle Practice division of DRT Systems, the first technical branch of Deloitte and Touche. Served as pre-sales technical advisor to sales teams. Formulated and presented data warehousing solutions to customers.

- ✓ Assumed responsibility for an on-going sales tool project for a major automotive manufacturer. Assessed project status and determined that the project had been under-scoped and incorrectly designed and would not achieve the client's objective.
- ✓ Redesigned the sales tool and user interface using Oracle Financial Analyzer and Oracle Express, meeting the client's requirements for gross sales data including quarterly, weekly, and YTD data on products, sorted by customers, regions, and sales persons. Reports included real-time, month-over-month performance comparisons accessible at any time from laptops.
- ✓ Launched the sales tool at company headquarters, temporarily relocating there to make modifications as needed and to migrate the client database housed on an IBM system to the Oracle Express Database.

Apple Graphics, Boulder, CO   April 1994 – December 1997
Database and Applications System Administrator, Employee of the Month Award
Executive Information Systems, Englewood, CO   March 1992 – April 1994
Project Coordinator/Technical Advisor
Performance Appliances, Inc., Denver, CO   May 1987 – November 1991
Data Center/Telecommunications Supervisor, Employee of the Year, 1990

EDUCATION AND TECHNICAL TRAINING

Front Range Community College, Computer Science

- Informatica PowerCenter
- Oracle Financial Analyzer Administrator
- Application Development with Oracle Express Objects
- Oracle Backup and Recovery Workshop
- Building Oracle Sales Analyzer Database using Data Loader
- Oracle 7 Performance Tuning

- Oracle Express Database Design and Control
- Oracle 7 Database Administration
- Oracle Applications System Administration
- Fundamentals of Solaris 2.X
- Executone Accelerated Digital Products Certification

Attended Oracle OpenWorld Conferences 1997 – 2002

COMMUNITY SERVICE

Sponsor for Habitat for Humanity, Arvada Safehouse for Women, and Valley High School, donating time and fencing materials.

Emerson Van Rensselaer

41141 Mulberry Square, No 11 • Chicago, IL 60699
O: 312 380 0169 • C: 872 349 5776
evanrensselaer@twil.rr.com

MARKETING AND SALES EXECUTIVE

— Expertise in Growing Revenue and Profits in Business-to-Business Companies —

Senior executive with extensive functional experience, including P&L responsibility. Consistent record of generating growth and profits through strategic and tactical marketing, supply chain analysis, new business and product development, and sales leadership. Successful at decreasing operational costs and improving profitability of existing businesses. Demonstrated ability to build and lead teams to heightened levels of achievement. Expertise in:

- Strategic Planning and Tactical Execution
- Branding/Marketing Communications
- Team Building and Management Development

- Strategic Account Acquisition and Management
- Market Research and Analysis
- Sales and Marketing Training/Compensation

Career successes in:

Marketing • Improved the profitability of a strategic business segment 15% through implementation of manufacturing, product specification, marketing, and distribution enhancements • Generated $125 million in revenue and $27 million in profit from new product launches over three years ($40 million from Asian markets) • Reduced marketing expenses 25%; improved sales support effectiveness and product mix performance

Sales • Increased sales $65 million (30%) in first year as Senior Sales Leader • Doubled sales volume in target market the first year – eventually grew business to over $100 million in revenue • Initiated relationship and closed $50 million strategically targeted account

---

PROFESSIONAL EXPERIENCE

CARAUSTAR INDUSTRIES, INC. [1999-2005]; Atlanta, GA / Chicago, IL
$12 billion paper/paperboard, packaging, office products, and specialty chemicals company
Vice President, Marketing – Packaging Resource Group • 2002-05
Member of the executive leadership team for $2.8 billion division. Led the division's strategic planning, business development, and tactical marketing efforts. Managed a staff of 18 and reported to the Division President.

- Drove sales volume in targeted aseptic, tobacco packaging, and printing businesses up to 20% annually in year-over-year sales.

- Led strategic repositioning of the $300 million packaging segment, uncovering growth opportunities with private label and contract packagers and retailers.

- Consolidated marketing functions and activities into a cohesive, effective group; evaluated personnel skill sets and set new organizational vision.

- Built and deployed division-wide, web-based product knowledge and marketing training programs that improved marketing and sales staff efficiency and effectiveness.

- Selected to be on task force that integrated distribution channel go-to-market strategy resulting from the merger between Mead and Westvaco corporations.

Manager, Marketing • 2000-02; Atlanta, GA
Provided leadership in business development, marketing communications, and sales support, as well as commercialization of new product and service innovations. Created and implemented marketing plans for product lines, monitoring results and taking corrective actions. Initiated product improvements to meet changing marketplace/customer needs. Directed a staff of 10.

- Reduced new product development cycle times up to 50%, and generated significant new product concepts and methodology.
- Led CEO-initiated corporate branding strategy implementation, resulting in a unified repositioning of the company based on its unique core competencies.
- Developed annual and long-range growth strategies; created and managed budgets and forecasts; managed marketing communications; gathered and analyzed customer satisfaction information.

Manager – U.S. Converting & Merchant Sales; Atlanta, GA • 1999

Charged with integrating the sales, marketing, and customer service and logistics functions following acquisition of Inland Eastex by MeadWestvaco. Managed 25-member, $300 million revenue sales team.

- Reduced manufacturing and transportation cost by $20 million annually as a result of implementing efficiency-based customer and product rationalization processes.
- Increased sales volume by 15% and revenue 12% over prior year.

COLBERT PACKAGING CORPORATION [1988-1999]; Lake Forest, IL
$5 billion subsidiary of A.B. Massa Paper Company
Vice President, Sales • 1996-99

Managed 100-person, $600 million sales and marketing organization. Responsible for P&L, strategic and business planning, account development, customer service, and logistics. Reported to the Executive Vice President. Caraustar Industries acquired division.

- Created and implemented a sales compensation system that moved the organization from revenue-motivated to profit-driven.

National Sales Manager – Commercial Printing Business; Suffield, CT • 1995-96

Full P&L responsibility for new business unit focused on high-profit market targeted for aggressive growth.

- Reduced overall service and distribution costs in commercial printing segment, improving delivery lead times from two weeks to 3-5 days.

Regional Sales Manager; Suffield, CT • 1993-95

Responsible for sales activities in $60 million region, managing a sales team of five. Sold products to office products, packaging, food service, and commercial printing industries.

- Consistently exceeded aggressive sales targets/revenue goals.

Senior Account Manager; Suffield, CT • 1988-92

GREEN BAY PACKAGING INC. [1984-1987]; Green Bay, WI
$3 billion firm with interests in paper and paperboard, packaging, and specialty chemicals
Sales / Sr. Sales Representative – Bleached Board Division • 1984-87
Management Trainee • 1984

EDUCATION & PROFESSIONAL DEVELOPMENT

KELLER GRADUATE SCHOOL OF MANAGEMENT – DEVRY UNIVERSITY - Milwaukee, WI
Master of Business Administration • 1983 *(Cum Laude)* – Major: **Organization & Management**

UNIVERSITY OF WISCONSIN – GREEN BAY, College of Environmental Science & Forestry
Bachelor of Science • 1980 – Major: **Wood Products Engineering**

Various internal Management Training and Development Programs • 2000-04

Visionary Leadership & Planning – Advance Associates • 1998-99

Colbert Leadership Development Programs • 1997-98

Colbert Quality Selling Skills Programs • 1996-97

Emerson Van Rensselaer — page 2
41141 Mulberry Square, No 11 • Chicago, IL 60699
O: 312 380 0169 • C: 872 349 5776
evanrensselaer@twil.rr.com

74

DIANE LYNN WEST

352-885-7345 • dwest@email.com

1814 Fort Knox Drive • Gainesville • FL • 32606

SALES AND MANAGEMENT PROFESSIONAL

Results-oriented **Management Professional** with a proven track record for enhancing service offerings, managing profitable relationships, developing and implementing programs, improving workflow processes, and generating increased revenues. Experience reflects consistent achievements and promotions to more visible leadership positions.

PERFORMANCE OVERVIEW

Account Development and Management ... Liaised with intradepartmental teams in overseeing enrollment and retention. Increased enrollments within the College of Nursing by almost 25% in a two-year period.

Customer Relationship Management ... Built long-term, profitable relations with local and state agencies and with business and industry leaders.

Marketing and Public Relations ... Conceived the marketing campaign encompassing direct contact, career fairs, trade journal and Internet advertising, and news releases that positively impacted enrollment. Produced a 25th anniversary promotional video.

Training and Development ... Collaborated with cross-functional teams to develop traditional curriculum, and videoconferencing and web-based distance learning programs. Presenter at the annual Lilly Conference on college teaching and adjunct professor.

Multi-Site Operations Management ... Managed four locations within a 9-county area, ensuring quality staffing, training, service delivery, and standards at each facility.

Visionary Leadership ... Catalyst in reorganizing and streamlining the academic services area resulting in a fully integrated system with increased efficiency, improved responsiveness, and enhanced service to internal and external customers. Championed web-based distance learning programs. Currently developing a paperless scanning system to reduce admissions processing time and improve accessibility.

Budgeting ... Administered over $600,000 annually in financial aid and awards.

Participative Management ... Fostered employee empowerment and participative management practices throughout the organization.

Consensus Building ... Demonstrated competency in consensus building, team building, and executive liaison relationships.

PROFESSIONAL EXPERIENCE

UNIVERSITY OF FLORIDA, College of Nursing, Gainesville, Florida
Assistant Dean – since 2001
Interim Assistant Dean – 1999 to 2001
Consultant – 1998

Recruited into a part-time consulting position. Recommended by the faculty and Dean to assume interim position, and promoted to Assistant Dean 21 months later. Direct a 10-person staff in managing policies, monitoring training programs, overseeing enrollment and retention, executing strategic marketing plans, and administering $600,000 in annual financial aid applications and awards.

UNIVERSITY OF FLORIDA, Academic and Student Services, Gainesville, Florida
Assistant Dean – 1996 to 1997
Director - 1991 to 1996
Associate Director – 1989 to 1991
Acting Associate Director – 1987 to 1989

Hired as an advisor and promoted through increasingly responsible management positions. As Assistant Dean, directed the development, implementation, and administration of all Arts and Sciences, Business, and Education programs for a student population of 1,100.

EDUCATION

Ph.D., Curriculum and Instruction, University of Florida, Gainesville, Florida
M.B.A., University of Miami, Miami, Florida
M.A., Guidance and Counseling, University of Florida, Gainesville, Florida

BRUCE CLAYTON

30 N. Stockade
Farmington Hills, MI 48330
248.878.0335
bruce26@aol.com

SALES AND MARKETING PROFESSIONAL

Top-Performing Professional with 17 years of progressively responsible business experience. Combines excellent sales skills with creative ways to increase market share and develop innovative and comprehensive solutions. A proven performer and leader who thrives on new challenges. Strong track record of successful sales and account management with the ability to accomplish objectives by focusing on essential activities. Effective communicator with excellent relationship-building skills.

- Account Development & Management
- Marketing Presentations
- Financial Management
- New Business Development
- Project Management
- Strategic Sales & Marketing
- Client Consultations
- Training & Staff Development
- Contract Negotiations
- Cost Reduction

PROFESSIONAL EXPERIENCE

GREAT LAKES LANDSCAPING, Northville, MI   1992 — Present
A residential & commercial design & build landscape company with 40 employees & annual revenues of $12 million per year.

DIRECTOR OF LANDSCAPING

Handle all aspects of overseeing entire projects. This includes conferring with customers, creating designs and drawings, estimating costs, leading customer presentations, purchasing materials, planning and directing all functions and sequences of work for residential customers, bidding on projects, and managing collections. Perform site follow-up for compliance with terms and specifications of contract.

- **Increased sales one year from $441,000 to $1.2 million**, completing state-of-the-art projects.
- Won "Gold" award from the Metro Detroit Landscape Association for an outstanding residential project over $100,000.
- Published in local newspaper as leading an outstanding project that received high acclaim.
- Acquired a huge referral base, cultivating a loyal client following by delivering innovative work.
- Designed and implemented total project, from start to finish, for the Detroit Symphony.

RON'S LANDSCAPING & NURSERY, INC., Union Lake, MI   1984 — 1991
LANDSCAPE DESIGNER

Performed client consultations and handled all steps in between to transform their vision into reality. Formulated proposals, made presentations, and closed sales. Scheduled work for implementation and provided follow-up for projects lasting from one day to several weeks.

- **Increased sales 100%**, presenting clients with designs that far exceeded their expectations.
- Won various prestigious awards for outstanding landscape design of residential properties.
- Oversaw residential projects for prominent Michigan figures such as William Milliken, Max Fisher, and Geoffrey Fieger.

EDUCATION

BA, *Landscape Architecture*, MICHIGAN STATE UNIVERSITY, E. Lansing, MI
ABA, *Business Administration*, OAKLAND COMMUNITY COLLEGE, Bloomfield Hills, MI

CHERI R. PIERRE

1434 Madison Boulevard Residence:
Orlando, FL 38917

Pierre2004@aol.com

Home: 954-621-9388
Mobile: 954-859-9060

CAREER OBJECTIVE AND SUMMARY

Passionate epicure seeking to transition to a career promoting the wine and food of France. Particular experience in the regional culinary and wine traditions of France. Write and speak expressively, in both English and fluent French, about the aesthetics that emerge at the nexus of wine, food, and culture.

Competencies in writing, editing, public relations, communications, management, strategy development, and marketing. Broad range of skills honed during a fast-track, 10-year public relations/communications career at industry-leading firms in the U.S. and France. Talented evangelist for products and concepts.

- **Lived, traveled, and worked in France / Toured 50+ French vineyards / Fluent French speaker**
- **Earned a diploma at Ecole Ritz Escoffier, School of French Gastronomy, Paris, France**
- **Authored article: "From the Heart of France: The Undiscovered Culinary Traditions of Auvergne"**
- **Studied Principles of Vinification, Appellation, Winetasting, and Wine Serving**
- **Completed coursework in Food Writing, Wines of France, and Wines of Bordeaux**

Available for relocation and international travel

TRANSFERABLE SKILL SET AND SELECTED ACHIEVEMENTS

Writing — Wrote bylined magazine and newspaper articles, press releases, proposals, and presentations.

Editing — Established and maintained high standards for all written materials.

Public Relations and Communications — Achieved positive press coverage in top media in the U.S., the U.K., and France, including *The Wall Street Journal* and *The New York Times*.

Relationship Building – Gained access to and forged positive relationships with influential industry players.

Management — Coordinated and directed international teams to achieve consistent messaging.

Marketing – Strategy Development, Branding, and Promotion— Managed a multimillion-dollar corporate positioning program for Big Four accounting firm; drove image-building for a top-40 French company.

Events Management – Designed a seminar on new media attended by 300 people, including top media CEOs.

PROFESSIONAL EXPERIENCE

SanteTechnologie, Paris, France
Multibillion-dollar medical software company. One of the top 40 companies in France.

Senior Manager, International Press Relations (2000 – 2005)

Managed business and trade press relations with U.S., U.K., and English-language media in Paris. Directed international media activities. Coordinated activities of 10 North American staff. Managed PR agencies.

- Secured positive press coverage on CNN and in *The Wall Street Journal, The New York Times, International Herald Tribune, Forbes, Fortune, Financial Times, Times of London,* and trade publications.
- Introduced company to 100 key media targets including 15 top-tier business publications.
- Worked closely with the company's Secretary General and the Director of Government Affairs to achieve recognition for the company's CEO as a "player" in a global technology study group.

78

BOWDITCH PUBLIC RELATIONS WORLDWIDE, New York, NY
Rapid promotion to VP at one of the world's largest independent PR agencies with 25 offices and $170 million in revenues.

Vice President, Corporate Affairs Group (1995 – 2000)

Managed major account relationships. Worked with the Executive Vice President and agency CEO to strategize and implement new business initiatives. Liaisoned with senior executives in client organizations. Managed up to 10 direct reports. Supervised global account teams on the larger accounts. Managed crisis communications.

- Managed $3.2 million global positioning program for a Big Four accounting and consulting firm. Developed strategic initiatives including media activities, roundtables, and high-level global seminars.
- Played a key role in creating a Professional Services Group that tripled the number of clients.
- Credited by a *Wall Street Journal* reporter with rescuing a potentially damaging story about a client company by exercising skills in diplomacy, communication, and analysis.
- Instrumental in securing multimillion-dollar accounts and in developing global PR programs.

PAINE & JONES, New York, NY
One of the top 60 law firms with 250 lawyers in six international offices.

Communications Manager (1992 – 1995)

Implemented marketing and communications program. Worked with partners and all 12 practice groups.

- Created all communication materials, including brochures for 12 practice areas.
- Instrumental in organizing a major 3-day conference on energy for 200+ industry executives.

EDUCATION, AFFILIATIONS, AND SKILLS

UNIVERSITY OF CALIFORNIA AT BERKELEY: B.A. in English – Emphasis on literature and writing (1989)

ECOLE RITZ ESCOFFIER, SCHOOL OF FRENCH GASTRONOMY, PARIS, France: Diploma (2002)

Foundations of the French Culinary Tradition	*Foundations of French Wine*
- Techniques of food and pastry preparation	- Degustation
- Product selection	- Appellation
- Presentation and service	- Vinification
- History of French gastronomy	- Wine serving
- Regional culinary customs and traditions	

THE NEW SCHOOL, New York, NY
- Basics of Wine Tasting (1998)
- Wines of France (1997)
- Wines of Bordeaux (1996)

PROFESSIONAL MEMBERSHIPS
- The Culinary Guild of New England
- The French-American Chamber of Commerce
- The American Institute of Food and Wine

RICK PHILLIPS

3823 Gunther Drive • Salt Lake City, Utah 84121 • 801.548.3698 • rphillips@hotmail.com

SENIOR SALES EXECUTIVE

Business Performance Turnaround & Revitalization ♦ Market Development & Growth

Advertorial / Media Scheduling / Vertical Publications / Brand Equity / B2B / SOHO / SME

QUALIFICATIONS PROFILE

High–performance Senior Executive with extensive experience and exemplary achievements in driving under–performing media businesses into profitable organizations. Influencer, driver, and a catalyst for change, laying the foundations for the development of market–leading companies. Exceptional business, marketing and staffing leadership/management competencies, strategic planning, development and execution of performance–enhancing and revenue–growth initiatives. Expertise verified within:

- Performance & Productivity Improvement
- System/Procedure Development & Review
- Organization Restructure & Process Redesign
- Negotiations, Presentations, & Consultations
- Customer Relationship Management
- Innovative Sales & Marketing Campaigns

- New Market Identification & Penetration
- Product & Brand Awareness Advertising
- Revenue, Profit, & Market Share Growth
- Staff Leadership & Performance Enhancement
- Coaching, Communication, & Interpersonal
- Analytical & Conceptual Problem Solving

PROFESSIONAL EXPERIENCE

CORPORATE & BUSINESS PRODUCT REVIEW   1992 to Present

Largest B2B direct marketing publication building a 200,000 national distribution base, an inventory of high-profile advertisers, and a 60,000 national subscriber base.

General Manager - Sales *(National Sales Manager; 1993 to1996 /Senior Sales Representative; 1992)*

Fast–track promotion to senior role, challenged to transform struggling business experiencing staffing and revenue lows into a successful business. Quadrupled revenues to top $8.2M in annual sales through numerous strategies and solutions to optimize efficiency and increase revenue and overall profitability.

Oversee diverse staffing functions including recruitment, training, supervision, and performance of internal staff/external contractors. Assist and collaborate with Managing Director, infusing creativity and expertise to continually appraise and enhance magazine/website design and structure. Direct creation and development of sales and promotional collateral retaining dynamism, professionalism, and leading marketplace status.

- Relaunched magazine in 2001 after revitalization into a visually dynamic and reader–friendly format in response to an aggressive market research campaign. Modernized image and enhanced magazine's profile to **capture significant market and advertorial revenue growth of 72%.**

- Professionalized entire level of service, monopolizing the marketplace by offering a "complete direct marketing service" to clients, including copyrighting, advertorial design, sales lead reports, website promotions, and permission email marketing newsletters.

- Forged and maintained key customer relationships with major, multi–divisional accounts, **capturing over $1.2M revenue,** becoming and retaining position as CBPR's top salesperson throughout the company's history.

- Evaluated, architected, and executed productivity–enhancing initiatives revolutionizing under–performing sales team into outstanding media sales professionals that **secured short-term sales growth of 85%** and subsequently **generated issue revenue of $1.8M.**

Continued...

- **Slashed excessive and costly discounts totaling around 58%** of issue revenue to single figures through championing creation and execution of a strategic rate code system.

- Introduced ACT! contact management software, transforming ad-hoc and impromptu reporting functions into a highly efficient mechanism, enabling staff to strategize and implement powerful customer relationship management techniques.

- Ongoing redesign of program to meet company's specific requirements, overseeing seamless integration with other powerful software systems to facilitate evaluation across the database, continued operational planning, and delivery of customer service excellence.

- Optimized public relations between BPR and clients by facilitating successful Client Breakfast Seminars on a national scale with marketing professionals as guest speakers.

- Restructured company's entire sales procedures/methodologies encompassing reporting, corporate profile, sales/promotion collateral and presentation material, creating a consistent, dynamic, and professional branding/corporate statement.

- Transformed sales team of 22 from a group of individual and unprofessional sales representatives to a team of dynamic, highly talented media sales professionals.

- Augmented national product and brand equity through introduction of new interactive website. Initiated permission email marketing newsletter, successfully driving reader traffic by 66% to both website/magazine.

PANORAMIC PRODUCTIONS   1990 to 1992

Independent television and film production house, developing television shows/documentaries within a specialized program format for domestic and international markets.

Senior Marketing Services Manager

Multi-faceted role accountable for maximizing operational efficiency and overall income through aggressive selling of on-air promotions. Targeted the hospitality industry, while maintaining/expanding client base to encompass food/kitchen equipment manufacturers and importers. Crafted client's campaign involving written proposals, negotiations, and initial pre-production planning.

Interfaced with clients, oversaw production while directing cameramen on location during filming of clients' on-air promotions, and represented clients' interests in the studio. Mentored sales staff in strategic selling techniques to significantly boost client buy-in and overall revenues.

- Exceptional track record for prospecting new business, while maintaining strong customer relationships with existing clients. Led high-level presentations and strategic negotiations with senior executive staff and advertising/PR agencies.

- Co-developed promotional strategies that catapulted the national TV show "Anne's International Kitchen" into the marketplace.

- Intervened and overcame intricate organizational challenges due to eclectic/eleventh-hour product/formatting variations in order to mediate and preserve strong client relationships.

- Increased company's public profile by attending numerous media functions and trade shows.

- Track record for achieving outstanding sales levels. Recognized on several occasions as the best salesperson in the company's history.

EDUCATION AND PROFESSIONAL DEVELOPMENT

M.B.A. — Sales, Marketing and Finance
B.A. — Marketing and Economics
Numerous sales and in-house management courses, including:
A-Z of Advertising and Newspaper Sales • Professional Selling with Great Results • Sales Pursuit •
Gain the Edge and Beyond

Marcia Orlando

1150 E. 27th St. #5D
Miami, FL 30014

395-873-9733
morlando@gmail.com

Summary of Qualifications

- Accomplished **Corporate Communications** professional with the ability to leverage unique combination of media and marketing experience.

- 10+ years as a reporter covering hard and breaking news provides proven ability to meet deadlines and creatively combine challenging content and style for print and the Internet.

- Thorough understanding of what makes an issue newsworthy, with excellent source development, story pitching, troubleshooting, interviewing, writing, and editing skills to produce quality communications.

- Ability to create effective newsletters, press releases, and direct marketing materials.

- High proficiency in Spanish (verbal and written) and computer literacy, including research using databases and Internet resources.

- Willing to travel and relocate.

Relevant Skills and Achievements

Writing and Editing (AP Style): Process, Range, and Excerpts (full text available on request)

After writing short news items about homeless people apparently committing suicide along train tracks, I followed with a larger story. The challenge was to speak with homeless people and experts who might be able to provide insight about the tragic trend. I also developed the story for radio.

"People who saw it said he did it on purpose. Just sat right down in the middle of the tracks and stared down the engine of the northbound train as it roared up over him…. It was over fast. And Richard Lewis, 60, became the 11th person killed on tracks this year in Broward County. Of the 11, eight were homeless men or women who simply stood, sat, or lay in the path of an oncoming train."

It was Sept. 12, 2001, and the world was consumed with the attacks in New York and Washington, D.C., when it was revealed that several of the hijackers had lived and trained in South Florida. Following a hunch several days later, I was the first reporter to learn that one of the hijackers had taken private martial arts lessons at a local gym. *team reporting*

"At least six men suspected of bringing down the World Trade Center and piercing the Pentagon had been in Broward and Palm Beach county fitness clubs. Among them: Mohammed Atta, thought to have been the cell leader of the 19 known hijackers, and who roamed extensively through South Florida."

Three weeks after the attacks, an FBI source passed me the document that agents had been compiling since. It contained details of some of the hijackers' activities just prior to the attacks. As a result, I was the first reporter in the U.S. to report those details. *team reporting*

"Only two weeks before the Sept. 11 hijackings, one of the suspected terrorists purchased three poster-board replicas of the control panel of a Boeing 767 as well as handheld global positioning satellite devices…The report, not made public before, adds detail to the picture that has been emerging of the 19 suspects…And it shows how they moved from city to city, apparently making preparations for the destruction that would leave 6,000-7,000 dead."

A beautiful teacher is strangled and beaten in her home. Police suspect her husband. On 24 hours' notice, I was sent to Puerto Rico to find and interview the victim's relatives. They didn't know I was coming. At the time, I spoke very little Spanish. I got an interview with the victim's father and reported details no other media outlet had.

"The day she died, Marie Noguera called home to Puerto Rico, something she did several times a week…. 'Hey, Mom, I'm looking for you. Call me back.' Those were the last words Juan and Diana Noguera would hear from their eldest daughter."

Relationship-Building/Source Development

- Developed and maintained relationships with difficult-to-cultivate sources that allowed for thorough and accurate coverage.

- Earned the trust of many law enforcement officers and community members, based on sensitive assertiveness and reliability, resulting in strong and productive alliances.

- Teamed with reporters and media partners to produce newspaper, radio, and television reports, garnering internal awards for teamwork and coverage.

Professional Experience

Reporter 2000–2005
The Miami Herald, Miami, FL
A major metro daily paper with a daily readership of 680,000 on weekdays and more than 1 million readers on Sundays.
Covered breaking news, crime, police, and general reporting assignments, working in one of the paper's two most competitive areas, going head-to-head with competitor, as well as six television stations. Often the front line on breaking news and accountable for getting the story to radio, Internet, and into print as soon as possible, writing 2-3 daily stories. Played a strong role in helping television news partners get their stories. Beat coverage also included weekend pieces and teamwork on large breaking stories, such as the Free Trade Act of the Americas (FTAA), human cloning, Haitian immigration, and Sept. 11 terrorists living in South Florida. Was embedded with law enforcement on dangerous street coverage during the FTAA Summit in Miami in 2003.

Marketing Director 1999
Your Renewal Catalog, Charleston, SC
Managed marketing and public relations for innovative catalog start-up company, selling recovery products to cosmetic and reconstructive surgery patients. Supervised direct mail campaign. Placed national advertising and oversaw advertising budget. Wrote copy for catalog and promotional literature, including national trade and consumer advertisements, brochures, press releases, and newsletters. Organized company's debut at the American Society of Plastic Surgeons trade show, resulting in exposure to thousands of attendees and new business.

Reporter 1993–1999
Rockland Journal News, Nyack, NY (96-99)
The Westchester Gazette, White Plains, NY (93-96)
Covered breaking and ongoing news stories on the crime beat, which encompassed multiple local, state, and federal law enforcement agencies. Covered county government, economic development, criminal trials and community cultural events with stories consistently appearing on section fronts. Researched and wrote stories for weekend editions and enterprise projects. *Won first place for business reporting and a third place for enterprise reporting from the New York Press Association.*

Assistant News Producer 1990–1992
Federal News Radio, Washington, DC
Produced studio recordings of news and features. Covered hearings and conferences on Capitol Hill and the National Press Club. *Won an award for Outstanding Newsroom Performance during the Gulf War.*

Education

Bachelor of Arts, English (Minor in Spanish) 1990
Georgetown University, Washington, DC

Ongoing Professional Development:
- Member, Public Relations Society of America — Present
- HTML and Basic Web Design — 2004
- Designated Victim Advocate Practitioner, Certified by the Florida Attorney General's Office — 2004
- **Six-Month Sabbatical in Mexico and Guatemala to study Spanish** — 2003

JED CONLEY

300 Fairgrove Ave
Seattle, WA 98900

Phone: 555.466.0000
conley88@yahoo.com

PUBLIC RELATIONS AND MARKETING PROFESSIONAL

Excellent communication skills, including oral, written, persuasive, and presentation ~ **Hi**story of effective interaction and relationship building with management, peers and the general public ~ **A**n out-of-the-box thinker with strong analytical and critical-thinking skills ~ **I**ndependent worker and team player, highly motivated and strongly committed to excellence ~ **B**uilds business relationships through performance and credibility ~ **E**stablishes priorities and manages multiple simultaneous projects ~ **T**rains and mentors others

Strengths include:

Creative market planning and execution...ability to envision innovative and effective sales and marketing programs...develops strategies and follows through on all details to ensure successful implementation.

Public Relations...created and executed successful plans for community involvement in order to increase company awareness, using various media channels...served as an advocate for the media, striving to build and maintain positive relationships with the public.

Sales...proficient in all stages of the sales process...proven ability to develop new business and to build and maintain positive customer relationships.

Perception...an excellent listener...talent for honing in on buyers' real motivations and needs.

PROFESSIONAL HISTORY

KNOC-TV, Seattle, WA
News Anchor/Reporter

2000 — Present

Delivers the evening news at 5:00, 6:00, and 11:00 p.m. Responsible for writing the stories, in addition to checking the accuracy of other reporters' stories.

- ➢ Improved station ratings, from poor to #1 in key demographics, in one year, due largely to community outreach and volunteer efforts (including Children's Miracle Network).
- ➢ Trusted by top management to handle the crime and court stories, making sure the facts are correct and the right people are acknowledged, in order to avoid libel suits.
- ➢ Effective in obtaining compelling news stories, getting the information accurate, and meeting tight on-air deadlines. Often must interpret and deliver news while on the air and without a script.
- ➢ Successful in getting interviews with families who have suffered a tragedy, treating them with empathy and respect.
- ➢ Voted the 2003 "Apple Valley Broadcasting Employee of the Year" by peers.

WTAG-TV, Cheyenne, WY   1999 — 2000
SPORTS DIRECTOR

Oversaw all daily sports coverage, including local games held on weekends.

➢ After one month of working there, station became the top rated station in the market.
➢ Initiated highlighting of local high school sports that led to increased ratings.

KPLT-TV, Provo, UT   1998 — 1999
SPORTS PRODUCER

Outlined and wrote sports stories for half-hour weekend sports shows.

➢ Created an award, presented on air, to outstanding local athletes to increase community outreach and visibility.
➢ Won AP award for *Best Sportscast* two years in a row.

SUN, INC., PROVO, UT   1998
SALES REPRESENTATIVE

Hired to sell computers to school districts and government agencies.

➢ Convinced decision makers at an Air Force Base to buy computer parts from Sun, becoming the first sales rep in the company to sell into the federal government.
➢ Adept at matching customers with the right computer models and packages to meet specific needs.

LIVING SCRIPTURES, Salt Lake City, UT   1994 — 1997
TELEMARKETER

Made cold calls to people via phone, persuading them to purchase videos.

➢ Sold more than $100,000 during tenure with the company because of ability to communicate well over the phone.

Previous employment: Worked on the family cattle ranch in Evanston, WY, training horses and irrigating 1,000 acres of meadow.

RELEVANT SKILLS

Public Speaking - Asked to speak at many community events.
Rodeo/Sports Announcer - Provided play-by-play commentaries at sporting events and rodeos.

EDUCATION

BS, *Broadcast Communications/Technical Sales*, UTAH STATE UNIVERSITY, Provo, UT

MARY ANNE WARNER
7822 Forester Road • Reston, Virginia 20191 • 703.716.3356 • mawarner@aol.com

GOVERNMENT RELATIONS MANAGEMENT

Effective strategist of governmental/public affairs initiatives that win legislative support, positive media recognition and favorable public awareness for manufacturing, healthcare and food-processing corporations.

Dynamic business professional, political and organizational spokesperson with proven strengths in crisis and project management.

Adept in articulate message development and delivery to address complex issues. **Possess a vast network of influential contacts** at the local, state and federal government levels.

2004 Fellow—Virginia Excellence in Public Service

RELEVANT EXPERIENCE & ACCOMPLISHMENTS

Governmental Relations / Public Affairs Management: Selected to lead a new department to combat negative perception at a global company. Creatively developed and leveraged political initiatives supporting Government Relations' goals.

- Partnered with Government Relations staff at the state level and played key role in devising comprehensive, internal communication strategies that defeated all legislative bans introduced against company.

- Turned around public perception in less than 2 years by designing and launching programs that educated all constituents and positioned company as a responsible corporate citizen. Company is now recognized as a leading corporate citizen in the environmental arena and winner of numerous awards.

- Forged strategic alliances and relationships with key groups, legislators and business leaders, as well as created grassroots lobbying campaigns that gained substantial legislative support.

- Executed initiatives that improved company's public image and effectively addressed concerns as a spokesperson for the organization at international conferences/meetings.

- Key contributor on team that innovated a highly recognized public relations coup and designed a new program that now operates as a stand-alone $1 billion program.

Community Relations Management: Planned, coordinated and implemented effective community relations and outreach programs that strengthened the image of a governmental bureau.

- Designed and educated community members countywide on vital information on the bureau's mission, services, projects and key accomplishments.

- Created programs to address fundamental concerns of senior citizens and produced informational brochures and other outreach materials to inform and promote key programs.

- Managed budget for community-relations projects and programs. Directed volunteer staff and provided training to new personnel on departmental procedures, programs and functions.

- Built relationships and served as primary contact with the media covering publicized events and cases.

Public Relations/ Marketing Communications Management: Conceived, designed and executed strategic marketing, sales, public relations and media programs for corporate clients. Project managed the development of creative promotions, advertising campaigns, product launches, special events, trade shows and collateral materials.

- Retained to assist in transitioning company's Canadian base of operations to the U.S., following financial reorganization and provided strategies for managing the U.S. Public Affairs Department.

- Designed new exhibit booth used at industry events nationwide for $100 million manufacturer that drove trade show revenues by $3 million over prior year.

- Instrumental role in winning $1 million account for the largest U.S. trade show producer. Planned and managed entire production of 13 international events, launching major product lines worldwide.

CAREER HISTORY

MAW ASSOCIATIONS, RICHMOND, VIRGINIA
Marketing & Public Relations Consultant (2003 to present)

MALLOY CORPORATION, RICHMOND, VIRGINIA
Manager, Marketing Communications & Events (1999 to 2003)

SOUTHLAND CORPORATION, RICHMOND, VIRGINIA
Public Affairs Manager (1996 to 1999)
Product Marketing & Communications Manager (1995 to 1996)

RICHMOND COUNTY STATE'S ATTORNEY'S OFFICE, RICHMOND, VIRGINIA
Community Relations Coordinator (1990 to 1995)

POLITICAL EXPERIENCE

VIRGINIA REPUBLICAN PARTY

Assistant Committee Member, Media Advisor, Caucus Judge and fundraiser for candidates in local, state and national elections.

Active member of Virginia Republican Committeewoman's Roundtable, Virginia Federation of Republican Women's Organization and Richmond County Republican Women's Organization.

COMMISSION ON THE STATUS OF WOMEN IN VIRGINIA

Appointed in a statewide selection process to serve as a commissioner on the 19-member board.

EDUCATION

UNIVERSITY OF VIRGINIA, CHARLOTTESVILLE, VIRGINIA
Master of Integrated Marketing Communications
Bachelor of Science in Education, with honors

PROFESSIONAL DEVELOPMENT

VIRGINIA EXCELLENCE IN PUBLIC SERVICE SERIES
2004 Graduate and Fellow

Awarded a fellowship for women pursuing political and government leadership roles. One of only 15 selected annually in a statewide, highly competitive process to participate in the 9-month educational program. Met with elected officials locally and in Washington D.C. Attended legislative hearings on the Hill and briefings with top White House officials, developing contacts with leaders of key governmental agencies.

Carolyn M. Slater

726 Cathedral Avenue
Nutley, NJ 07110

Home: 973-284-2692
Mobile: 973-284-0085
cjslater@comcastnet.net

EVP / EXECUTIVE DIRECTOR
Market Positioning / Category Management / Change Management

- **Creative, visionary marketing, and business development professional with MBA** – 20+ years' experience providing ROI services to business-to-business (B2B) and business-to-consumer (B2C) clients, primarily in retailing, manufacturing, trade associations, and government consulting.

- **Builder, developer, and manager** with track record of designing and leveraging ground-breaking marketing programs to drive revenues, while maximizing budgets and controlling costs. A savvy team player and leader, experienced in spearheading high-impact strategic and tactical programs to establish branding and market dominance. Seasoned trade show and conference presenter and moderator.

- **Proven analytical and organizational skills,** with expertise in market analysis and research. Author of nationally published market-research publications, including award-winning industry *Factbook,* utilized by industry executives, consultants, government officials, and Wall Street analysts.

AREAS OF EXPERTISE

- Quantitative & Qualitative Research
- RFPs & Proposal Development
- Client Relationship Management
- Competitive Market Positioning
- Corporate Market Research

- Program Development
- Category Management
- Focus Group Research
- Strategic Solutions
- Revenue Generation

- New Product/Service Launch
- Trade Show Presentations
- Team Building & Motivation
- Market Development
- Competitive Analysis

PROFESSIONAL EXPERIENCE

CONSTRUCTION INDUSTRIES ASSOCIATION (CIA) – New York, NY   1984-present
(FKA Construction Equipment & Services Association) International construction equipment trade association with 6,000 members and $7.6 million in annual revenues. Premier global construction industry association, delivering research publications, training seminars, conferences, annual trade show, lobbying, business development tools, technology standards, international trade program, and cost saving services to its members.

Director, Aftermarket Industry Development (2003-present)
Challenged to boost growing Category Management program, generate new revenues, and achieve cost reductions. Manage budgets of $500,000. Member, Strategic Planning Committee. ***Key Accomplishments:***

- **Strategic Visioning.** Built pioneering Category Management program, establishing revolutionary business process based on construction industry collaboration, rather than distrust. Secured $100,000 in industry contributions in less than six months to offset cost of program development. Collaborated with national research firm in 2003 to build first industry-distribution model forecasting sales by channel.

- **Business Development.** Attained membership growth of 150% (from 2,500 members in 1999 to 6,000+ members in 2004) by propelling Category Management and Market Research programs, with annual revenues of $520,000, to industry and media prominence, and capturing Wall Street's attention.

- **Leadership.** Select and oversee workgroups comprised of volunteer members: senior-level industry executives from companies such as Internationale Constructione, American Construction Products, and ConstructionWorld, as well as consulting firms (U.S. Auditing Group, Kline & Company, BTRG Marketing).

- **Project Management.** Stage and manage sell-out events: annual trade show Category Management Forum, annual Presidents' Forum (40 industry executives), and category management training seminars.

- **Cost Savings & Reductions.** Initiated and delivered $159,000 in cost savings over three years, reducing costs by 25% to 63% for diverse expenditures, such as equipment rental, printing, training costs, and promotional mailings, as well as by renegotiating vendor contracts.

Senior Director, Market Research (1997-2002) and
Executive Director, Foundation for Aftermarket Industry Research (1984-1998)
Promoted through progressively responsible positions (Managing Director to Director of Market Research 1984-1996) to senior management. Hired, trained and supervised four analysts. *Key Accomplishments:*

- **Program Development.** Conceptualized and developed best-in-class industry Market Research program and profit center ($240,000 annually) that identifies major market shifts, industry trends, and opportunities. Program attained status of "most important" member benefit by majority of membership. In 1999, introduced Category Management process (first-ever industry point-of-sale data-sharing initiative).

- **Market Research & Publications.** Created award-winning industry *Factbook,* with industry size and trend information for domestic and international markets, as well as 100+ consumer-driven studies, reports, and training manuals/CD-ROMs. Market segmentation research accurately predicted third-world market growth.

- **Market Analysis.** Laid foundation for national consumer products program by analyzing market potential, target audience, and key program concepts. Gained national media attention in pre-launch phase.

PREVIOUS EXPERIENCE

Business Analyst, DAVID GROGAN & ASSOCIATES (Boutique Consulting Firm) – New Paltz, NY
- **Government Contract Compliance.** Uncovered more than $1 million in non-compliance discrepancies by participants in American International Business Development's commodity marketing program.

- **Center for Commerce.** Wrote and published two in-depth case studies (still used in major universities' MBA programs) of public policy programs at Bradley Corporation and USARM. Developed pivotal marketing plan for client, which led to media campaign strategy to increase sales.

Department Manager / Assistant Buyer, MYERSON'S (Upscale Specialty Retailer) – New York, NY
- **Retail Management.** Held P&L responsibility while managing merchandise departments with $800,000 in annual sales. Doubled and tripled sales goals through on-target consultative sales training (supervised 11 sales staff), and by creating innovative merchandising and promotions programs.

EDUCATION & TRAINING

Master of Business Administration – Marketing, New York University, New York, NY
Bachelor of Science – Psychology, Carlow College, Pittsburgh, PA

Continuing Professional Development:
Advanced Category Management Training, BTRG Marketing, Atlanta, GA (2001-2004)
Focus Group Moderator Training, Garrison Group, New York, NY

Technology Summary: Windows 2003/NT, MS Office 2003 (Word, Excel, PowerPoint), MS Outlook, SPSS

MEMBERSHIPS

- International Marketing Association – past Membership Vice President
- Construction Industry Marketing Research Council – past Chairman of Statistics Committee
- Who's Who in Professional and Executive Women

TESTIMONIALS

"The Category Management program is one of the best we have at CIA and is one of the reasons the association is such a big success." – **CIA Chairman of the Board,** Board Meeting, 2004

"The association is at an all time high, the best we have ever had. We have programs we've never had before, like the Category Management program, that's helping our members in these tough times. We have every major company in the country on this committee." – **Incoming CIA Chairman of the Board,** 2004

CARL E. HARTWIG
6972 Orchard Lane, Basking Ridge, NJ 07920
(609) 683-7787 Home • (609) 683-2711 Mobile • chartwig@comcast.net

Senior Executive – International Business Development
Building Corporate Value and Increasing ROI

Results-driven management career, building top-performing U.S. and international business units. Proactive leader with 18 years' management and P&L experience spearheading complex start-up, turnaround, and high-growth cycles, as well as developing profitable business relationships. Degrees in Business Administration, Finance, and Law. Skilled in cross-cultural communications and cross-border transactions. Expertise in:

- Strategic Business Planning
- Competitive Market Positioning
- Acquisitions, Start-Ups, Mergers
- Corporate Purchasing
- Quality Improvement
- Cost Containment
- New Business Development
- Multi-Site Operations
- Staffing & Development

An experienced international liaison who protects company interests and projects a professional, mature image. Fluent in English, French, and German; familiar with Spanish. E-marketplace and e-procurement savvy (EDI, XML, Elemica). Lived in Asia, Europe, Africa, Middle East - now based in the US / NJ with Green Card.

PROFESSIONAL EXPERIENCE

CHEMCOM INC., Basking Ridge, NJ (corporate headquarters)   1986-present
Leading multi-billion dollar global chemicals manufacturer with production facilities in 29 countries. Promoted through six assignments in four countries. Key player in providing guidance and stability in acquisitions, mergers, start-ups, business-unit internationalizations, and strategic alliance scenarios.

Purchasing Director – Raw Materials, Chemcom NA, Basking Ridge, NJ (1999-present)
Chosen by Executive Committee to revitalize Purchasing and to lead transition from local-zone management to global organization. Oversee raw materials purchasing for 22 domestic sites as well as worldwide raw materials purchasing for surfactants (total $500 million). Lead team of six direct and 10 indirect reports, and manage 400 suppliers worldwide. Member of WW Raw Materials Purchasing Committee ($2 billion spend).

- Challenged to transition organization from transaction style of former management team to industrial-marketing orientation. Facilitated transformation by external and internal recruiting for entire team. Won Chemcom award "Winning Spirit" (2002, 2003) for management change initiatives and team spirit.

- Led unification and global expansion of Purchasing unit: increased NA action perimeter from $220 million to $500 million spending budget through $85 million acquisition, transfer of worldwide purchasing from Germany, and transition of domestic purchasing from Business Division to Purchasing Corporate. Absorbed acquisition made in 2001 without adding staff, achieving "quick wins" savings.

- Initiated "reverse-marketing" concepts and introduced cutting-edge database technology as viable tool for measuring savings vs. market prices, Key Value Drivers, and price forecasting.

- Spearheaded innovative e-procurement project (EDI, XML, Elemica exchange) to reduce transaction costs, and initiated increase in business negotiations through e-marketplace (e-auctions and e-trading).

- Streamlined transaction-procurement function and consolidated domestic purchasing at 22 plants from 60 purchasing agents to 20. Created Business Council to approve purchasing initiatives, savings, and resources, resolving potential tensions between shared services and business units.

- Developed and implemented new partnership-oriented global supplier-management tool focusing on common expectations for existing and future deals, and defining return-on-investment (ROI) goals. On target to decrease number of suppliers by 38% (from 400 to 250) by aggressively challenging existing contracts, re-negotiating global deals, and globalizing action plans.

- As member of Human Resource Committee, conduct 200 performance-based evaluations semi-annually for shared services, identifying high-potential employees and strategizing succession planning.

PROFESSIONAL EXPERIENCE

Business Director – Precipitated Silica, Chemcom Inc. – USA, Edison, NJ (1997-1999)
Senior Operating Executive brought in to manage start-up of $50 million production plant. Reported to VP of U.S. Division. Controlled $1 million in annual capital / plant investments. Supervised two facilities with 40 employees. Full P&L, strategic planning, operations, finance, marketing, HR, and MIS responsibility.

- Orchestrated development of three-year strategic plan, achieving consensus throughout Europe, Asia, North America, and South America on turnaround vision and implementation strategies.

- Launched aggressive reengineering of existing operations to reduce fixed costs, develop new business, raise quality, define safety standards, and build technology service.

- Developed dynamic organizational infrastructure responsive to constantly changing market as well as financial and customer demands. Invested $2 million in market-oriented application lab and conducted in-depth market analysis based on segmentation and competitor analysis.

- Recruited new marketing, industrial, and R&D staff in turnaround effort. Introduced new human resource development and sales-incentive plans, pioneering employee process ownership, team building, and participative management strategies.

- Spearheaded quality relationship management program with customers and suppliers. Signed long-term contracts ($3 million-$10 million), optimized logistics costs, and started e-procurement.

- Brought plant to full capacity operation with sales in NA and exports to Germany and Japan. Delivered revenue improvement: from minus $3 million at start-up to $1 million+ within first year. All financials managed with new management tool KVD (Key Value Drivers).

- Achieved sustainable sales growth based on new products and technology transfer from Germany. Grew from minor import business to 10% market share without price destruction.

- Realized targeted 5% annual fixed cost reduction through capacity / process management optimization and re-negotiation of allocated corporate assets. Met ROI objective of 12%.

- Developed new R&D programs, adapting and improving European technology to meet North American needs. Achieved 10% capacity increase through continuous process improvement.

Strategic Planner, Chemcom Germany, Berlin, West Germany (1994-1996)
Promoted to plan and orchestrate Chemcom's global strategic planning and business development initiatives across five continents for precipitated silica and metal organics industries.

- Created statistical models and reports of competitive market intelligence for products, potential markets, technologies, and service in $400 million feasibility analysis sales study.

- Championed corporate development initiatives including mergers, acquisitions, strategic alliances, and joint ventures. Planned and proposed strategies to expand focus throughout emerging markets worldwide, and negotiated internal / external growth investment plans.

- Fully integrated Korean joint venture, obtained corporate authorization for new facility in China and expansion in Europe, and acquired two global customer contracts which financed $80 million in proposed investment plans.

PROFESSIONAL EXPERIENCE

Export Sales Manager, SOKOGER (JV Chemcom Korea), Seoul, South Korea (1993-1994)
Chosen to manage export sales from joint venture. Given full P & L authority for two manufacturing plants with 330 employees and $90 million in annual sales. Management responsibilities included sales, marketing, and international business development.

- Organized and negotiated international takeover, and recruited and introduced new management team.

- Guided market research, market expansion, and channel development efforts throughout emerging Asian marketplace. Company subsequently became primary export production site in Asia for Chemcom.

- Established strong voice for this start-up international division within U.S. corporate headquarters.

Director, Chemcom Korea, Seoul, South Korea (1991-1993)
Senior-level management position directing strategic planning and business development for this trading company with 30 employees and $80 million in annual sales. Full P&L responsibility for controlling, reporting, investments, and sales exports to Japan and Taiwan.

- Authored 10-year strategic plan, including investment recommendations, for Chemcom in South Korea. Identified and received approval from corporate HQ for two prime acquisition candidates.

Export Area Manager - Basic Chemicals, Chemcom Germany, Berlin, West Germany (1989-1991)
Challenged to spearhead business development and basic chemicals sales in English-speaking Africa and Eastern Europe (pre- and post-Berlin Wall fall).

- Adapted Chemcom's sales and marketing management tools in countries emerging from socialized economy to free-market environment. Achieved $70 million in sales annually.

Financial Manager, Chemcom Switzerland, Bern, Switzerland (1986-1989)
Recruited to head tax control system and implement uniform group procedures in newly acquired European division. Responsible for financial control, financial and government reporting, credit management, and technology development in international subsidiary with 50 employees and $30 million in sales.

- Reassessed, restructured, and consolidated local Chemcom subsidiaries (Film, Ag, Chemical divisions), reducing legal entities from six to two core businesses.

- Introduced and implemented initial computer system as well as new management tools.

EDUCATION
Degree in Business Administration / Finance – MSTCF
University PREMIERE Berlin, West Germany (1986)

Degree in Law, University PREMIERE Berlin, West Germany (1985)
(Each degree equivalent to 4-year college degree)

PROFESSIONAL ASSOCIATIONS
Drug and Chemical Allied Trades DCAT
National Association of Purchasing Management
New Jersey Chemical Association

Willing to relocate / travel

CHAPTER 5

Best Resumes for Transitioning Into Finance, Administration, and Human Resource Careers

Building the Foundation

Transferability of skills is the foundation upon which every effective career transition resume is written. Your challenge, therefore, is to identify the skills, qualifications, experiences, and competencies you have that will be of value in your new job, career, or industry. Those skills then become the key points in your resume around which everything else is written.

To help you get started with identifying your transferable skills, review the brief listing below of *some* of the skills, qualifications, and competencies that companies and recruiters look for in candidates seeking positions in finance, administration, human resource, or related career tracks. (*Note that this is only a partial listing of the countless different skills that companies look for in qualified candidates.*)

Carefully review the keywords and keyword phrases to identify those that accurately reflect skills you possess and which are transferable into your new position. Then, be sure to incorporate those words into your resume, your cover letters, and any other career marketing documents that you create. They will capture a prospective employer's interest and open the door to interviews and opportunities.

Acquisitions & Divestitures
Asset & Liability Management
Banking
Capital & Operating Budgets
Cash Management & Optimization
Continuous Process Improvement
Corporate Administration
Debt & Equity Analysis
Employee Benefits
Financial Planning & Analysis

Financial Reporting
Organizational Development
Policy & Procedure Development
Program & Project Management
Recruitment & Retention
Performance & Profit Improvement
Risk Management
Staff Training & Development
Strategic Planning
Treasury

Sample Career Transition Resumes

Following are nine sample resumes for individuals transitioning into finance, administration, human resource, and related careers. Each of these resumes was written by a professional resume writer with extensive experience working with, writing for, and positioning individuals in career transition. Full contact information for each of these writers is in the Appendix. To understand why these resumes were written and designed the way that they were, it is critical that you read the following information, which explains the specific objective of each of these job seekers and the particular strategy that was used to prepare their resume.

Resume: Martin Sherman (page 97)
Writer: Louise Garver
Objective: To transition out of retail management and into a career in accounting/finance management.
Strategy: Crafted a strong introduction highlighting relevant skills, degrees, certifications, and capabilities. Used brief job descriptions to demonstrate functions and communicate accomplishments only related to finance, accounting, and management.

Resume: David F. Leavitt (page 98-99)
Writer: Susan Guarneri
Objective: To transition from 15+ years as a principal of his own company and a leading bankruptcy consultant into an executive-level corporate finance career.
Strategy: Showcased unique financial expertise and accomplishments in headline and summary, and followed with strong job descriptions emphasizing financial achievements and cross-functional knowledge. Included community affiliations to demonstrate executive-level "character."

Resume: Noreen Stanley (pages 100-101)
Writer: Vivian VanLier
Objective: To transition out of the small business sector and into a much larger corporation in a senior-level finance and administrative management position.
Strategy: Demonstrated outstanding cross-functional skills and contributions in a powerful summary, and then broke down her most recent achievements in her current position into two sections to demonstrate dual expertise in finance and investment management. Virtually no mention of any industry-related specifics to position her for any one of a variety of industries.

Resume: Paul Johnston (pages 102-103)
Writer: Vivian VanLier
Objective: To transition out of banking/legal career and into a top-level financial management position in any industry.

Strategy: Combination of strong career summary followed by key accomplishments section clearly minimized his positioning as a "banker" and instead communicated the message that he is a senior financial executive. Job descriptions focused on general banking and finance functions as would be related to corporate affairs.

Resume: James H. Nicholson (pages 104-105)
Writer: Diane Burns
Objective: To transition from IT/enterprise integration in the nonprofit sector into executive-level business management with a for-profit company.
Strategy: Wrote a powerful headline and summary section demonstrating his cross-functional, executive-level management competencies and highlighted recent master's degree from a prestigious university with high GPA. Job descriptions focused on management, leadership, and results.

Resume: James A. Katz (pages 106-107)
Writer: Michele Haffner
Objective: To transition out of 20-year career with a major public school system and into a senior-level administrative/business management position in the private sector.
Strategy: Highlighted business accountabilities and organizational culture transitions he orchestrated, renamed functional responsibilities to reflect private-sector counterparts, and put a strong emphasis on bottom-line achievements.

Resume: Michele R. Layman (pages 108-109)
Writer: Cindy Kraft
Objective: To transition out of academic counseling and program management and into a position in training and development within corporate human resources.
Strategy: Designed a unique summary section to introduce her career contributions as they relate to training and development, recruiting, interviewing, public speaking, program management, and more. Included third-party testimonials from colleagues verifying her capabilities.

Resume: Arlene Kahlenberg (pages 110-111)
Writer: Susan Guarneri
Objective: To transition out of 20-year administrative management career into a corporate human resource management position.
Strategy: Used headline and summary to showcase HR competencies, experience, and keywords. Began each bullet of job descriptions with a one- to three-word phrase in bold print to draw further attention to her most related skills and value.

Resume: Gerald A. Dixson (page 112)
Writer: Roberta Gamza

Objective: To transition from a career as an actuary and into a position as an employee benefits specialist.

Strategy: Focused resume on his knowledge, skill sets, and contributions as they relate to benefit and retirement plans, and downplayed irrelevant actuarial responsibilities. One-page format provides just enough information to demonstrate his strong qualifications.

MARTIN SHERMAN, C.P.A.

87 Regatta Lane		Mobile: 914.662.7835
Tarrytown, New York 95807	msherman@yahoo.com	Home: 914.618.3499

CORPORATE ACCOUNTING • PUBLIC ACCOUNTING • TAXATION

Certified Public Accountant with a Master's Degree in Accounting and Taxation and management experience.

Proven analytical and financial management skills. Critical thinker and creative problem solver with excellent planning, organizational, and supervisory strengths.

Technical skills: MS Office (Word, Excel, Access, and PowerPoint), JD Edwards, and Peachtree Accounting.

Key Competencies

General and Cost Accounting
Financial Modeling
Financial/Business Analysis
Asset and Liability • Management Cost/Benefit Analysis • Risk Assessment • Working Capital

---

CAPABILITIES – ACCOUNTING/FINANCE
Education and training provided a solid foundation in:

- Setting up balance sheets, income statements and cash flow statements in compliance with GAAP.
- Analyzing financial performance of business operations; tracking and analyzing costs; creating and implementing cost control systems to achieve corporate objectives.
- Developing and administering budgets; familiar with capital budgeting process. Versed in the different types of corporations, consolidations, and tax advantages.
- Determining valuation of business assets, stock and bond prices, depreciation schedules, and pro-forma statements. Creating capital asset pricing models and financial models.
- Calculating P/E ratios, DCF, EPS, discounted cash flow, and beta for equity security analysis.
- Devising portfolio asset allocation strategies and conducting risk assessments; developing business plans.
- Developing financial management and investment strategies for both individuals and companies.

EDUCATION

FORDHAM COLLEGE, NEW YORK, NEW YORK
M.S. in Accounting and Taxation, 2004
B.S. in Business Administration with concentration in **Finance**, 1994

Relevant Courses: Advanced Accounting, Intermediate Accounting, Managerial Accounting, Governmental Accounting, Auditing, Finance, Business Law, Cost Accounting, Tax Accounting

Certified Public Accountant – State of New York, 2003

BUSINESS MANAGEMENT EXPERIENCE

VALUE STORES, INC., New York, New York (1992 to present)
Manager (1995 to present) / **Assistant Manager** (1992 to 1995)

Promoted to manage the financial and day-to-day operations of $3 million business. Scope of responsibilities encompasses P&L management, auditing, financial records, payroll, cash management, inventory control, inventory, account reconciliation, and human resources management. <u>Accomplishments</u>:

- **Significantly improved store's financial performance, bringing it from 10% under budget to 3% above budget** within the first month as manager by:
  - Assessing and realigning employee skills with appropriate tasks/functions.
  - Improving inventory levels and product mix on sales floor.
  - Reducing turnover by recruiting, training, and developing quality candidates.
- **Boosted profits by 20% over prior year, sales by 4% annually,** and budgeted profit forecasts by 6% per year.
- **Winner of 3 Paragon Awards out of 15 managers** in the district for achieving excellence in customer service and exceeding profitability/sales targets. Tapped as mentor, developing and training 25 new store managers.

David F. Leavitt

1635 McKinley Blvd., North Bergen, NJ 07047
(201) 854-2575 Home ▪ (201) 921-7721 Mobile ▪ dleavitt@optonline.net

CORPORATE FINANCE EXECUTIVE
Debt Analysis & Restructuring / Chapter 7, 11, 13 Bankruptcy / Business Reorganization

Financial Consultant and **Court-Appointed Trustee/Receiver** with 20 years of financial and legal experience in bankruptcy proceedings, business restructuring, trust administration, operations management, and real estate development. Clients include Fortune 500 companies, law firms, accounting firms, banks, importers, restaurants, schools, contractors, developers, realtors, and nonprofit organizations. Expertise in:

✔ Strategic Business Finance Planning
✔ Real Estate Development & Management
✔ Pro Forma Analysis & Due Diligence

✔ Business/Enterprise Turnarounds
✔ Operations & Financial Analysis
✔ Investments & Development Funding

Proven financial management results, conceptualizing and implementing innovative "rescue plans" for million-dollar-plus businesses in distress (99.9% success rate). Consistently restructure and revitalize problem organizations – expert in bankruptcy codes and solving tax-related and insurance issues. Computer skills: Excel, Word, Bloomberg, Quicken, Westlaw, Lexis, Nexis, bankruptcy software, Windows OS.

Professional Experience

U.S. HARDWARE CO., St. Louis, MO (bankruptcy headquarters)   1997-present
Bankruptcy Consultant / Bankruptcy Court Representative
Consult on legal cases that often span 12-month period. Provide financial loss analysis and bankruptcy expertise, as well as data analysis, risk management, and debt restructuring skills. Assemble, sort, track, and investigate voluminous financial and legal data, and determine creative solutions for bankruptcy cases.

- Manage and track progress of complex, multi-state Chapter 7 bankruptcy proceedings in six federal courts. Serve as expert witness in Superior Court proceedings in three states. Successfully negotiated double-digit, million-dollar bankruptcy settlements favorable to U.S. Hardware.

- Administer, coordinate, and implement terms of triple-digit, million-dollar settlement between U.S. Hardware and the United States Attorney General and the Federal Trade Commission.

DAVID F. LEAVITT, LLC, North Bergen, NJ   1989-present
Principal, Reorganization Firm (Chapter 7, 11, 13)
Financial and business restructuring consultant to 15 real estate limited partnerships, two limited liabilities, and two corporations ($7 million aggregate value). Perform cash flow and forensic analysis, and review books and records (asset transfers, tax returns, state filings, bank statements, real estate deeds, stocks, etc.)

- Consulted to 17 law firms regarding Chapter 7, 11, and 13 bankruptcy proceedings ($8 million value). Collaborated in strategic financial planning, researched and wrote action plans, negotiated new loans, and served as expert witness, attending and analyzing court proceedings relevant to bankruptcy case. **Result:** All plans confirmed by court and all clients emerged from bankruptcy.

- Court-Appointed Receiver to Private School (capital assets of $3 million). Managed school under terms of court order, wrote Chapter 11 bankruptcy financing plan, developed funding, and testified in legal hearings. **Result:** Won court-approved financing plan, negotiated $600,000 bank loan, and successfully settled legal matters before Attorney General of New Jersey – client emerged from bankruptcy.

- Administered insurance claims for seven apartment buildings and one restaurant (claim value of $2.5 million). **Result:** Successfully negotiated and/or litigated with six separate insurance companies, achieving favorable settlements on behalf of client companies.

98

DAVID F. LEAVITT, LLC – continued

- Retained as financial and management consultant to 175-seat restaurant ($1.25 million annual sales) experiencing economic downturn. Devised and implemented multi-faceted business reorganization:
  - ✓ Negotiated with New Jersey Division of Taxation for re-payment of $100,000 in back taxes.
  - ✓ Raised $750,000 in private stock offering to buy stock, pay off negotiated indebtedness, and provide $100,000 in critically needed renovation capital.
  - ✓ Oversaw restaurant renovation, as well as recruiting, hiring, and training of 30 new staff, achieving restaurant re-opening on schedule and within budget.
  - ✓ Favorably negotiated forward labor and vendor contracts (valued at $600,000).

- Oversaw daily operations, while also managing dissolution of seven distressed companies (through sale or negotiated transfer). Used Chapter 11 as business reorganization tool with three business enterprises.

- Raised $3 million in private capital for business restructuring of distressed or bankrupt companies. Purchased several businesses in buy-out deals, and directed daily operations with up to 100 employees.

AMERIFUNDS LTD., North Bergen, NJ   1989-present
President / General Partner / Rental Manager
Own and operate up to 30 apartment buildings (multiple-family units), as well as two commercial buildings (condominium office suites) in New Jersey. General Partner of six Limited Partnerships.

- Rehabbed all 30 apartment buildings, overseeing $2 million budget. Serve as Rental Manager for 150 tenants and manage in-house staff of seven, as well as local carpenters' union contract. Represent firm in landlord/tenant litigation in NJ Special Civil Court. Expert in New Jersey landlord/tenant law.

- Raised $1 million in development funding and won housing assistance contracts with Section 8 housing, Bergen County Board of Social Services, Trenton Board of Social Services, Catholic Charities, Red Cross, Sheltered Homes, and Edison Crisis Ministry for 100+ families.

Previous Career: VP of Business Reorganization, Dykas Management in New York, NY (1985-1987) and Trust Officer, Estate & Trust Administration, United Bank & Trust in Eatontown, NJ (1982-1985).

Education

NEW YORK UNIVERSITY, New York, NY
Master of Arts / Juris Doctor (JD), Diplomacy / Law – anticipated Spring 2006
Courses completed in: Globalized Telecommunications, International Criminal Law, United Nations and World Politics, Cultural and Ethic Diversity, and Peace Making.

Bachelor of Science (BS), Business Administration – Stern School of Business, NYU

Continuing Professional Development: financial forecasting, debt analysis and restructuring, real estate law, banking law, and bankruptcy law. Institute for Continuing Legal Education (ICLE) courses: Advanced Strategies in Chapter 11 proceedings, Consumer Bankruptcy Practice.

Community Involvement

- ✓ Family Community Center, North Bergen, NJ – Negotiated real estate contract, raised development funding, and attained 401c3 tax-exempt status for nonprofit agency – 1996
- ✓ Recipient of Richard and Edna Bowles Fellowship (Edison Rotary Club) – 1996
- ✓ Treasurer, Edison Township Memorial Scholarship Fund (1993-1997)

NOREEN STANLEY
noreen_stanley@email.com

12345 Greenbrier Drive
New York, NY 10024

Residence (212) 849-3862
Mobile (917) 211-9083

SENIOR FINANCE & ADMINISTRATION MANAGER

Contributed Millions of Dollars to Bottom-Line Profits
Start-Up / Turnaround / High-Growth
MBA Degree

Results-oriented Senior Executive with 15+ years' progressive experience across diverse industries. Excels in strategic planning, with proven ability to identify and capitalize on opportunities to drive revenues, streamline operations, optimize working capital, and slash operating expenses. Skilled communicator and leader with reputation for forging strong business partnerships and motivating cross-functional teams to succeed in achieving company and personal business goals.

—*Core Competencies*—

Strategic Business Planning • Project Management • Cross-Functional Team Building & Leadership
IT/IS • Human Resources Affairs • Employee Benefits • Risk Management • Hiring, Training & Coaching
Negotiations • Research & Analysis • Financial & Business Modeling • Finance & Portfolio Management
Acquisitions & Divestitures • Operating Policies & Procedures • Inventory Management • JIT / MRP

EXECUTIVE PROFILE

Chief Financial Officer • 2000–Present
EAST COAST TRADERS INTERNATIONAL, LTD., Newark, NJ

Recruited to direct all operating, finance, HR, risk management, purchasing, and IT functions for $60 million manufacturer of nationally branded personal products. Report directly to President/CEO with P&L responsibility.

Corporate Finance Management

- Orchestrated strategic plan that reversed years of declining sales, generating $6 million revenue increase and 200% gain in profit contributions.
- Instituted reporting process that improved cash receipts and DSO by $1.5 million annually (200% gain).
- Improved inventory turns from 5 to 9 per year by introducing inventory purchasing controls of min/max inventory levels, JIT, cycle counting, product sales review, and monthly inventory purchase requirements.
- Streamlined and expedited month-end closing by fully automating all aspects of accounting system.
- Negotiated lease concessions that included generous tenant improvements allowance, directly impacting bottom line and offsetting future facilities expenses.

Portfolio/Investment Advisement

Advise company owner on broad range of private and public equity investments and loans; manage portfolio and track additional business holdings. Review and make recommendations regarding stock purchase agreements, options, warrants, liquidation preferences, voting rights, etc.

- Analyzed and provided recommendations pertaining to $5 million purchase agreement. Assessed shareholder positions and authored sales proceeds distribution agreement.
- Prepared and maintained promissory note documentation including security agreements and UCC-1 filings with Secretary of State.
- Conducted in-depth reviews of prospective business deals encompassing real estate, emerging technologies, financial services, lending (such as convertible debentures), and industrial businesses.

100

Chief Financial Officer • 1998–2000
ANDANTE, INC., New York, NY

Recruited to spearhead company growth and direct finance and operations functions for small chain of specialty stores. Full P&L accountability.

- Spearheaded strategic business plan and formulated financial model that drove revenues from $2 million to $9.5 million during tenure.
- Fine-tuned day-to-day operating policies and procedures, optimizing profitability.
- Instituted controls and introduced incentive system that reduced shortage from 5% to less than 1%.
- Completed negotiations for four new locations.

Vice President Finance & Operations • 1988–1998
OUTRAGEOUS INTERNATIONAL, INC., New York, NY

Promoted after two years from Controller to direct finance and operations functions for multi-million dollar cosmetics company. Planned and oversaw day-to-day operations including budgeting, risk management, manufacturing, facilities, IS/IT, human resources, etc.

- Orchestrated and managed comprehensive strategic financial operating, and manufacturing plan that took company from $1 million to $15 million in revenues.
- Fully integrated accounting and reporting processes, including sales order entry, purchasing, inventory, etc.; instituted MRP and JIT inventory management.
- Fully automated manufacturing process, capturing 20% decrease in labor costs.
- Improved cash flow and working capital, enabling company to increase credit line at favorable rates from under $500,000 to over $1 million.
- Pioneered incentive plan that improved morale and motivated sales force to achieve aggressive targets.
- Transitioned from purchasing to leasing capital equipment, conserving capital, improving balance sheet position, and reducing tax burden.

EDUCATION

MBA—New York University, New York, NY
BS—Florida State University, Tallahassee, FL

ADDITIONAL INFORMATION

Computer Skills—Windows, Microsoft Word, Excel, PowerPoint, ACT, PeopleSoft

Hobbies—Golf, Tennis, Sailing

Community Activities—Youth Soccer and Football Coach, Boys and Girls Club of America

—Available for Travel and/or Relocation—

PAUL JOHNSTON
555 Hitching Post Drive * Lancaster, CA 93534

Phone (661) 789-3625
Mobile (661) 561-8989

Office (818) 222-1906
pauljohnston@email.com

CHIEF FINANCIAL OFFICER / VICE PRESIDENT OF FINANCE

Senior Finance and Accounting executive with extensive experience building, leading, and advising companies through complex turnarounds as well as high-growth cycles. Combines expert strategic and tactical financial expertise with strong qualifications in general management, MIS, human resources management, and transaction structuring/negotiations. Key team member in structuring and negotiating complex public and private financing.

Expert Qualifications Include:

Financial Planning and Analysis / Cash Management and Optimization
Debt and Equity Management / Systems Development / Budgeting (Capital and Operating)
Cost Reduction / General Accounting / Banking and Treasury Functions
Financial Reporting (Shareholder and SEC) / Performance and Profit Improvement

---

KEY ACCOMPLISHMENTS

- Instrumental in raising $102 million in stock rights offering for major Southern California financial institution.
- Facilitated private placement of $10 million capital infusion for $25 million company.
- Key member of expense reduction taskforce reducing overhead by 25% in two-year period for $6 billion company.
- Restructured and consolidated infrastructure of $500 million company, realizing savings in excess of $250,000 per year.
- Implemented complex systems conversions, including investment accounting, budget/planning, and billing/case management software.

PROFESSIONAL EXPERIENCE

Controller * 2000–Present
ADAMS, CARSON, SWIFT & WHITE, Lancaster, CA

Recruited by independent consulting organization to join, plan, and implement financial turnaround of troubled multi-office law firm.

- Redesigned core financial processes, budgeting, cash management, treasury, banking, and long-range investment planning.
- Re-engineered financial operations and reduced staffing requirements by 25% within 18 months.
- Initiated outsourcing of accounts receivable collections management, significantly improving receivables turnover.
- Orchestrated aggressive cash management policies increasing value of pension and firm investments by over 30%.

Controller * 1997–1999
WEST COAST FINANCIAL, Santa Monica, CA

Recruited by Chief Financial Officer to re-engineer $15 million financial services company and successfully position it for acquisition.

- Directed cash management functions, installed fixed assets accounting system, and improved accuracy of financial reporting systems and asset accounting procedures.
- Developed business plans, participated in financial strategy and planning, and coordinated preparation of financial statements and liquidity analysis.
- Created timelines, labor allocation resource management, and weekly status reports for new operating segment of company.
- Improved physical inventory controls.

Sr. Vice President/Controller * 1985–1996
PACIFIC NATIONAL BANK, Beverly Hills, CA

Achieved fast-track promotions through positions of increasing challenge and responsibility for highly respected community bank serving high net worth individuals and business clientele.

- Key player in successful stock rights offering, raising $102 million in new capital.
- Implemented complex system conversions, including investment accounting and budgeting/planning.
- Created and implemented budgeting and forecasting reports, consolidated unit budgets into divisional/corporate budgets, and provided management with estimates of future impact of business decisions.
- Coordinated effectively with executive management, branch, department, and division managers, audit committees, outside auditors, and corporate counsel.
- Led numerous special projects, collaborating with cross-departmental/cross-functional teams, that introduced new products, elevated customer care, and generated significant gains in niche market penetration.

EDUCATION AND PROFESSIONAL DEVELOPMENT

UNIVERSITY OF CALIFORNIA AT LOS ANGELES
Bachelor of Arts Degree in History

Additional post-graduate studies include Accounting, Finance, Statistics, Taxation, Organization Behavior, Economics, Project Management, Business Law, and Marketing at UCLA Graduate School of Management and Loyola Marymount University

COMPUTER SKILLS

Windows, Lotus 1-2-3, Microsoft Excel, Microsoft Word, Peachtree Accounting, MAS 90, Great Plains, Quick Books Pro, TimeSlips, TimeMatters, and Microsoft Projects. E-mail and Internet proficient.

COMMUNITY AND PROFESSIONAL AFFILIATIONS

Volunteer—Boys and Girls Club of America, Special Olympics
Member—Rotary International, High Desert Professional Association

6070 Constantine Road
Anaheim Hills, CA 92807

JAMES H. NICHOLSON

714-998-4509 (h)
jameshnich@verizon.net

CAREER FOCUS

EXECUTIVE-LEVEL MANAGEMENT / BUSINESS STRATEGIST
Corporate Financial Services Operations and Solutions

PROFESSIONAL AND PERSONAL VALUE OFFERED

Management Professional and Respected Authority / Consultant with uncommon combined expertise in
Financial Planning · SEC Reporting · Business Acumen · GAAP, FAR, & CAS Regulations · Customer Relations
· IPO Preparation · Venture Capital Acquisitions · Program Management for Large-Scale ERP Implementations ·
Software and Infrastructure Development · Analysis · Budgeting Acquisitions · Divestitures ·
Treasury and Internal Information Functions · Corporate Financial Reporting

- Optimize investments with effective business, financial, and IT operational solutions to deliver cost-efficient and heightened productivity. Develop, establish, and implement financial infrastructures including corporate disaster recovery plans and programs.

- Skilled financial analyst, processes planner, and technical expert — provide functional guidance on multifaceted projects for fast-paced services companies, federal government contracts, and associated commercial operations in multi-location, multi-state, and international environments. Effectively manage six or more simultaneous projects worth up to $12 million each, with up to 45 personnel per team.

- Conduct advanced systematic reviews to formulate and execute business strategies, reducing risk and enhancing customer satisfaction. Recognized by customers as a Financial System Implementation and Integration Expert. Maintain knowledge of current and emerging technologies.

- Report to steering committees and clients. Excellent interpersonal skills. Comfortable public speaker.

- Build talented teams, promote consensus, and establish a working environment conducive to optimum production. Determine manpower and resources needs, serve as a hiring official, enforce EEO procedures, and foster a diverse workforce. Supervise direct-report operational division managers during projects.

EDUCATION AND PROFESSIONAL DEVELOPMENT

Master of Science in Management (GPA: 3.85), University of Southern California (USC), 2004
Bachelor of Science in Business Administration, California State University (Fullerton), 1993
Certified Public Accountant, 2001
Professional IT Development Training and Financial Applications Training (Oracle and Microsoft.Net)

PROFESSIONAL EXPERIENCE

Gamzon Systems, Irvine, CA   07/2000 — Present
Manager of Financial Applications   07/2001 — present
* Gamzon is a nonprofit organization with 1,240 employees, serving the public interest consulting to federal, state, and local entities with mainframe systems, regarding IT asset procurement, IT Architectures, Biometrics, Chemical Demilitarization, and Biological Warfare. Manage and consult on diverse IT projects for external clients and internal implementations:

Representative Projects

- Project Manager for up to $26 million in capital investments for delivery and deployment of a data warehouse and a contracts module. Project completion is slated in three phases during three years.

- Developed a five-year plan to integrate the organizational enterprise application systems (architecture of hardware, software, web development, and network upgrades), providing the best technology advancement path for the organization.

Projects Continued…

- ❏ Project Manager: Oracle Financial Application Upgrade from release 10.7 to 11i. Captured project costs according to regulations for the capitalization of software development projects. Completed the upgrade three months ahead of schedule and more than $700,000 under budget. Oracle financial modules included G/L, project accounting, F/A, A/P, A/R, procurement, and contracts.

- ❏ Directed the conversion of the Oracle database software from Oracle version 7.3.4 to Oracle 8i. Successfully mitigated a required change of server configurations from Sequent servers over to Sun Solaris server platforms for the entire corporate financial system enterprise.

- ❏ Coordinated with operational departments during implementation of a storage area network solution (SANS) to increase and enhance financial system storage capabilities.

- ❏ Installed and configured Oracle migration and development tools including PVCS Tracker and Professional, Chain Link migration software, Oracle OEM, configuration management tools, Oracle Web DB, Oracle Developer 2000, and Oracle Applications Desktop Integrator.

- ❏ Analyzed, for government customers, financial system implementation program plans and budgets, and reported findings and recommendations directly to each organization's VP of IT.

- ❏ Currently working on development and prototyping activities for various Biometric device and database implementations for federal security implementation.

Accounting Manager and Financial Systems   07/2000 — 07/2001

- ❏ Managed and streamlined corporate project accounting, A/P, and payroll departments.

- ❏ Directed a full life-cycle upgrade and implementation of Oracle Financials (Character version 9.4 to 10.7 Smart client), CSTAR, and Jamis Systems to address Y2K compliance issues. Managed a $4 million project budget and team functions for 30 documenters, testers, system engineers, and software trainers.

- ❏ Managed a Quality Assurance Review for a PeopleSoft upgrade and rollout procedures.

- ❏ Reported bi-weekly to corporate officer steering committees and coordinated rollouts for all of the projects.

- ❏ Promoted after one year to Manager of Financial Applications.

Concept Seven Systems, Inc., Pomona, CA   03/1998 — 07/2000
Director of Finance

- ❏ Recruited from Imaging Ink to establish the financial and IT infrastructure for Concept Seven to pursue venture capital and become IPO. Managed the corporate merger and acquisition.

- ❏ Thoroughly experienced in all phases of the full life-cycle of developing and implementing advanced software systems solutions, working within a wide range of development, supporting company-wide systems, client-server environments, and application domains.

- ❏ Hired to manage all corporate budgeting functions, due diligence, daily financial needs, cash management, and investor relations. Established corporate accounting in-house using Perl IV software and internally developed server configurations including Perl IV modules for G/L, project accounting, F/A, A/P, A/R, procurement, asset tracking, and a payroll interface.

- ❏ Developed a WAN to support fiscal and infrastructure reporting requirements. Analyzed and developed a corporate-wide timekeeping system that directly interfaced with developed accounting applications.

- ❏ Interim Director of Accounting: Managed the hiring and establishment of a 10-person accounting and finance group. Managed corporate treasury needs, risk assessment, and preliminary accounting development for a corporate IPO.

Accounting Manager, Imaging Ink, Orange, CA, 03/1996 — 03/1998
Controller, Linko Systems, Huntington Beach, CA, 02/1994 — 03/1996

JAMES A. KATZ

163 Kingsbury Street
Chicago, Illinois 60610

jamesakatz@yahoo.com

Home: (312) 273-4786
Mobile: (312) 878-5485

PROFILE

Senior-level executive with a 20-year track record of successful organizational leadership and performance-based program management, transitioning into private-sector employment. Proven ability to manage large, diverse organizations and lead the financial/business planning process, providing strategic direction and detailed metrics/analysis to support business decisions. Master of Business Administration degree; completing Master of Science degree (Human Resources – May 2005).

Visionary and dynamic with experience leading staff through complex organizational and technological transitions. Highly effective planning, organizational, and communication skills. Demonstrated ability to motivate employees (at all levels), instill a common vision, and develop productive teams.

Core competencies/areas of expertise include

- Strategic & Tactical Business Planning
- Budgeting, Planning, & Forecasting
- Continuous Process Improvement
- Total Quality Management

- Procurement & Strategic Sourcing
- Performance-Based Contracting
- Labor Relations & Practices
- Community & Public Relations

PROFESSIONAL EXPERIENCE

CHICAGO PUBLIC SCHOOLS – Chicago, Illinois   1985 to Present
The largest school district in the state of Illinois with 539 schools serving over 200,000 pre-kindergarten through 12th-grade students.

DIRECTOR OF BUSINESS SERVICES (1999 to Present)
Oversee district-wide business administration and operations services including Purchasing/Procurement, Facilities Maintenance, Food Services, Transportation Services, and Technology. Full profit and loss accountability for a $325+ million annual budget (representing 12% of total district budget). Position reports to the Chief Operations Officer with authority for a staff of 1,500 with eight bargaining units.
DIRECTOR OF PARENT AND STUDENT SERVICES (1992 to 1999)
DIRECTOR OF PUPIL TRANSPORTATION (1987 to 1992)

Cross-Functional Accomplishments
- Led the CPS 12-person executive leadership team through the strategic planning process and execution of district initiatives. Assumed responsibility for district policy and compliance with federal, state, and local regulations. Restructured operations to align with district decentralization efforts and achieve a business enterprise orientation/culture.
- Expedited the design and implementation of the CPS Strategic Technology Plan to deliver voice, video, and data communications to 14,800 classrooms. Leveraged school funds by obtaining governmental and private grants totaling $60 million annually.
- Marketed business services to outside school districts and nonprofit agencies; increased revenues by $2.1 million.

Purchasing/Procurement, Warehousing, and Logistics
- Integrated strategic sourcing into the transaction-oriented process. Ensured high customer satisfaction while delivering low cost of ownership as benchmarked against purchasing groups ($46 million annual goods and services purchasing volume).

Continued

CHICAGO PUBLIC SCHOOLS

Purchasing/Procurement, Warehousing, and Logistics (continued)
- Develop and negotiate major contracts in compliance with competitive restrictions, contractor ratings, terms, conditions, and performance metrics to ensure achievement of expected outcomes.

Facilities and New Construction
- Manage the maintenance, repair, environmental control, regulatory compliance, leasing, and new-construction activities for 378 facilities and recreation sites.
- Managed the development and passage of a $198.4 million school building initiative to add 11,000 classroom seats over a five-year period. Employed an extensive community outreach effort to obtain legislative and community approval.
- Developed systematic, fact-based deferred maintenance program (70% of facilities were built prior to 1930). Received recognition as having one of the best school district physical plants in the United States.

Food Services
- Manage the preparation of more than 250,000 meals per year. Ensure compliance with health/safety regulations, as well as federal funding programs.
- Instituted focus group taste testing to remain current with changing tastes and cultural diversity. Implemented ala carte meal programs in the middle- and high-school grades to provide additional revenues.

Transportation Services
- Initiated performance-based transportation service contracts resulting in $11.8 million in cost savings and a 66% reduction in accidents since 2002.

Marketing and Public Relations
- Developed full marketing campaign for school choice program utilizing direct mail and public service announcements. Completed within a limited budget.

SB TRANSPORTATION CORPORATION – Canton, Ohio   1976 to 1985
Purchased by Circle Software Group in 1996. A leader in transportation software technology, SB Transportation was the first company to develop map-based redistricting and bus-routing solutions for the school bus transportation industry.

ACCOUNT EXECUTIVE
- Managed 30 key accounts nationwide; assigned the most critical clients. Authority included customer relationship management and full lifecycle project management: needs analysis, budget/timeline development, installation, testing, and customer support.
- Achieved a 90+% account renewal rate.

EDUCATION

MS (HUMAN RESOURCES), NORTHWESTERN UNIVERSITY – Evanston, Illinois   May 2005
MBA, NORTHWESTERN UNIVERSITY – Evanston, Illinois   1989
BA, OHIO STATE UNIVERSITY – Cleveland, Ohio   1976

PROFESSIONAL AFFILIATIONS

The Council of Great City Schools
Society for Human Resource Management

MICHELE R. LAYMAN

713–330–3338
mlayman@email.com
19 Plantation Oaks Dr., Houston, TX 77003

HUMAN RESOURCES PROFESSIONAL
Training and Development …Recruiting and Retention … Mediation

Reba Garth, Director of Student Support Services

"Her organization skills and recordkeeping are superb."

Michael Tooke, Assistant Director, USF Career Center

"Not only does she motivate and encourage her charges, she goes a step beyond and empowers them with the confidence, skills, and knowledge of policies and procedures that result in a success story."

Mack Davis, Program Director

"Among Michele's most favorable attributes is her ability to anticipate and offer solutions to potential problems. Through open and honest discussion, she presents her ideas and suggestions in a manner that is thoughtful and reflective."

Sylvia Salter, Director Academic Advising

"She quickly became a competent facilitator, adroitly coordinating the complex, sensitive issues …."

CONTRIBUTIONS

Chaired the 6–person search committee tasked with **recruiting, interviewing, and recommending the candidate** to fill the Student Affairs Coordinator position.

Selected to serve on the Student Affairs Faculty Market Equity Committee developing a formula for the distribution of salary equity funds. **Personally tasked with acquiring data related to distance from market (DFM).** The formula on DFM, Longevity, and Performance/Merit was **accepted and implemented by the Provost.**

Coordinated the themed Annual Awards and Scholarship Banquet fundraising event, **raising $160,000+ in scholarship funds (more than twice the prior year's amount).**

Served as the Department Representative for the Texas State Employees' Charitable Campaign. Directed advertising and solicitation activities, distribution and collection of pledge cards, and reporting functions. **Achieved a 100% participation rate with a 45% increase in contributions.**

Revitalized a program falling short of the Department of Education (DE) performance objectives and jeopardizing financial aid and grant money. **Improved the percentage of students in good standing at the end of the academic year from 73% to 90% within a 3–year period.**

Halted spiraling retention rates by providing structure, resources, and educational seminars. **Reduced the 2002 dropout rate of 50 to 16 in 2003, and averaged a 51% graduation** rate versus the DE-approved performance objective of 15%.

PROFESSIONAL EXPERIENCE

UNIVERSITY OF TEXAS, Houston, Texas
(Multi–campus national research university)

Counselor/Advisor and Instructor *(Student Support Services)* – current
(SSS is a federally funded retention program supporting 220+ students annually; $283,730 annual operating budget.)

Graduate Counselor/Advisor *(Personal Excellence Program)* – 1997 to 1998

Selected to provide academic advising and monitoring, individual and group counseling, seminars, social and cultural enrichment programs, and activities to broaden career perspectives.

- Recruited, hired, trained, and supervised six peer counselors for the Summer Peer Counselor Program.

- Developed the highly successful recruitment program brochure and newsletter.
- Created the "Leadership Development Series" workshop that included topics on self–development, understanding self, group behavior, organizational design, ethics, and teamwork.
- Conducted leadership training and teambuilding activities for SSS Club members.

Norma Cano, Counselor / Advisor SSS Program

"She shares her sense of humor with all of us and keeps our office free of the particles that could contribute to bad feelings with anyone."

DOMESTIC SHELTER OF GREATER HOUSTON, Houston, Texas
(Texas's largest certified domestic violence shelter)

Children's Program Specialist – 1994 to 1996

Hired to develop domestic violence intervention curriculum with an emphasis on violence prevention, anger management, conflict resolution, and safety.

- Created and presented domestic violence intervention curriculum to over 900 inner-city children.
- Speaker at the National Association for the Education of Young Children Annual Conference.
- Trainer and facilitator for 20+ domestic violence prevention and intervention workshops.

Marie Austin, Coordinator

"Michele is always willing to take the time to fully understand the needs and context of a person, assignment, or problem, subsequently matching the appropriate action with the situation."

UAHC CAMP CHRISTINA, Chattanooga, Tennessee
(Summer live–away camp for children ages 6–10)

Unit Head – 1993 to 1994

Oversaw a 30–person staff in developing and executing programs and activities targeting child development, stress management, and peer relations.

- Recruited, hired, trained, and supervised 30 counselors; created and directed staff orientation.
- Introduced ropes course training to build trust, communication, leadership skills, and teamwork that lead to increased productivity.

Shalandria Wright, SSS Program Assistant

"Her teamwork approach along with her passion for education allows her to be an excellent role model for our students."

EDUCATION AND TRAINING

University of Texas, Dallas, Texas
Master of Arts – College of Education, Counselor Education – 1998
Bachelor of Arts – 1994

Leadership Development for Supervisors – Leading by Choice
Team Building and Staff Development
Anger Management / Conflict Resolution

COMMUNITY AFFILIATIONS

Co–Facilitator, Teen Support Group – Houston AIDS Network
Counselor, Child Life Unit – Shriner's Hospital for Children

Arlene Kahlenberg

299 Wesley Road, Souderton, PA 18964
(215) 660-2811 Home ▪ akahlenberg@newfrontier.net

Human Resources Manager / Human Resources Generalist

Dual-degreed human resources professional with 13 years of HR management experience in administration, recruiting, hiring, training and development, benefits administration, employee relations, compensation, performance appraisals, and downsizing. Master's degrees in Counseling and Criminal Justice. Expertise in:

✓ Wage & Salary Administration	✓ HR Project Management	✓ HRIS Conversion
✓ Management & Staff Development	✓ Organizational Development	✓ Hiring & Staffing
✓ Performance Management Process	✓ Strategic HR Management	✓ Personnel Policies

Senior court manager / administrative manager with leadership in complex multi-branch, multi-level government environments. A savvy team leader and proactive decision maker, skilled in building and sustaining cooperative working relationships for productivity and change management initiatives. Strong needs assessment, group presentation, and platform communications foundation. Experienced in transitioning to updated HRIS programs.

PROFESSIONAL EXPERIENCE

PENN COUNTY VICINAGE, Philadelphia, PA   1999–2005
Court Executive
Managed 60 Probation staff in 2 locations, supervising 6,000 cases and collecting $793,000 annually. Liaison with judicial / non-judicial agencies as well as national, state, and community organizations, including unions.

- **HR Management.** Instituted and led first management team in Penn County Probation Adult Supervision Division. Introduced bi-weekly staff strategy sessions to increase productivity, as well as communications, coaching, motivation, and planning skills. Mentored and coached staff, establishing goals and objectives, and provided guidance and direction. New performance appraisal process launched at this time.

- **Training and Development.** Established training and development programs that aligned strategic leadership, staffing, training, and performance management processes to ensure highest competency levels and uniform performance standards. Led new hire orientations, assessment, curriculum design, lesson plan development, and training for state and local vicinage staff – many training programs adopted statewide.

- **Presentations.** Created, wrote, and presented training modules for entry-level Probation training programs, co-training select modules with Labor Relations managers and attorney. Updated and delivered interactive training sessions on managing diversity, sexual harassment, and performance appraisals for managers and supervisors. Presented "Performance Appraisal" workshops at national and state conferences.

- **Administration.** Created and implemented strategic plan for Adult Supervision operations, as well as contributed key components in Probation Division and Penn County Courts Strategic Management Plan. Oversaw staff supervision, disciplinary, and recognition activities using CAPS automated supervision system. Directed development and implementation of workload and performance standards.

- **Project Management.** Spearheaded mission-critical change management projects, such as introduction of statewide-automated tracking and accounting system which increased efficiency and results. Initiated strategic operating procedures and policies to increase compliance with court orders, as well as maximize resources. Updated performance appraisal standards for supervisory, probation, and clerical staff.

- **Revenue Enhancement.** Researched court collections process and wrote court collections guidelines which were implemented in Penn County Vicinage. Resulted in increase in court collections in Penn County Probation from 17% below goal in 1999 to 18% above goal in 2000 and 24% above goal in 2001.

ADMINISTRATIVE OFFICE OF PA COURTS (AOC), Philadelphia, PA   1996–1999
Administrator IV – Probation Supervision Services

- **Training and Development.** Created and delivered group and one-on-one staff and management training presentations, including specialized computer training and new hire orientations. Coordinated Curriculum Development Group and actively participated on statewide and regional training advisory councils.

- **New Training Initiatives.** Introduced diverse new training programs for Probation staff, as well as management, including topics on Ethics, Legal Issues in Violation of Probation, Managing Diversity, Sexual Harassment, Improving Court Collections, Time Management, and Performance Management.

- **Performance Appraisal Development.** As member of AOC Judicial Training Advisory Council, developed Performance Appraisal training components to introduce new Human Resources system (Performance Management Process) in Pennsylvania. Conducted well-received trainings statewide 1800+ participants.

- **Operations Improvement.** Conceptualized, developed, introduced statewide, and monitored Probation Division's "Best Practices" including "Violation of Probation Standards, Guidelines and Formats" and "Curriculum Design for Supervision Training", improving court operations, uniformity, and results.

WESTMORELAND VICINAGE, Pittsburgh, PA   1984 –1996
Supervising Probation Officer (1991–1996)
Principal Probation Officer II (1990 – 1991), **Senior Probation Officer** (1984 – 1990)
Provided administrative management for Probation Division in largest PA vicinage (360 staff) with caseloads of 81,000 and annual collections of $58 million for Adult Supervision and Child Support programs.

- **Administration.** Oversaw training and staff development, human resources, budget, policy development and writing, annual reports, statistics, automated and manual record keeping, attendance, purchasing, research, annual report publication, and college internship program.

- **Employee Relations.** Conducted performance reviews and salary administration for union and non-union employees. Managed employee relations in policy enforcement, disciplinary action, retraining, and exit interviews. Facilitated employee communications, utilizing process improvement analysis and coaching, contributing to employee retention and team building.

- **Operations Improvements.** Increased efficiency by creating inter-divisional workflow tracking system, expanding collaboration and reducing delays. Receiving documents intake sped up by 200%.

EDUCATION
M.A., Criminal Justice, Pennsylvania State University, Philadelphia, PA
M.A., Counseling (Focus: Drug & Alcohol Studies), Rutgers University, New Brunswick, NJ
B.A., Psychology, Thomas Edison State College, Trenton, NJ

PROFESSIONAL CERTIFICATIONS
Criminal Justice Counselor, Addiction Professionals Certification Board of Pennsylvania – December 2001
Certified Fellow of Court Management Professionals, National Center for State Courts – May 2000

GOVERNMENT APPOINTMENTS
Pennsylvania Diabetes Council, State of Pennsylvania Executive Appointment (January 2002-present)
Local Advisory Committee on Drugs and Alcohol, Westmoreland Co. Executive Appointment (1990-1996)
Westmoreland Juvenile Conference Committee, Westmoreland Co. Executive Appointment (1977-1988)

Gerald A. Dixson

567 S. Dublin Street, Centennial, CO 80015
303.555.1234   gadixson@mymail.com

EMPLOYEE BENEFITS SPECIALIST

** High-Impact/Cost-Effective Benefits Plans with Improved Return on Investment **
** Aligning Benefits Strategies with Business and Financial Objectives **

An innovative and critical thinker capable of serving as a catalyst for breakthrough benefits strategies and programs that contribute to revenue and profit objectives while improving employee satisfaction. Accurately performs challenging tasks with precision and attention to detail. Excels at organizing and setting up new procedures, troubleshooting, and reversing adverse situations. Impeccable ethics and integrity. Willing to roll up his sleeves and work relentlessly when duty calls.

EXPERTISE / KNOWLEDGE / ABILITIES

- Market Research/Intelligence
- Issue Identification/Resolution
- Data Management
- Pension Plans
- Executive Compensation

- Tax Code Implications
- Regulatory Compliance
- Vendor Relations
- Health and Welfare
- Pay-For-Performance

- HIPAA Regulations
- ERISA
- Individual/Group Insurance
- Personal Financial Planning
- Economic Analysis

Proficient with Microsoft Office applications, Microsoft Access, project management software, and pension administration software.

Able to impact the bottom line by:

- Developing strategies and implementing new programs using project management methodologies to reduce overall benefit expenses and increase employee appreciation.
- Improving reporting information to participants with new/enhanced record-keeping processes.
- Ensuring accurate enrollment of plan participants, billing, and legal compliance.
- Renegotiating existing contracts and finding new, more competitive providers.

PROFESSIONAL EXPERIENCE / EMPLOYMENT HISTORY

Applied a combination of analytical skills, business knowledge, and understanding of human behavior to design and manage programs that controlled risk. Evaluated the likelihood of future events and designed creative ways to reduce the likelihood of or decrease the impact of undesirable events.

Administered over 70 different pension plans, managing and reviewing them for regulatory compliance, accurate valuations, data integrity, and forecasting precision. Identified and eliminated gaps in client services and ascertained need for additional services. Performed certified actuarial work.

Actuary, Power Pension Group, Denver, CO	January 2004 – August 2005
Certified Retirement Plan Services	January 1998 – November 2003
Consulting Actuary, Englewood, CO	
Senior Plan Administrator, Milwaukee, WI	
Assistant Actuary, Robert F. Burge, ASA, Orlando, FL	August 1995 – January 1998
Actuarial Assistant, Wiggins Watson Worldwide, Orlando, FL	January 1989 – June 1995

PROFESSIONAL DESIGNATIONS AND AFFILIATIONS

CEBS and Fellow, International Society of Employee Benefit Specialists
Enrolled Actuary, 2001
Member, American Academy of Actuaries
Member, American Society of Pension Actuaries

EDUCATION

M.S.   **Economics**, Michigan State University, East Lansing, MI
B.S.   **Biology**, North Carolina State University, Raleigh, NC

CHAPTER 6

Best Resumes for Transitioning Into C-Level Positions and Opportunities

Building the Foundation

Transferability of skills is the foundation upon which every effective career transition resume is written. Your challenge, therefore, is to identify the skills, qualifications, experiences, and competencies you have that will be of value in your new job, career, or industry. Those skills then become the key points in your resume around which everything else is written.

To help you get started with identifying your transferable skills, review the brief listing below of *some* of the skills, qualifications, and competencies that companies and recruiters look for in candidates seeking C-level positions and opportunities. *(Note that this is only a partial listing of the countless different skills that companies look for in qualified candidates.)*

Carefully review the keywords and keyword phrases to identify those that accurately reflect skills you possess and which are transferable into your new position. Then, be sure to incorporate those words into your resume, your cover letters, and any other career marketing documents that you create. They will capture a prospective employer's interest and open the door to interviews and opportunities.

Acquisitions & Divestitures	Joint Ventures
Board of Directors Affairs	New Business Development
Business Transformation	Operating Management
Change Management	Organizational Development
Competitive Market Intelligence	Organizational Leadership
Emerging Ventures	Profit & Loss Management
Executive Liaison Affairs	Risk Management
General Management	Strategic Alliances
Global Market Expansion	Strategic Planning
Intellectual Property	Turnarounds & Revitalizations

Sample Career Transition Resumes

Following are eight sample resumes for individuals transitioning into C-level positions and opportunities. Each of these resumes was written by a professional resume writer with extensive experience working with, writing for, and positioning individuals in career transition. Full contact information for each of these writers is in the Appendix. To understand why these resumes were written and designed the way that they were, it is critical that you read the following information, which explains the specific objective of each of these job seekers and the particular strategy that was used to prepare their resume.

Resume:	Marcus Winston (pages 117-118)
Writer:	Beverly Harvey
Objective:	To transition from a senior VP position in the electronics industry into a C-level position with a Fortune 100 corporation.
Strategy:	Developed executive profile highlighting the breadth and depth of his executive-level qualifications, his UCLA MBA degree, and his fluency in several languages. To emphasize his candidacy for a C-level position, grouped his job titles together, segmented his accomplishments by C-level competencies, and added subheadings to emphasis his accomplishments in each competency.

Resume:	James Andrews (pages 119-120)
Writer:	Diane Burns
Objective:	To transition from his career in nonprofit association marketing into a C-level position in general management, operations management, and/or organizational leadership.
Strategy:	Highlighted recent MBA degree and achievements on various boards of directors and his 18-month assignment as an Interim COO. Created perception of a well-rounded, executive-level skill set by emphasizing dual expertise in business operations and marketing leadership.

Resume:	Earl S. Rossman (pages 121-123)
Writer:	Susan Guarneri
Objective:	To transition from successful sales and marketing management career into a CEO or other high-level executive management position.
Strategy:	Started with strong headline to clearly communicate objectives and value; followed with comprehensive summary highlighting core executive qualifications. Job descriptions focus on impressive accomplishments (including graphic representation) in business development, leadership and process improvements, sales/marketing, and technology.

Resume:	Erik Lierson (pages 124-125)
Writer:	Vivian VanLier

Objective: To transition out of the apparel industry and into another manufacturing industry in a C-level position.

Strategy: Crafted powerful professional highlights section to demonstrate his value to any manufacturing organization and emphasized broad scope of client mix in most recent consulting experience. Background in the apparel industry not mentioned until page two of his resume, after a strong case has already been made for his candidacy.

Resume: Bill Steadman (pages 126-129)
Writer: Deborah Wile Dib
Objective: To transition from the vice-presidential tier to the C-level tier in corporate security.

Strategy: Began with a powerful skills-based profile that focused on corporate accomplishments in security and management, with strong positioning of his unique educational credentials, and clear presentation of all keywords relevant to his industry and expertise. Presented accomplishments under each company and wrapped accomplishments around bottom-line result when possible.

Resume: R. Ross Tuthill (pages 130-131)
Writer: Lorie Lebert
Objective: To transition out of an executive leadership position with a nonprofit and into a C-level, corporate position in the medical, pharmaceutical, and/or health care industries.

Strategy: Created strong summary section demonstrating cross-functional executive management skills and core competencies. Followed with detailed job description highlighting all relevant skills and a track record of strong financial contributions. Used military career background to further accentuate leadership talents.

Resume: George A. Stockhausen (pages 132-133)
Writer: Michele Haffner
Objective: To transition out of senior management career in training and educational services into a C-level position with a for-profit corporation.

Strategy: Extrapolated relevant executive-level skills and characteristics and showcased in the profile section. Followed with job descriptions which reflected strong leadership, management, financial, executive liaison, strategic planning, and other related skills. Leveraged past military experience to further substantiate leadership capabilities.

Resume: Kyle Lawrence (pages 134-138)
Writer: Deborah Wile Dib
Objective: To transition out of career in the failed dot.com industry and capture a C-level position with a strong, stable, technology-driven corporation.

Strategy: Wrote an extensive profile section to clearly communicate his personal brand and executive attributes and focus the reader on his skills and not his most recent work history in consulting. Proved his abilities in the corporate world by referencing his past successes and demonstrating bottom-line impact by showing high-value contributions throughout his career.

Marcus Winston

257 S.W. 99th Lane
Miami, Florida 33186

mwinston@earthlink.net

Home: (305) 388-1477
Mobile: (305) 582-9857

SENIOR OPERATING & MANAGEMENT EXECUTIVE

Strategic Planning and Leadership • New Business Development • Consumer, Corporate, and B2B Marketing
Corporate Finance and Treasury • Organizational Development • Partnership Management • M&A

Start-Up Ventures, Turnarounds, Reorganizations, High Growth Environments, Fortune 100 Corporations
U.S. and International Markets

Seasoned executive with over 18 years of senior management experience and a proven track record of success. Combine strong operating and financial management skills with excellent marketing, branding, and product launch talents. Built highly profitable businesses in volatile and competitive environments. UCLA MBA.

Fluent in English, Spanish, Portuguese, and French.

PROFESSIONAL EXPERIENCE

Quasar Electronics Corporation
1993–Present

One of the largest distributors of IT products and services worldwide. Quasar grew from $1 billion to $15 billion in ten years.

Senior Vice President, Corporate, and President, Latin America (April 2000–Present)
Senior Vice President, Latin America (February 1997–April 2000)
Vice President, General Manager, Latin America Sales (May 1993–February 1997)

Executive Officer leading a division with locations in five countries plus an export business unit in the U.S. Full responsibility for P&L, $40 million SG&A budget, operating management, and functional areas including strategic planning, human resources, technology, business development, marketing, sales, warehousing, logistics, finance, accounting, credit, legal, and treasury.

Manage a team of nine direct reports supervising up to 571 employees. Report to President Worldwide.

Operating Management & Leadership Accomplishments:

- Started and built Latin American (LA) division into one of the company's most profitable international divisions with revenues in excess of $700 million. Achieved profitability in fifth month of operation.
- Developed and oversaw relationships with 15,000 resellers and 250 vendors including Intel, Microsoft, Cisco, and IBM.
- Initiated and led negotiations for the development of a strategic alliance with one of the largest computer companies in the world to capitalize a start-up in Brazil.
- Leveraged U.S. infrastructure and economies of scale to rapidly grow LA division from a sales organization to a fully functioning, self-standing business unit.
- Led integration of four concurrent acquisitions in Argentina, Chile, Peru, and Uruguay. Drove competitive positioning for market share dominance. Turned around two acquired companies from $7 million loss to $2 million profit position.
- Established operational infrastructures. Built management teams in the U.S. and abroad. Developed and implemented detailed business plans for each business unit.
- Negotiated and led divestiture of the Argentine subsidiary (2002) while aggressively minimizing balance sheet exposure and maintaining subsidiary's position as number one distributor in the country.

Revenue, Profit, & Financial Accomplishments:

- Launched Margin Improvement Task Force. Initiated competitive analysis process, instituted margin holds, renegotiated major vendor agreements, increased freight recovery, and increased margin on low velocity SKU's. Applied priced-at-sold-for monitoring and customer activity-based-costing (ABC). Results: Five out of six units' margins were higher than the previous year by an average of 1.28%.
- Led right-sizing initiatives for the region and exceeded 2002 targets despite turbulent year and 25% drop in sales. Achieved 1.67% operating income and 2.01% PBT.
- Reduced in-country average inventory days from 34.9 in FY01 to 22.5 in FY02. Delivered 55% improvement of in-country inventory reserves. Delivered 2.5-day reduction in regional cash outlays. Reduced vendor receivables with reserves dropping from 20% in FY02 to 4% in FY03.
- Led intense vendor meetings and negotiations resulting in over $2 million in exposure recoveries.

117

Marketing & Customer Service Accomplishments:

- Signed thousands of new customers and developed tailored service offerings.
- Developed/launched integrated sales and marketing campaigns. Consistently achieved higher-than-market growth.
- Spearheaded a greenfield operation that positioned Brazil as a leading distributor in the largest market in South America. Launched e-commerce initiative that drove 40% of all transactions through the website within 10 months.
- Gained consistent recognition from customers, vendors, trade magazines, and competitors for the most service-oriented team and the best back-room operation.

Human Capital Accomplishments:

- Recruited to pioneer company's first foreign market entry outside of North America and lead start-up operations for this new international division. Grew the organization from one associate to over 500. Led various talent upgrades and reorganizations as the business evolved.
- Implemented a capacity planning tool and led a 46% regional reduction in workforce without any lawsuits or contingencies. Led a 60% RIF in Brazil while improving live answer rates by 6%.
- Established recognition and incentive awards, training programs, team-building activities, and employee relations programs. Maintained personal contact with employees at all levels of the organization.

ExcelCard, Latin America Division   1982–1993

Began as a Marketing Analyst and progressed through increasingly responsible leadership positions pioneering numerous initiatives and new product developments.

Vice President, Cardmember Marketing (June 1992–April 1993)

Headquarters leadership role for ExcelCard's most profitable, $5 billion International Division.

- Developed and launched "one-to-one" direct response and loyalty building strategy.

Regional Vice President, Consumer Financial Services (July 1990–May 1992)

Led start-up of new division with activities in 40 countries. Held general management responsibility. Created legal framework, developed core systems, designed new product strategies, and shaped brand identity.

- Launched 51 new products.
- Spearheaded database development, modeling, and telemarketing to develop cross-selling strategies.
- Identified and restructured non-performing assets to create a bank.
- Increased net income by 66% over 1990.

VP, Marketing, Sales & Strategic Planning, Cards (August 1988–July 1990)

Led marketing, sales, and public affairs of a $5 billion unit. Managed network of 50 representative offices, 2,200 bank branches, and 6 service centers. Directed research and planning to shape long-term strategy.

- Exceeded new card targets by 20% while reducing cost per card by 15%.
- Developed and introduced new card and electronic data capture program.

Director of Marketing (April 1986–August 1988)

Managed trade, consumer, and bank marketing of ExcelCards.

- Launched new card, services, programs, and insurance products.
- Built one of the company's most cost-effective marketing teams, with 30% of staff and 50% of budgets allocated to comparable business units.
- Exceeded previous year's results by 48%.

Earlier career included additional positions in sales, marketing, and general management in Europe.

EDUCATION/PROFESSIONAL DEVELOPMENT

University of California at Los Angeles (UCLA), **MBA, Finance/Marketing**

Harvard Business School, **BS, Political and Diplomatic Sciences – Magna cum laude** (Top 1% of Class)

University of Virginia, The Darden School, **– Mergers & Acquisitions – Leadership for Extraordinary Performance**

JAMES ANDREWS

3489 Palo Alto Drive * Irvine, CA 92806
714.555.7890 *jamesadrew@Comcast.net

CAREER FOCUS

~ EXECUTIVE LEVEL ~
BUSINESS DEVELOPMENT · ORGANIZATIONAL LEADERSHIP · TRANSFORMATIONAL LEADERSHIP

EXECUTIVE PROFILE

- Talented, high-performance Product/Services Business Strategist with 14+ years of progressively responsible executive-level experience refining and managing critical marketing efforts. Cross-functional expertise in products and services marketing, brand identity, multimedia communications, fundraising, business acumen, publications management, and special events planning and promotion.
- Demonstrated success building strategic alliances and partnerships to bridge the cultures between corporations, nonprofit, and government organizations to achieve organizational initiatives. Meet with city officials, financial institutions, various businesses, and agencies to solve needs. Strong leader and staff manager.
- Spearhead successful marketing communications, public information, and fundraising programs for nonprofit organizations. Specific knowledge of academic and educational programming (seven+ years), health care systems (two+ years), and city government (seven years). Successfully manage multiple projects under tight deadlines.
- Direct corporate-wide communication platforms and strategies. Expertise leading, managing, and developing long-range marketing/public relations plans, strategies, operational tactics, and budgets (worth $250,000).
- Hands-on experience and knowledge of organizational communication and the integration of publications, photography, videos, and the Internet to create a successful multimedia communications program. Broad-based publications writing/editing/design expertise, including grant writing.
- Superior negotiation, organizational leadership, and management skills. Build talented teams and rally consensus. Accomplished public speaker and corporate spokesman. Define target audiences. Adept at developing, composing, and presenting key messages. Created messages and wrote speeches for the Mayor.

PROFESSIONAL EXPERIENCE

CHIEF OF PUBLIC INFORMATION AND MARKETING   1999 — Present
Fullerton Management Corporation
*A nonprofit corporation (supported by $80 million in federal funding) operating eight community centers. To date, the corporation has partnered with more than 300 businesses to create over 4,000 jobs, arranged for employment for another 4,000 city residents, and helped 600 people become homeowners. Additionally, promote after-school enrichment programs including reading and math, vocational assessments and training, etc. **Assumed responsibilities of Interim COO for 18 months directing a staff of 35 and managing daily operations. Report directly to the CEO and President.***

- ❑ Recruited as part of the senior management team to create and execute plans to improve distressed areas of the region as part of a federal initiative. Joined management team during company start-up to develop and drive strategic communications platform to create awareness, inform, educate, and garner support for objectives from hundreds of businesses and thousands of citizens.
- ❑ Created a centralized identity through development of business plans and marketing tools. Initiated radio announcements, billboards, telephone campaigns, and brochures, successfully penetrating target audiences.
- ❑ Conduct regular liaison and build effective relationships with influential business contacts throughout the community. Attend Board meetings and serve as Secretary to Board of Directors with fiscal responsibilities. Sign contracts and payables. Determine financial commitments.

Continued...

❑ Develop and manage annual marketing budget integrating print communications, special events, and electronic media for increased public visibility of the organization, its initiatives, and services. Determine cost-effective marketing schemes. Designed initial/start-up marketing materials.

❑ Created and implemented a telephone hold message and telephone dialing scripted messaging program to reach the community. Track and monitor the effectiveness of calling promotions.

❑ Company spokesperson: Communicate the mission and accomplishments in external and internal forums, including the Mayor's office and official testimony for the U.S. Congress and Senate.

❑ Implemented a successful media relations plan. Developed relationships with local, regional, and national media that generated more than 20 positive news or feature stories per year.

❑ Planned and executed as many 45 special events per year, including press briefings, ribbon cuttings, business openings, and community meetings.

MARKETING AND PUBLIC RELATIONS MANAGER   1997 — 1999
Fullerton Medical System, Fullerton, CA

Developed and executed an aggressive marketing plan, responsive to the rapidly changing health care industry, for this $30 million community health organization. Marketing plan focused on patient retention, new patient acquisition, and name recognition/community awareness. Accomplishments included:

❑ Established internal communications strategy to promote Total Quality Management. Created company brochure and advertisements. Generated feature stories to support campaign objectives.

❑ Developed and executed monthly "Patient Satisfaction Surveys" to monitor patient care and guide improvements in patient care and services.

DIRECTOR OF PUBLICATIONS AND PUBLIC RELATIONS   1990 — 1997
Hudson School, Orange, CA (*A private elementary and secondary school*)

Recruited to direct internal and external communication strategies to achieve marketing, fundraising, and enrollment goals during a period of rapid growth and change. Developed and created publications (where none previously existed), public relations, media relations, advertising, and development communications from concept through project completion. Worked closely with the admissions director to review student enrollment statistics.

❑ Worked with development staff to conceptualize, develop, and implement all special events.

❑ Orchestrated a successful annual giving campaign that raised nearly $1 million, and an alumni event that grossed more than $60,000.

❑ Conducted liaison and oriented marketing materials to secure funding for a new middle school and a new computer lab.

EDUCATION/TRAINING
❑ **MBA in Management and Transformational Leadership, University of Southern California, 2002**
❑ **BA in Mass Communications/Public Relations and Marketing, University of Riverside, CA, 1989**
❑ **Mayor's Executive Leadership Forum.** *Selected to participate in this prestigious 6-month leadership program as a team of 20 from a pool of 150 nominees. Curriculum included modules in Technology Integration, Improving Business Practices, Team Building, Effective Communications, and Marketing, 2004*

PROFESSIONAL MEMBERSHIPS
▪ Greater Anaheim Committee

▪ Greater Anaheim Technology Council

▪ California Association of Nonprofit Organizations

▪ Anaheim Workforce Investment Board

EARL S. ROSSMAN
5635 Baker Lake Road, Eatontown, NJ 07724
(732) 927-2345 Home ▪ (732) 927-7762 Mobile ▪ rossman@netcom.com

---

Career Target: Senior Management Executive / CEO / COO
Operations Management ▪ Business Development ▪ Change Management

Versatile executive with experience in revitalizing companies and product lines, and increasing revenues and profit margins while reducing costs. Decisive leadership merging expertise in strategic planning and development with P&L management, sales and marketing, and project management.

Solid analysis, organizational development, and problem-solving skills combined with fresh insights into attaining market share dominance. Restructured Sales Incentive Program (SIP), recharging sales team to exceed sales quotas, with no resulting turnover. Demonstrated track record of success in:

☑ Strategic Alliances / Reseller Partnerships	☑ Strategic Planning / Process Improvement
☑ New Product / Business Development	☑ Risk / Safety Management
☑ Staff Development / Management	☑ Strategic / Tactical Marketing

---

PROFESSIONAL EXPERIENCE

GENERAL CASUALTY COMPANIES (subsidiary of Amerinet), Woodbridge, NJ   2000-present
Provider of auto claims and risk management services, primarily for Fortune 1000 companies in the US, Canada, and Puerto Rico, as well as outsourced services for insurance carriers.

National Director of Sales & Marketing
Senior Management Executive with full P&L responsibility for the Fleet Risk Services and Insurance Services divisions, as well as marketing and help desk operations (8 direct reports and 17 in the chain-of-command). Charged with strategic planning, development, operations, sales and marketing, public relations, advertising, sales force automation, C-level sales, reseller management, customer service, client accounts receivables, human resources, administration, and technology performance.

ACCOMPLISHMENTS

Challenged to transition stagnant business units into profitable business entities servicing major accounts nationwide. Controlled sales and marketing operating budget of $3.6 million. Spearheaded revitalization, explosive growth and profitability (demonstrated by the following financial metrics):

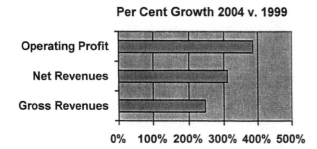

2004 v. 1999
Gross Revenues: $91 million v. $37 million
Net Revenues: $25 million v. $8.1 million
Operating Profit: $2.7 million v. $700K
EBITDA: $2.4 million v. 20K
Employee Growth: 135% (168 employees)

Page 1 of 3

Business Development
- Grew business units to company-high levels: 738,000 total Fleet Division vehicles and Insurance Service vehicles under management for 534 customers representing diverse industries such as pharmaceutical, industrial manufacturing, health care, energy, communications, transportation, business services, leasing and financial services, as well as government agencies and non-profits.

- Teamed with CEO in negotiating favorable terms for acquisition of $33 million book of business from GE Capital Fleet Services. This acquisition has increased 2004 gross revenues by 60%.

- Negotiated major strategic partnership, a 3-year renewal agreement with the company's largest reseller (representing more than 22% of gross revenue production in 2003).

Leadership & Process Improvement
- Developed and introduced Client Economic Modeling to increase operational efficiency and ROI by providing a common service platform, along with greater company scalability.

- Revitalized unprofitable business units by instituting cost-neutral customer service processes, increasing fee structure, and re-aligning target markets. Gross revenue increases up 48% in first year. Initiated and hosted Client Advisory Council for revitalized Insurance Services business.

Sales & Marketing Development
- Increased gross margins by 50% and boosted 2001 gross revenues through the creation and development of a new transformational selling system for entire sales cycle, bundling claims and safety services into one monthly fee plan (replacing one-time, transactional fee structure).

- Targeted new market niche – government agencies – and won first sale (Washington State government) in 2003. This sale alone represented twice the new business written in 2002.

- Created and implemented first formal sales and marketing strategy, identifying target markets with associated products, revenue and sales projections by business unit, competitive market intelligence, quantitative value proposition, pricing, and promotions.

- Upgraded marketing promotions by creating new advertising campaigns, new trade show booth featuring web-based services, and bi-weekly employee newsletter. Redesigned safety newsletter and won company award for "Most Improved Publication".

Technology / Online Services
- Pioneered web-based applications with operational infrastructure redesign to expand product offerings. Added safety and risk management services to core accident claims services in 2001. IT investment recouped within 5 months with no need to hire full-time service employees.

- Led sales force automation (SFA) rollout in 2001, increasing lead generation by 248% and new business unit sales by 221% in 2002. Played key team role in design and introduction of low-cost customer claim service and safety service web tools, which positioned company to capture market share and dramatically increase revenues.

CEP UNDERWRITERS (Member of Acme Financial Group), Eatontown, NJ   1988-2000
Regional Sales Manager
Oversaw property and casualty insurance, banking, credit insurance, vehicle service contract, and life insurance products. Full P&L responsibility. Managed and motivated team of 25 providing sales, underwriting, claims, and risk management services. Given autonomous decision-making authority.

- Revitalized failing business unit (ranked 25th out of 28 offices nationwide) bringing it to 6th place in production and 3rd place for total book of business within 16 months. Achieved highest market penetration in the nation (41%) and the largest premium development per account ($74,000).

- Delivered strong financial results in extremely soft market (1998): net increase of 9% in written premium, as compared to company loss of 4% of written premium to competition. Identified, developed, and led rollout of new financial product for New Jersey market in 1999.

- Created income development program, tied to Finance & Insurance products, which increased sales by 359% and was adopted nationwide by the company within the first year (1993).

- Spearheaded team that developed national standards and methodologies for recruiting and training new Account Executives, which successfully addressed the issue of high turnover.

Previous Career History:
Began career with start-up independent insurance agency (**Rossman & Company**) that grew from concept to $2.5 million in premium in 2 years. Recruited to **Wagner Insurance** to launch new agency in B2B sales of life, health, group, and mutual fund products – won awards for production and agency building. Transitioned to **Ads Insurance** (1984-1988) to re-introduce and market B2B commercial lines insurance. Rapidly built book of business to $1 million, winning company awards.

EDUCATION & PROFESSIONAL DEVELOPMENT

Connecticut College, New London, CT
Master of Science, Financial Services – 1998, Bachelor of Science, Insurance – 1989

Continuing Professional Development:
Kellogg Executive Program, Strategic Management, New York University – 1998
Dynamics of Selling Program, National Council of Insurance Marketing – 1998

Licenses & Certifications:
Property / Casualty and Life / Health Insurance Licenses ▪ Finance & Insurance Professional (AFIP)
Registered Financial Planner (RFP) ▪ Registered Health Underwriter (RHU)

PROFESSIONAL AFFILIATIONS

Association of Finance & Insurance Professionals ▪ Registered Financial Planners Institute
National Association of Fleet Administrators ▪ Risk & Insurance Management Society
National Association of Health Underwriters

ERIK LIERSON

eriklierson@email.com

5555 Magnolia Lane
Encino, California 91326

Residence (818) 632-7682
Mobile (818) 799-3297

SENIOR EXECUTIVE

Operations / Manufacturing / General Business Management / Sales and Marketing
Experienced in Offshore Sourcing and Manufacturing / Customs Issues

Senior Manufacturing Manager with 20+ years experience in all aspects of garment industry, including operations, production, plant/facility management, inventory control, purchasing, quality assurance, and financial management. Track record of consistent contributions to increased production, quality, cost effectiveness, and profitability. Persuasive leader, team builder, and negotiator. Key contributor to strategic business planning process.

- ✓ Manufacturing and Production Planning
- ✓ Inventory Management
- ✓ Facilities Management
- ✓ Quality Assurance
- ✓ Cost Reduction and Controls
- ✓ Budgeting

- ✓ Recruitment, Training, and Supervision
- ✓ Vendor Negotiations
- ✓ Team Building and Leadership
- ✓ Health and Safety Regulations
- ✓ OSHA Compliance
- ✓ Offshore Operations

——KEY PROFESSIONAL HIGHLIGHTS——

- ✓ A key management team member contributing to the revenue growth of start-up company to $120 million annually in highly competitive industry.

- ✓ Supervised cross-functional/cross-department teams of 300+. Fostered team-based environments which promoted high morale.

- ✓ Developed and managed multi-million dollar company/division budgets.

- ✓ Achieved highest factory evaluation score with national mass merchandiser.

- ✓ Implemented purchasing and production systems, and negotiated delivery schedules with global and local trading partners, to ensure quality concurrent with timely and cost-effective product delivery.

- ✓ In-depth experience working with U.S. Customs and custom brokers.

- ✓ Negotiated and managed contracts with leading retailers (available upon request).

- ✓ Initiated and negotiated purchase contracts for raw materials and finished products globally.

- ✓ Instituted technology to increase production and improve delivery dates.

PROFESSIONAL EXPERIENCE

President/Consultant • 2000–Present
ESVL CONSULTING, INC., Los Angeles, CA

Provide management, manufacturing, international/domestic production, and sales/marketing expertise to clients across diverse industries. Examples include:

- Retained by start-up company to develop lines, create cost sheets, design production schedules, and advise on sales force development.
- Traveled throughout Mexico and Guatemala to identify new production resources and/or negotiate pricing and ensure appropriate manufacturing processes.
- Introduced clients to new services and products.
- Retained to serve as interim senior management to complete processes and recruit new management replacements

General Manager • 1992–2000
WEST COAST STYLE INC., Los Angeles, CA

Key member of management team involved with strategic planning and corporate direction. Directed entire operation of multi-tiered apparel manufacturer, overseeing production process involving staff of 300+. Established production priorities, monitored costs and revamped quality standards. Ensured on-time delivery of raw materials through expert supervision of supply chain management process.

- Managed revenue growth from $21 million to $48 million.
- Achieved sales increase of 15% concurrent with sales cost reduction of 5% by hiring a factory representative instead of a traditional salesperson.
- Awarded *Vendor of the Year* by (major retailer).
- Improved on-time delivery to 97%; reduced damages to less than 2%.
- Introduced of state-of-the-art computerized systems that streamlined production processes.
- Innovated quality control program to accommodate stringent requirements of key customers.

Vice President/Partner • 1982–1992
CELEBRITY STYLES INDUSTRIES, Los Angeles, CA

Member of start-up team and board member, instrumental in driving success of junior sportswear manufacturing company. Implemented strategic direction and management plan, distribution center, quality assurance, facility management, and inventory control for four sales divisions.

- Grew annual revenues to $120 million, including $70 million import business.
- Built distribution center from initial 5,000 sq. ft. to 200,000 sq. ft.
- Managed multi-million dollar budgets.
- Marketed off-price merchandise at an annual volume of $8+ million.
- Coordinated with trading company to direct offshore manufacturing in four Asian countries.

ADDITIONAL INFORMATION

Education—Philadelphia College of Textiles & Science, Philadelphia, PA / Temple University

Computer Skills—AS/400; PC & Macintosh; Microsoft Word, Excel, Outlook, Lotus 1-2-3; Internet

Foreign Languages—Working conversational Spanish

Professional Affiliations—Coalition of American Apparel Manufacturers; California Chamber of Commerce,

BILL STEADMAN, CPP

CORPORATE EXECUTIVE ● CHIEF SECURITY OFFICER

"Security is always too much...until it's not enough."
— Daniel Webster

Experienced in dynamic large-cap & mid-cap enterprises doing business in diverse industries.
Improve profitability, enhance operational performance, eliminate/mitigate risks, identify/close security gaps, and protect executives, personnel, and property. Internal and external clients have included West Side Arena, major sports teams, Lyman Recital House, the Metropolis Plaza, and many others in communications, entertainment, and retailing.

Deliver consistent bottom-line results.
Make high-stakes decisions, attack complex security issues, provide expert advisory services, and manage large-scale projects. Design, implement, and enforce comprehensive, technologically sophisticated, yet fiscally conscientious, corporate security programs and solutions.

EDUCATION & DEVELOPMENT

MA, INDUSTRIAL SECURITY BUSINESS MANAGEMENT ● BA, CRIMINAL JUSTICE ADMINISTRATION
Cooper University, Bayside, MD (1986)

ADJUNCT PROFESSOR, CRIMINAL JUSTICE & SECURITY ADMINISTRATION (Master-level teaching)
Cooper University, Bayside, MD (1989 to present)

CERTIFIED PROTECTION PROFESSIONAL (CPP)
National Society for Industrial Safety—NSIS

AREAS OF EXPERTISE

SECURITY MANAGEMENT

Corporate Security
Executive & Employee Protection

Security Force Oversight
Asset Protection & Loss Prevention
Investigations Management
Intellectual & Proprietary Property Protection
Travel & Event Security
Facility Security
Regulatory Affairs & Compliance
Pre-Employment Screening & Investigation

STRATEGY & EXECUTION

Strategic & Countermeasure Planning
Vulnerability Assessment & Risk Management

Competitive Intelligence Countermeasures
Crisis Response & Emergency Preparedness
Business Process Design & Reengineering
Executive Decision Support
Internal & External Consulting
Business Continuity Planning & Implementation
Disaster Recovery Planning & Implementation
Project Planning & Management

EXECUTIVE OVERSIGHT

Vision, Strategy, & Execution
Financial Planning, Analysis, & Reporting
P&L/Operations Management
Turnaround & Change Management
Budgeting & Cost Control
Team Building, Mentoring, & Leadership
Contract Negotiation & Supplier Relations
Corporate Communications & PR
Internal & External Customer Relations
IT & HR Solutions

CAREER ADVANCEMENT

CLEAR CABLE CORPORATION, Brookhurst, MD
1994 to 2005

Vice President, Asset Protection, 1998 to 2005
Director, Corporate Security, 1994 to 1998

Senior-level executive in Fortune 1000 corporate security team, reporting directly to SVP of Security with solid line to CEO. High-profile corporate holdings in communications and entertainment include *CLEAR CABLE* (cable television services); *Matrixx* (commercial telephony); *West Side Arena; Lyman Recital House; KC HOOPS; WA PUCKS; SD LAZERS; METRO Media Holdings* (television programming/production); *WIRED* (electronics retailer); and *Movietone Cinemas* (movie theaters).

MANAGEMENT ACHIEVEMENTS

- *Served as Head of Security for all of CLEAR CABLE's corporate entities.* Devised/executed strategies and managed programs, projects, budgets, and teams for Executive Services, Intelligence Services, Asset Protection/Facilities Security (for corporate headquarters) and two corporate subdivisions (Matrixx and Metro Media Holdings). Delivered corporate-based security consulting to West Side Arena, Lyman Recital House, WIRED, and Movietone Cinemas.

- *Administered and controlled $7 million capital and expense budget.* Monitored security services budgets of other CLEAR CABLE holdings — $24+ million. Provided technical direction/managerial leadership to three senior managers and indirect oversight to 800+ employees.

25 Bristol Road, Smallville, MD 29408 ● Home: 609-893-2838 ● Cell: 212-382-9383 ● E-mail: bstead@verizon.net

Career Advancement / CLEAR CABLE / Management Achievements, continued

- *Played principal role in improving company's security strategy/practices* and effecting enterprise-wide culture change. Successfully evolved perception of corporate security from "corporate cop" to "employee protector and aide."

- *Instrumental in achieving $1.2 million cost saving* in losses from employee turnover and theft — by upgrading corporate pre-employment screening practices and leveraging CLEAR CABLE's relationships with vendors to encourage them to implement/upgrade employee screening/hiring systems.

- *Created/led Intelligence Services Group* to mitigate and/or avoid employee/vendor security issues. Justified/obtained funding, recruited/trained staff, established strategies/procedures, and managed organizational infrastructure integration.

- *Produced accurate physical inventory figures—key in major M&A (WIRED) negotiations—*in only four days.

- *Contributed to corporate image enhancement* by serving as liaison to local and national law enforcement. Obtained funding for high-profile corporate sponsorships, and represented company at security planning and crisis management events. Leveraged internal communications to profile new image/service offering of the corporate security force.

KEY SECURITY STRATEGIES, INTERVENTION, & PROJECTS

- *Managed installation of complex security systems.* Wrote specifications, negotiated contracts, provided technical/ managerial oversight at corporate headquarters (three buildings, 1.5+ million sq. ft.), satellite communication/control stations, professional sport teams training facility, corporate childcare facility, and chief executives' residences.

- *Achieved 12% to 15% reduction in labor costs* — while ensuring 24 / 7 / 365 security services coverage — by designing an algorithm for determining FTE staffing requirements and a scheduling system to align with the staffing formula.

- *Authored business and technology plan* for transitioning access control from multiple disjointed stand-alone systems to centralized system linked with HR employee database. Solution closed security gaps/related employee accessibility.

- *Contributed to 15% reduction in shrinkage* at WIRED — 60 retail outlets throughout MD, DE, and VA.

- *Protected company's main data center* by recommending and project-managing $1 million installation of Inergen (Ansul) suppression gas system. Enabled fire recovery within hours vs. seven-plus days with traditional water system.

- *Contributed to post-9/11 security planning/implementation* — at West Side Arena and Lyman Recital House for permanent security improvements during events, and at BCB's "Salute to America" star-studded extravaganza honoring Lyndon City's police officers, firefighters, and emergency responders.

- *Positioned CLEAR CABLE as first non-medical public corporation to utilize defibrillators.*

- *Principal architect of security design for Lyman House Lassies' Travel Group's* four-week engagement in Mexico City ("The kidnap for ransom capital of the world"). Security Team Leader for Senior GMA Tournament sponsored by Lightpath.

STEADMAN ASSOCIATES, INC., Smallville, MD   **Security Consultant**
1990 to 1994

Consulting firm specializing in security operations, guard force management, facility security design, IT/HR solutions, contingency planning, and crisis management. Managed strategy, finance, business development, contract negotiation, and relationship building. Representative engagements included:

- **METROPOLIS PLAZA** — Reorganized 700-member, unionized guard services force following 1993 bombing. Within 90 days, devised plan enabling 12% reduction in headcount and $900,000 reduction in related costs on $19 million contract, while improving competency and performance of security force.

- **SECURITY INSPECTIONS** — Performed comprehensive vulnerability and risk assessment of facilities, cash-handling procedures, banking systems, and transportation personnel, policies, and procedures of current and potential clients of a major international insurance carrier of armored car services companies in North America.

Career Advancement / continued

LOSS PREVENTION CORPORATION, Beechurst, MD   **Vice President**
1986 to 1990

Key executive team member of this private investigation firm representing large national and regional retailers, and world-class production, manufacturing, and warehouse/distribution corporations. Led team of four investigator supervisors, managed office manager and administrative staff, and indirectly supervised 30+ undercover operatives. Provided technical, fiscal, and managerial oversight to all investigative projects. Achievements included:

- *Contributed to accelerated growth*, enterprise-level vision, strategy, decision making, and problem solving.

- *Improved cash flow and profit margins* by automating investigative findings and reporting process.

- *Reorganized back-office operations.*

- *Teamed with Owner/President in developing and presenting 2-day training program* for new undercover operatives.

SMALLVILLE DEPARTMENT OF CORRECTIONS, Smallville, NJ   **Warden, 1985 to 1986**
1978 to 1986   **Deputy Warden, 1980 to 1985**
                                                    Assistant Deputy Warden, 1978 to 1980

Earned performance-based promotion to chief operating officer in facilities housing as many as 1,600 inmates and employing 700+ uniformed officers. Built, mentored, and led management teams (civilian and uniformed) and auxiliary personnel. Administered operating budgets in excess of $50 million.

Held full accountability for all operations — staffing, budgeting, financial reporting, security operations, policy formation, resource management, food service, facilities, risk management, regulatory compliance, and internal/external communications/relationships — for Lyndon Correctional Facility, North Facility, and Lyndon House of Detention (with Maximum Security Housing Unit).

- *Achieved path from officer to warden in shortest time* and at youngest age in DoC's history (at the time).

- *Met operational performance, quality, and regulatory compliance objectives* despite serious constraints — over-population, budget cuts, occupational stress/burnout, etc.

- *Shored up security gaps and reduced operating costs by $278,000* by restructuring inmate housing and reorganizing inmate movement within the facility.

- *Led development of Internal Audit Department* to analyze business processes and financial reporting systems, implement best practices, and identify and resolve mismanagement, impropriety, and fraud.

- *Improved relations and related consulting/legal fees* by virtually eliminating subjectivity of the employee evaluation process through design/implementation of a fact-based performance model.

- *Reduced accounting errors by 12%, and slashed lag time from eight months to a reliable six weeks,* by developing and implementing an IT solution for calculating/generating overtime and night shift differential payroll checks.

PROFESSIONAL ACTIVITIES

PROFESSIONAL MEMBERSHIPS

National Society for Industrial Safety — NSIS
(Former Chair, Long Island Chapter)
Electronic Crime Task Force
(Government and private enterprise coalition)

Smallville Coalition for Workplace Violence Awareness
National Law Enforcement Associates, Inc. — NLEA
National Academy for Certified Law Enforcement — NACLE

PUBLICATIONS AND PRESENTATIONS

"Public Law Enforcement and Private Security," *Safe and Secure*, magazine of the National Society for Industrial Safety

"Transitioning Skills from the Public Sector," keynote address, Association of Crime Prevention Officers' Association

"The Benefits of Volunteer Leadership," keynote address, National Society for Industrial Safety

25 Bristol Road, Smallville, MD 29408 • Home: 609-893-2838 • Cell: 212-382-9383 • E-mail: bstead@verizon.net

BILL STEADMAN, CPP

"Security is always too much...until it's not enough."
— Daniel Webster

RESUME ADDENDUM • CRITICAL LEADERSHIP INITIATIVES

Greatly reduced investigation costs, lawsuits, and other risks/liabilities at CLEAR CABLE.

Created and led Intelligence Services Group — hired, screened, and managed researchers and analysts; established sophisticated software and data sources; benchmarked the organization against industry standards. Introduced and managed in-house pre-employment screening — including a 3-tiered, easily understandable hiring authorization structure.

Results   Virtually eliminated potential grievances and lawsuits related to hiring — an additional 3% of applicants were denied employment for undisclosed criminal convictions, previous acts of impropriety, and misrepresentation on resumes/ applications. Gained 100% compliance to utilization of pre-employment screening model among all CLEAR CABLE entities.

Impact   *"I consider Bill to be a key asset in problem solving, and I seek his input as often as possible. [The Intelligence Services Group] is an extremely successful and growing operation that has garnered enterprise-wide praise."*
--Phil Greene, S.V.P., Corporate Security, CLEAR CABLE

Drove culture change by design—an evolutionary, not revolutionary, process—with enterprise-wide impact.

Upgraded training programs to include customer service skills, CPR, utilization of defibrillators, emergency auto repair, and impaired driving prevention/solutions. Reoriented security team to view role as customer service providers, yielding a positive change in employee perception.

Results   Gave security officers an image and performance standard to live up to, with a positive impact evidenced by personnel's morale and incentive in recruiting new security officers. Changed corporate citizens' view of the security function and teams from "corporate cop" to "employee protector."

Impact   *"Bill, I don't claim to know anything about security [people]. But I've always heard that you know you have the best when they are undetectable, yet on the spot when needed. That's exactly my impression of your team. Thanks."*
--Len Starr, Senior Executive, CLEAR CABLE IS Department

Provided post-9/11 comprehensive, proficient, cost-effective NY metro-area corporate security services.

Performed ongoing analyses of existing security operations and related controls, staffs, and business processes. Designed algorithm based on operational requirements, budget projections, and historical staffing data to determine FTE requirements. Followed with development of scheduling solution that met security coverage requirements while controlling costs.

Results   Achieved a world-class security operation — perimeter, facilities, access control, proprietary and intellectual assets, personal property, and executive/employee protection — by contributing to refining strategies, upgrading programs, and mentoring teams. Delivered 12% to 15% reduction in labor costs and turnover rates.

Impact   *"Bill has implemented some creative ideas for improvements in function, streamlining processes and reducing costs. He seeks opportunities to conserve resources and reduce costs without compromising quality."*
--Phil Greene, S.V.P., Corporate Security, CLEAR CABLE

Earned reputation as valuable executive, and knowledgeable, technically competent security professional.

Developed/executed security strategies for multiple operational units and several large-scale correction facilities. Served as internal consultant on virtually every aspect of the corporate security function. Founded and managed a successful security consulting firm and, as its sole consultant, represented corporate clients doing business in diverse industries.

Results   Succeeded in meeting complex security services requirements for high-profile, large-scale organizations, venues, events, and personalities — CLEAR CABLE Corporate, CLEAR CABLE Cable Television Services, CLEAR CABLE executives, Metro Media Holdings, Lyman Recital House, West Side Arena. Achieved "no-incident" performance under demanding security situations — post-9/11, large corporate citizenship, large inmate populations, large public events, international travel, etc.

Impact   *"I feel confident that under Bill's continued leadership, the security responsibilities [at CLEAR CABLE] will continue to outperform industry standards and fully support the objectives of each [internal] business unit."*
--Phil Greene, S.V.P., Corporate Security, CLEAR CABLE

---

25 Bristol Road, Smallville, MD 29408 • Home: 609-893-2838 • Cell: 212-382-9383 • E-mail: bstead@verizon.net

R. ROSS TUTHILL

rrtuthill2@maxmail.com

C: 703 380 6101 • H: 703 349 5776

Senior Executive – Medical, Pharmaceutical, & Healthcare Industries

Expertise in Business Development & Growth • Turnaround Operations • Strategy Planning & Implementation

Career leader with executive-level experience in top management positions in government and private sector organizations. Significant contributions in every position through strong qualifications in relationship management, P&L accountability, strategic planning/tactical deployment, and team building.

Record of successful cooperation in building consensus and driving collaborative relationships with staffs, boards of directors, government agencies, and business partners. Strong qualifications in:

Policy & Procedure Development • P&L / Budgeting / Financial Management • Public Relations / Branding
Government Relations • Fundraising / Conferences • Strategic Alliances / Partnerships
Board / Committee Affairs • Recruiting / Team Management

MBA, MIPA, BS credentials • Registered Pharmacist • USAF Colonel

---

PROFESSIONAL EXPERIENCE

PHARMA-CARE ASSOCIATION OF AMERICA (PCAA)   *1996-2005*
Executive Vice President & Chief of Staff • 2000-05
Member of Executive Management Team providing visionary, strategic, operational, and financial leadership for national trade group with representation throughout the U.S. and its territories. Key decision maker in daily business operations including P&L, forecasting, strategic fiscal planning, and management. Managed $25 million budget and a 40-person staff; reported directly to the Board of Directors.

Made a significant impact on the organization by turning the vision and mission around to be more comprehensive; raising awareness through marketing and branding to improve the image in the industry; streamlining operations for efficiency; and delivering a robust organization that stands alone on its own resources.

- Led organizational restructuring and expanded membership 300% to include member and associate categories; realigned resources to accommodate the association's growth and development.

- Increased income from alternate resources to represent 35% of total revenue and achieved a 68% rise in vendor memberships by creating improved opportunities for participation.

- Orchestrated relocation of the Association from Alexandria, VA to Washington, DC to improve relationships on the "Hill" as well as with member companies and organizations. Worked with real estate, architectural, and construction planners to locate property, update and expand association's physical space to functional and attractive office environment on Constitution Avenue.

- Built the Government Affairs Department leading to major impact at the state and federal level; defeated 98% of all detrimental state issues over a nine-year period and paved the way for increased roles for the organization in federal issues, including the Medicare Prescription Plan.

- Solicited grants and special sponsorships amounting to $12 million between 2001 and 2004.

- Spearheaded an awards program for outstanding achievements in improving healthcare delivery, and established industry guidelines, standards, and policy statements on relative issues.

- Cultivated strategic alliances with other associations. Organized and coordinated activities of seven committees and councils to promote networking and create viable goals and objectives for the association.

- Expanded annual conference attendance four-fold and increased conference revenues from a mere 10% to a lucrative 55%. Tripled the Annual Conference Exhibit Program.

- Led initiatives to advance published monthly and online newsletters. Evolved the website to share data on association initiatives, foster member recruitment and retention, and promote profitability.

- *Promotion record:* Secretary of Administration, 1996; Vice President of Administration, 1998; Executive Vice President, 2000.

Colonel & Director, Health Personnel Policy & Programs • 1990-96

Led USAF pipeline medical specialty forecasting and training requirements at the US Air Force Surgeon General Headquarters at Langley Air Force Base in Virginia. Directed staff of ten which managed corporate personnel issues and education/training programs for 120+ healthcare specialties and disciplines within the HR department of the US Air Force Surgeon General Office. Areas of specialty included recruitment, training, assigning, and facilitating career development for 18,000+ doctors, nurses, and ancillary professionals of the US Air Force, serving in 250+ USAF medical treatment facilities and medical centers worldwide. Also involved in healthcare post-graduate degree programs; medical, nursing, and ancillary healthcare personnel promotions.

- <u>Exceeded recruiting and retention goals</u> for all medical specialties every year. Exceeded quotas for placement of candidates for each specialty requirement in residency training in Air Force-sponsored program and the National Residency Matching Program (NRMP) every year. Met quota for healthcare participation in reduction-in-force initiative mandated by Congress in 1990.

- <u>Provided critical input</u> by participating in the Deardon Commission Study to determine appropriate income and allowances for physicians and other healthcare personnel to be equitable to that of civilian counterparts. Worked to achieve goals for 100% equity in pay for military physicians compared with civilian counterparts.

- <u>Championed the Health Professional Scholarship Program</u> and other medical, nursing, and ancillary healthcare personnel training and education programs.

- <u>Implemented joint nursing and medical continuing education programs</u>, and introduced special wages for hard-to-recruit specialties (i.e., optometrists, pharmacists).

- <u>Recipient of</u> the USAF Meritorious Service Medal and the USAF Distinguished Service Medal. *"Recognized for his extraordinary leadership and management skills in improving healthcare for military beneficiaries throughout his USAF career, Colonel Tuthill was awarded the USAF Legion of Merit, Department of Defense and USAF Distinguished Service Medals, and USAF and Department of Defense Meritorious Service medals."*

Colonel & Director • 1986-90

Managed a team of 40 tri-service healthcare professionals in development of requirements for the Composite Health Care System – a fully integrated IT system to support 800+ US medical treatment facilities worldwide. Sited at the Pentagon in the Secretary of Defense for Health Affairs, Defense Medical Systems Support Center in Washington, DC.

Chairman, Department of Pharmacy • 1981-86

USAF Academy, Colorado Springs, CO. Received the Hospital Administrator of the Quarter Award, Outstanding Administrator of the Year Award, and Department of the Year Award.

EDUCATION & CERTIFICATION

Master of Business Administration –*University of Richmond*

Master of Systems Pharmacy Practice – *University of North Carolina at Chapel Hill*

MARDIE – YOU HAVE MASTER'S ABOVE IN TWO DIFFERENT WAYS. CORRECT?

Bachelor of Science in Pharmacy – *University of Texas at Austin*

Registered Pharmacist

AFFILIATIONS/MEMBERSHIPS

National Council on Patient Information & Education (NCPIE) – Member, Board of Directors • 1998-2005

United States Pharmacopoeia – Delegate • 1999-2002

Rho Chi Pharmacy Academic Honor Society Fellow

Greater Washington Society of Association Executives

American Society of Association Executives

American Pharmacists Association (APhA)

American Society of Health-Systems Pharmacists

American Council on Pharmaceutical Education (CE Administrator for CPE/CME Approved Provider)

GEORGE A. STOCKHAUSEN

gastockhausen@yahoo.com

1114 Turner Lane
New Berlin, WI 53133

Home: (414) 862-7095
Mobile: (414) 333-7095

PROFILE

Senior-level executive with a 20-year track record of successful strategic and tactical leadership and program development within public education, state government, and the United States military. Master of Education (Secondary Education) with more than 50 credits earned toward Doctorate in Education.

Visionary and creative with a positive attitude and steadfast commitment to excellence. Expertise developing and implementing successful educational programs and processes for all age levels. Specialty is at-risk youth.

Entrepreneurial leadership style with highly effective planning, organizational, and communication skills as well as a solution-oriented approach to problem solving. Demonstrated ability to instill a common vision and develop a dynamic team based on trust and mutual respect.

Core competencies/areas of expertise include:

- Strategic & Tactical Organizational Planning
- Visionary Leadership
- Budgeting, Planning, & Forecasting
- Continuous Process Improvement
- Organizational Development
- Team Building & Team-Based Culture

- Curriculum Development & Administration
- Staff Training & Professional Development
- Instructional Resource Selection
- Crisis Planning & Emergency Preparedness
- Collaborative Community Efforts
- Special Events Planning & Fundraising

EDUCATION ADMINISTRATION EXPERIENCE

STRATEGIC LEADERSHIP TRAINING CENTER – Madison, Wisconsin   1999 to Present
Nonprofit, non-instrumentality charter school operating through a contract with Madison Public Schools and serving an at-risk student population in grades 5 through 10. Provides rigorous classroom and project- and community-based educational opportunities for young people who have not experienced success in traditionally structured school settings

BOARD PRESIDENT (1999 to Present)
FOUNDER/CHIEF EXECUTIVE OFFICER (1999 to Sept 2004)

- Conceptualized, developed, and implemented nonprofit charter school combining academic learning and leadership development with job and technical skills training. Placed unique emphasis on military principles of discipline, pride, and persistence.
- Recruited and organized board of directors consisting of high-profile community members, parents, and human service professionals. Raised over $200,000 in contributions to support start-up and capital expenditures.
- Recruited and directed a full-time academic and support staff. Developed curriculum emphasizing tactile learning and the "three A's" of attitude, attendance, and academics.
- Opened doors in 2001 with 40 students; grew enrollment to 125 within three years. Achieved the following benchmarks: Attendance 92%; norm tests show full-year gains in reading and math.

STATE OF WISCONSIN DEPARTMENT OF CORRECTIONS, DIVISION OF JUVENILE CORRECTIONS,
LEADERSHIP TRAINING CENTER – Madison, Wisconsin   1995 to 1999
State-sponsored two-phase incarceration program for juvenile offenders.

SUPERINTENDENT

- Selected by the Adjutant General to serve as a consultant and liaison to the state Department of Corrections (DOC) in the development of an innovative juvenile offender rehabilitation program (prior to 1995 during active military duty).
- Appointed by the DOC upon military retirement to Superintendent accountable 24/7/365 for the in-residence rehabilitation of 120 boys, ages 13 to 19.
                                                                                    Continued

LEADERSHIP TRAINING CENTER (continued)
- Recruited and managed a staff of 44 academic and human service professionals.
- Developed 11-week training program incorporating military "basic training" and high-school equivalency academics. Grew enrollment from 120 students per year to 250.

BURLINGTON HIGH SCHOOL – Burlington, Wisconsin   1982 to 1986
Public high school serving 1,100 students in grades 9 through 12.

ASSISTANT PRINCIPAL/ATHLETIC DIRECTOR
- Developed and implemented "master teacher" concept for skill improvement. Created multi-faceted staff evaluation tool incorporating student input. Encouraged staff creativity, self-improvement, and ongoing professional development.
- Directed 17 varsity and five sub-varsity athletics programs. Established codes of conduct at all levels. Fostered inclusive mentality: all sports are part of the athletic program without exclusivity. Administered 30 state, district, regional, and county tournaments. Managed multi-million dollar sports complex.
- Fostered strong community relations through special events, public relations, and parent/school committee participation.

RED RIVER HIGH SCHOOL – Red River, Illinois   1980 to 1982
Public high school serving 500 students in grades 6 through 12.

PRINCIPAL
- Chaired curriculum review committees. Reconstructed vocational educational programs. Established unique one- and four-year curriculum plan for all students. Ensured curriculum met all accreditation standards.
- Expanded curricula through the development of co-operative agreements with neighboring school districts.
- Developed *Life Skills* courses for junior- and senior-high school students.

MILITARY LEADERSHIP EXPERIENCE

AIR NATIONAL GUARD – Madison, Wisconsin   1986 to 1995

COMMANDER – 246th Tactical Control Squadron (1989 to 1995)
DETACHMENT COMMANDER/DIRECTOR OF OPERATIONS – 246th TCS (1986 to 1989)
- Recruited to full-time position directing a team of 23 full-time civilian and 70 military personnel.
- Established and executed continuous improvement initiatives that dramatically improved unit retention and operational support response. Recognized as achieving the best retention rate within the state.
- Organized and directed first-ever national radar unit commander's seminar for long-range vision, mission, and strategic planning. Results included training specialty combinations and a 33% reduction in radar force.
- Motivated all unit personnel to work, think, and act as a team, which led to 10 of 12 areas receiving a rating of "Excellent" or better in the Tactical Air Command (TAC) Operational Readiness Inspection (ORI). This was a first for a TAC Forward Air Control unit.
- Requested by higher echelons to plan, organize, and host ORI conferences and seminars to assist other guard units in preparing for the TAC ORI.
- Designed and implemented asset exercise for KC-135 aircraft. Developed unique training scenarios and one-on-one learning; earned acclaim from the Air Force and a lead article in the *National Guard* magazine.

EDUCATION

M.S. ED., SOUTHERN ILLINOIS UNIVERSITY – Carbondale, Illinois
Completed 57 credits toward Ed.D. in Secondary Education.

B.A. (BUSINESS), NORTHWESTERN UNIVERSITY – Evanston, Illinois

KYLE LAWRENCE

C-LEVEL BUSINESS LEADER
BUSINESS & COMMERCIAL DEVELOPMENT EXPERT

234 Mill Pond Road
Walnut Grove, NJ 09801
910-890-3663
klawrence@juno.com

EXECUTIVE PROFILE

Executive Leadership

Vision, Strategy, & Execution

Development & Leadership

Startup, Turnaround, Change

Divisional & Regional Leadership

Capitalization Strategy

*Deal-Making –
Financing, Strategic Partnerships*

Venture Financing

*Global Sales, Marketing, &
Distribution*

*Process & Performance
Improvement*

Product Development

Product Rollout & Management

Consumer & Institutional Sales

Team Building & Leadership

Channel & Account Management

Technical & Clinical Affairs

Regulatory Compliance

Relationship Management

Internal Relations

Customer Relations

High-performance C-level executive with Fortune 100 / advanced technology experience.

Consistent success in maximizing corporate performance. Drive growth, generate revenues, capture market share, improve profits, and enhance value in domestic and international markets. Mentor, motivate, and lead high-performance business, sales, marketing, product management, and development teams. Value proposition includes:

Effective and wholly accountable in high-profile executive roles.

Overcome complex business challenges and make high-stakes decisions within fast-paced, high-pressure environments using experience-backed judgment, innovation, strong work ethic, humor, and irreproachable integrity. Respected as motivational, lead-by-example manager, change agent, and proponent of empowerment and accountability.

Visionary thinker with global perspective and entrepreneurial drive.

Key contributor to enterprise-level planning and decision-making. Valued advisor and requested consultant to board members, investors, and top-tier executives. Recently conceived and executed corporate strategy, raised funds, and secured in/out technology license agreements for capturing lead market position in the emerging proteomics arena.

Strong orientations in operations and finance.

Participate in high-level operational initiatives—infrastructure design, process reengineering, turnaround, reorganization, business/product integration—for stand-alone businesses, subsidiaries, divisions, and strategic business units—startup, rapid growth, and culture change.

Corporate and business development expert. Marketing strategist and tactician.

Secure feasibility, development, and commercial partner agreements. Spearhead successful market penetration/product launches for emerging technology companies and multinational Fortune 100 R&D, manufacturing, and global distribution enterprises Open new markets/accounts, launch products, drive growth, generate revenue, win market share, improve margins, and manage teams' peak performance.

Experienced in advanced technologies and product development.

Instrumental in identifying, designing, leading development, and marketing technology products in drug discovery/life sciences, medical devices, and medical diagnostics, including domain expertise in laboratory instrumentation, oncology, infectious disease, organ transplantation, and therapeutic drug monitoring. Biomedical technology education and experience.

CHRONOLOGY

PRO-SCX, Inc., Elliott, NJ   **2003 to Present**
CBO — CHIEF BUSINESS OFFICER

Corporate officer/core management team member for this early-stage, venture-backed life science company involved in developing and commercializing technologically advanced tools for comprehensive, quantitative analysis of proteins.

- Report directly to CEO with dotted line reporting to chairman and founder. Contribute to enterprise-level vision, strategy, problem solving, and leadership.

- Manage several crucial areas of operations — business development, strategic partnering, product development and commercialization, marketing, and public relations. Partner with CEO in fundraising and investor relations.

- Attract, hire, and direct talented team of professionals including Senior Directors of Product Development, Business Development, Scientific Affairs, and Regulatory Affairs.

134

CHRONOLOGY/ PRO-SCX

MANAGEMENT ACHIEVEMENTS

- *Strengthened company's credibility as a high-potential player* in the emerging protein array market through expertise in strategy and business development augmented by strong technical background.

- *Virtually transformed and renewed firm's viability and momentum.* Brought renewed focus to corporate strategy by redefining and accelerating product commercialization plan/cycle.

- *Reduced burn-rate by 30+%* by spearheading an organizational restructuring initiative. *Cut headcount from 75 to 51,* reengineered business processes, redesigned commercialization plan, and instilled urgency for financial discipline.

- *Contributed to successful completion of Series C financing* by teaming with the CEO to secure $19.5 million in new funding (venture, angel, and corporate financing).

NEW BUSINESS DEVELOPMENT & MARKETING RESULTS

- *Created a $1.5+ million revenue pipeline* (compared to less than $75,000 on arrival) by targeting, negotiating, and securing agreements with strategic global partners: Mitsui Trading (Tokyo, Japan), National Cancer Center (Tokyo, Japan), Merial (Lyon, FR), Beckman Coulter (Fullerton, CA), and NCI (Gaithersburg, MD).

- *Created a global market channel* by negotiating an international distribution agreement with Mitsui Trading. *Leveraged this relationship to secure $2.5 million investment note.*

- *Acquired necessary technology platforms and instrumentation* by securing agreements from leading proteomic array companies for development of PRO-SCX's breakthrough protein capture aptamer technology.

- *Inspired new energy and confidence companywide* by demonstrating personal enthusiasm and providing strong, decisive leadership to newly recruited business and product development teams of proven "startup athletes."

Consultants Inc., Del Norte, AZ	**2001 to 2003**

CONSULTANT — MANAGEMENT & BUSINESS DEVELOPMENT

Provided corporate strategy, business development, product commercialization, and strategic/tactical marketing consulting to startup and high-growth technology companies. Analyzed needs, determined scope of work, developed strategies, executed action plans, completed deliverables, and built/strengthened relationships. Key engagements included:

CHIEF BUSINESS OFFICER (interim), CONGLOMERATION MEDIA ● Restructured Del Norte-based, venture-backed web design company. Reengineered business model, changed culture, and shifted focus toward Fortune 1000 customers with offerings designed to "connect brands to youth through digital channels" targeting 14- to 21-year-old consumers. Secured intro engagements with such clients as Cisco and Microsoft.

CALVERAS COMMUNICATIONS ● Retained by venture-funded Internet enterprise targeting Internet-based medical transcription services in the health care field. Charged with rationalizing and expanding value of core technology — Centrally Managed Asynchronous Communications (CMAC) — within financial services, retail, and automotive vertical markets.

Isotech, Inc., Hillsdale, VA	**1999 to 2001**

VICE PRESIDENT — SALES & MARKETING

Corporate officer/key management team member of medical device company involved in development, commercialization, and marketing of proprietary, point-of-care, "lab-on-a-chip" clinical diagnostic technology with applications in osteoporosis, diabetes, and home pregnancy testing.

Reported directly to President and CEO, leading team of four professionals in marketing, sales, PR, and administrative support roles. Challenged to drive product rollout, build relationships, carve out partnerships, and generate/grow revenue. Teamed with President in planning and executing high-level corporate leadership initiatives: restructuring company, redeveloping and presenting corporate strategy to board, and raising funds.

MANAGEMENT ACHIEVEMENTS

- *Credited with contributions to re-inspiring investors and BOD* by bringing focus and momentum to company facing need to rationalize core technology in revenue terms by deploying products while controlling burn-rate and raising funds.

- *Partnered with CFO on roadshows and succeeded in securing $5+ million in funding* (including $1.5 million to finance point-of-care information technology spin-off, SigmaCare). Presented at 100-investor, 1999 Corporate Annual Meeting.

CHRONOLOGY/ Isotech

- *Created rational, highly structured, yet flexible corporate strategy wrapped around breakthrough technology* having unlimited potential for revenue and market share in the global medical diagnostic marketplace.

- *Validated viability of platform technology and secured new development funding* (including next-generation home pregnancy test) by closing deals with major medical diagnostic and pharmaceutical companies.

- *Strategy has been validated as Isotech recently gained FDA approval* to launch first home monitoring kit for analysis of HbA1c, a critical measurement of diabetes disease progression.

NEW BUSINESS DEVELOPMENT & MARKETING RESULTS

- *Led spin-off of Isotech's point-of-care IT platform* by creating/securing term sheets from key medical device and venture firms.

- *Succeeded in launching and hitting first-year sales targets* for osteoporosis point-of-care product line through a principal commercial partner (Ostex) and worldwide distribution agreements — US, Europe, and Asia.

- *Defined product specifications, developed FDA, NGSP, and HCFA approval strategy, and selected/negotiated agreements* with global distributors for HbA1c-NOW (POC test for diabetics), the second Isotech product to market.

Pitkin Diagnostics, Pitkin Laboratories, Morgan, IN	**1984 to 1999**
REGIONAL SALES MANAGER — MedTech (Subsidiary of Pitkin Diagnostic Division)	1997 to 1999
SENIOR WORLDWIDE PRODUCT MANAGER — HIV/Hepatitis Diagnostics	1996 to 1997
US MARKETING PRODUCT MANAGER — Cancer Diagnostics	1995 to 1996
TRANSPLANT DIAGNOSTIC SPECIALIST	1990 to 1995
ACCOUNT EXECUTIVE — Chicago Sales Region	1987 to 1990
GROUP LEADER — Rare Reagent Operations	1984 to 1987

Managed key products in new, mature, and intensely competitive national and global markets, for this Fortune 100 health care enterprise. Built and led regional sales organization for newly acquired subsidiary. Hired, motivated, and led teams of up to 15 sales, marketing, and administrative professionals.

MANAGEMENT ACHIEVEMENTS

- *Managed complex post-acquisition transition and integration phases* of newly acquired subsidiary, MedTech.

- *Doubled size of Pitkin's transplant business* ($7 million to over $15 million within three years) by partnering with key worldwide transplant centers, Fujisawa, Novartis, NIH, and UNOS (United Network for Organ Sharing).

    Played significant role in transplant diagnostic product line development, planning, clinical trials, and launch efforts for such products as CsA, FK506, MEGX.

- *Managed and grew Pitkin's $300 million product line across global HIV and hepatitis markets* in high-profile role of Senior Worldwide Product Manager.

- *Successfully defended $100+ million PSA business* by diplomatically, yet assertively, navigating complex affairs with FDA to retain Pitkin's significant business with reference lab, hospital, and clinic-based customers.

SALES & MARKETING RESULTS

- *Ranked #2 in revenues vs. goal and first in sales/representative for Pitkin-MedTech integration. Team exceeded sales goals by targeting VA health system accounts throughout western US.*

- *Achieved 130% of goal for blood glucose consumable sales within hospital* sector (YE 1997) while taking market share from entrenched competitors (J&J, Roche). *Delivered $4.3 million revenue* vs. $3.3 million target for YE 1998.

- Led global product launches (HCV, HIV, P24 Antigen). Product sales resulted in average of *120% of revenue target with minimal cannibalization from existing products. Generated $20+ million in combined new business* within first year of product launches—introduced automated infectious disease testing (HCV) to Asian market.

- *Marketing Team of the Year, 1995; Defensive Marketer of the Year, 1994; President's Club, 1993*

EDUCATION

BS — Microbiology, Larimer University, Larimer, AK, 1985

Continuing education includes leadership, marketing, technology, and negotiation skills training at Hopkins University, University of Jefferson, and others. Details available upon request.

KYLE LAWRENCE

CORPORATE STRATEGIST & C-LEVEL BUSINESS LEADER
BUSINESS DEVELOPMENT EXPERT

234 Mill Pond Road
Walnut Grove, NJ 09801
910-890-3663
klawrence@juno.com

CRITICAL LEADERSHIP INITIATIVES

Recalibrated and restrategized business, setting stage for millions of dollars in deals and funding.

*Isotech, an early-stage medical device company had raised $20 million and begun several development projects without regard to commercial value or degree of difficulty. As **Vice President of Sales and Marketing**, challenged to develop a realistic strategy and recalibrate business and product development.*

Solutions
- Assessed technology vs. available market opportunities as well as current product development programs vs. products' criteria for success in the market.
- Recommended two basic projects—in home pregnancy and diabetes markets.
- Worked to create partnerships and secure continued funding for program completion.
- Change-managed new thought transition for internal and external constituencies and evangelized high-value potential of ongoing projects in development.
- Caused team to reassess several deals to accommodate new thinking.
- Sold board and specific shareholders on viability of new plan (300 investors, several institutions, angels).

Impact
- Firm launched diabetes product (HbA1c), received FDA approval in 2001, and authorized for over-the-counter clearance in 2002.
- Isotech laser focused on R&D activities and secured deal around a pregnancy opportunity with Warner Lambert (now Pfizer) for $2.5 million (1999) in upfront and milestone payments.
- New strategy drove $25 million in additional funds from reputable VCs.
- Company is now marketing only rapid, fully disposable, glycosolated hemoglobin test for home use.

Analysis
I strategically lead innovation through the twists and turns of the needed trade-offs, win teams' hearts and minds, and then take the needed risk to secure the right pay-off.

Refocused teams on value creation activities leading to critical partnerships.

*As **CBO, PRO-SCX**, challenged to re-focus company on basics of value creation by bringing together the right team, positioning the right technology, and addressing the right market opportunity.*

Solutions
- Given control of commercial, product, and business development activities by founder.
- Built high-performing team to access technology and assess potential market opportunities.
- Looked to near-term revenue producers—opportunities that demanded fewer breakthroughs and were more readily accessible.

Impact
- Company is far more focused and has executed critical partnerships needed for revenues.
- Now have co-development efforts with large, validating partners such as Beckman and Perkin Elmer, and can trace a potential path to market.

Analysis
I can lead a team with immature technology and put the company on the right R&D and commercial trajectory, while attracting new investors to our overall value proposition.

continued

137

CRITICAL LEADERSHIP INITIATIVES

Instrumental in gaining foothold and propelling company into $2 billion marketspace.

*As **Regional Sales Director, Pitkin–MedTech**, challenged to help enter $2 billion/year blood glucose testing market after Pitkin acquisition of MedTech ($900 million). As one of three regional managers assigned to orchestrate hospital market entry (from $0 sales platform), was given P&L responsibility, and charged with delivering 4- to 5-year ROI target. Fundamental challenge was to rapidly gain market share vs. established competitors with minimum expenditure while leveraging Pitkin's strong presence in the hospital lab testing sector.*

Solutions
- Analyzed competition (Roche, Bayer, and J&J), and devised attack plan based on product differentiation.
- Determined key to product adoption to be data integration of glucose monitoring results into the LIS (lab info system). Hired several specialists in data integration.
- Successfully wrapped services into offerings and pulled together vendors, collateral, target list, and regional implementation budget.

Impact
- Reached 120% of goal each year — the second of three regions.
- Led competition by launching and differentiating ancillary services into strategic VA hospital market.
- Created data integration services position, adopted by MedTech throughout US.

Analysis
I synthesize innovative strategies that become corporate best practices, and attract and retain a great team of sales and marketing athletes, while positioning team structure, function, and discipline, setting the stage to get products off to a fast start.

Positioned and grew divisional product line to over $18 million in sales / 65% profit within three years.

*As **Transplant Diagnostic Specialist, Pitkin Diagnostics**, challenged to assume role as firm's first and only transplant diagnostic specialist. Tasked with formulating a revenue-producing product development plan for current and future products. Faced $4 million in sales product line, no sign of increasing sales trend, and a business unit with no understanding of organ transplantation.*

Solutions
- Immediately learned everything possible about organ transplantation, spent time with the top surgeons and transplant teams in world's top centers, and saw every nuance of process and clinical challenges.
- Determined needed strategies to jump-start business and requested funding.
- Established relationships with drug companies serving transplant patients, and became experienced with regulatory issues with NIH, FDA, and UNOS (United Network for Organ Sharing).
- Accelerated sales of current products by proving efficacy in clinicals, and funding new product trials with NIH, drug companies, and highest profile transplant centers.
- Secured an advisory board and attracted the best surgeons and physicians.

Impact
- Grew business to over $18 million in three years of tenure, with profit margins of over 65%.
- Business now produces over $50 million and offers over 25 products to transplant centers globally.
- Came to understand organ transplantation so well, from a technical and clinical side, that frequently presented at "grand rounds."
- Gained great respect from the transplant community, sat on the steering committee at UNOS, and orchestrated a $25,000 Pitkin donation to UNOS.

Analysis
I combine business development, sales, relationship skills, research, and product development abilities to develop and sustain a thriving business.

138

CHAPTER 7

Best Resumes for Transitioning Into Technology Careers

Building the Foundation

Transferability of skills is the foundation upon which every effective career transition resume is written. Your challenge, therefore, is to identify the skills, qualifications, experiences, and competencies you have that will be of value in your new job, career, or industry. Those skills then become the key points in your resume around which everything else is written.

To help you get started with identifying your transferable skills, review the brief listing below of *some* of the skills, qualifications, and competencies that companies and recruiters look for in candidates seeking positions in technology or technology industries. (*Note that this is only a partial listing of the countless different skills that companies look for in qualified candidates.*)

Carefully review the keywords and keyword phrases to identify those that accurately reflect skills you possess and which are transferable into your new position. Then, be sure to incorporate those words into your resume, your cover letters, and any other career marketing documents that you create. They will capture a prospective employer's interest and open the door to interviews and opportunities. Most important, be sure to include all of your specific technical knowledge (e.g., hardware, software, operating systems, applications, programming languages, networks, development tools).

Applications Development
Data Mining & Warehousing
Database Design & Administration
E-Commerce & E-Trade
Help Desk
Information Risk Management
Intellectual Property
Knowledge Management
Technology Development & Testing
Telecommunications Technology

Lifecycle Management
Network Protocols
Project Administration
Project Milestones
Software Development
Systems Administration
Systems Security
Technical Documentation
User Training & Support
Wireless Communications

Sample Career Transition Resumes

Following are six sample resumes for individuals seeking to transition into technology positions and/or industries. Each of these resumes was written by a professional resume writer with extensive experience working with, writing for, and positioning individuals in career transition. Full contact information for each of these writers is in the Appendix. To understand why these resumes were written and designed the way that they were, it is critical that you read the following information, which explains the specific objective of each of these job seekers and the particular strategy that was used to prepare their resume.

Resume:	Matt Riley (pages 142-143)
Writer:	Debra O'Reilly
Objective:	To transition from IT career focused on system administration and into a higher-level IT position in web development/management.
Strategy:	Led resume with his newly earned and extremely relevant credentials along with a strong endorsement of the added value he brings to his workplace daily. Focused job descriptions on solid technical achievements and their long-term performance improvement results.

Resume:	Marissa Whitney-Byrne (pages 144-145)
Writer:	Lorie Lebert
Objective:	To continue in a high-level IT management position while transitioning out of the insurance industry and into a higher-growth industry.
Strategy:	Clear and crisp presentation of her skills, experience, and project management expertise summarized succinctly on page one. Page two dedicated to brief summaries of education and other relevant experience, from technical expertise to professional honors and awards.

Resume:	Catherine Peterson (pages 146-147)
Writer:	Michele Haffner
Objective:	To move up the ranks in the field of IT management.
Strategy:	Titled summary as "General Management Profile" and used summary to highlight wealth of general management, project management, and operating management qualifications. Demonstrated strong performance and record of achievement in each position and highlighted combined accounting, marketing, and IT educational credentials.

Resume:	Harold Baker (pages 148-149)
Writer:	Beverly Harvey
Objective:	To transition from senior-level IT management to C-level IT management regardless of industry.
Strategy:	Developed executive profile highlighting his most impressive qualifications, diverse range of experience, and most notable core competencies. Used current position to explain the diversity of his responsibilities and functions;

used key phrases for earlier positions to indicate broad scope of functional accountability and most notable projects and achievements.

Resume: Stanley Gregson (pages 150-152)
Writer: Don Orlando
Objective: To bring to the forefront his previous experience in rocket science and technology to facilitate his transition from the military into a mid- to senior-level civilian technology career.
Strategy: Crafted a modified CV format to showcase his background and the two most important elements: his expertise in problem-solving and solutions delivery and his proof of performance as a talented scientist, technologist, and senior executive. Followed with impressive listing of educational credentials, technology skills, publications, and professional presentations to clearly demonstrate his value and reputation.

Resume: Mary Carlson (pages 153-155)
Writer: Don Orlando
Objective: To transition out of traditional technology career and into the newly emerging field of knowledge management in a CKO-level position.
Strategy: Portrayed leading-edge skills and competencies in new technology discipline and immediately connected that expertise to her bottom-line financial and performance contributions. Showcased fast-track career promotion and notable achievements with emphasis on quantifiable results. Solidified value with short list of presentations, publications, and "capabilities that leverage the power of IT."

Matt Riley, PCLP

25842 Munson Drive   Waterview, CT 06005   mattt.riley@yahoo.com   **203-929-7690**

SOFTWARE & APPLICATION DEVELOPER / WEB PROGRAMMER
Lotus Notes / Domino Development / System Administration
Top Three Priorities: People - Process - Performance

The "go-to" person: Fast-track advancements throughout high-tech career, including more than 5 years in information technology. **R5 & ND6 Principal Certified Lotus Professional** (PCLP) in **Lotus Notes / Domino development.** Currently working in Notes **system administration.** Dedicated to making the organization better today than it was yesterday.

- ✓ Expertise in the creation, implementation, and support of web technologies including dynamic web sites and Lotus Notes database systems.
- ✓ Experience in the full System Development Life Cycle (SDLC), from requirements gathering and client needs analysis through design, development, testing, and implementation, to system maintenance, upgrade, and support. Skilled in writing system requirements and other technical documentation.
- ✓ Demonstrated ability to build consensus between business and IT, producing win-win solutions that enhance productivity and increase profitability.
- ✓ Strengths in process reengineering/operational improvement, team leadership, workflow management, performance evaluation, organizational change, and customer relationship management.
- ✓ Extensive technical background in the nuclear power industry.

Technical Skills:

Languages/Databases: Lotus Notes @Formula, LotusScript, JavaScript, HTML, XML, Java, Java Servlets, JSP, JDBC, Eiffel, SQL, PL/1, JCL, Fortran
Applications: Remedy, Primavera P3e, MS Office Suite, Dreamweaver3, Lotus Notes, Endevor
Operating Systems: Windows 95/98/2000/XP, AS/390, UNIX
Development Tools: Percussion Software's Notrix Enterprise Data Integration Tool

PROFESSIONAL EXPERIENCE

Connecticut Power Utility, Bridgeport, CT   1993–Present
Lotus Notes System Administrator, IT Department (2004–Present)
  Recruited to this position. Coordinate all activities of the Groupware/E-Mail infrastructure. Assess and meet data recovery, maintenance, data integrity, and space requirement needs to optimize space allocation and maximize system performance. Write technical system requirements for all application development projects.

Accomplishments:
- ✓ Automated Disk Quota Increase process, facilitating first-level support; saved 20 labor hours per week.
- ✓ Automated Corporate Information Security renaming process, saving 5 hours per week.

Business Application System Developer, IT Department (1999–2004)
  Planned, designed, developed, tested, coordinated, implemented, and maintained computer business applications to meet client needs. Developed enhanced technology solutions for functions including scheduling, charting, reporting, and billing. Served as **Lotus Notes QA Reviewer**.

Accomplishments:
- ✓ Created browser-based, intranet reimbursement program system to track and manage requests for educational programs and reimbursement processing. Reduced Human Resource labor expenditure by 30 hours weekly. Tools: JavaScript, HTML, NotesView, ActiveX, Lotus Notes, and Java.
- ✓ Special assignment: IT Account Executive for Environmental Health & Safety Department (9/03–12/04). Conducted needs assessment and created high-level cost-benefit analysis. Served as business-IT liaison and ombudsman. Assessed business strategies and created technology solutions to optimize performance and profitability, ultimately resulting in ISO 14001 certification.

✓ Created and implemented software application to track and quantify team work requests. This application also serves as a software engineering management tool. Benefit: It has proved so effective that it was adopted by three other IT groups.

✓ Selected as member of Software Engineering process improvement committee. Continue to lead work group toward formalized project documentation process.

✓ Developed Environmental Incident Reporting system. Introduced Lotus Notes Connector to create real-time connections to RDBMS, execute stored procedures, and process dynamic results. For the first time, senior management receives real-time reports consolidated from a variety of previously isolated sources.

✓ Developed Lotus Notes application to track claims and automatically generate response letters to insureds, using MS COM.

✓ Leadership activities have included:
- Organized/hosted local-area Domino Users Group meeting; one of 3 company-sponsored presenters.
- Chairman of and presenter to Lotus Notes Special Interest Group (SIG) on subjects including Lotus Connector Classes, XML, and Java.
- Organized and hosted combined utilities Best Practice meeting (9/04). Conducted presentation on topic of Lotus Notes Application Development Best Practices.

In 1999, transitioned from nuclear power technology to information technology, quickly establishing a reputation for proficiency in the development, implementation, and maintenance of business application systems and the positive leadership of technical teams.

Engineering Technologist, Nuclear Power Plant Operations (1998–1999)
Reactor Operator/Plant Equipment Operator (1993–1998)

Following six years of steady advancement to increasing responsibilities at two nuclear power plants, was ultimately promoted to direct and evaluate plant operators/operations. Implemented quality assurance procedures to maintain safety, quality, and compliance with federal and company requirements. Previously managed start-up, operation, and shut-down for nuclear steam electric plant equipment. Also acted as Equipment Safety Tagger.

Accomplishments:
✓ Authored major revisions to reactivity control procedures, refueling procedures, and technical specification surveillances.
✓ Liaison to Nuclear Regulatory Commission (NRC) examiners for validation of power-plant operator license examination.

MILITARY SERVICE

U.S. Army: E4, Honorable Discharge   1987–1989

EDUCATION/PROFESSIONAL DEVELOPMENT

Principal Certified Lotus Professional (PCLP) in Application Development (R5, R6/ND6)

M.S. Computer Science, Rensselaer Polytechnic Institute	2003
B.S. Nuclear Engineering Technology, Fairfield College	1998
A.S. Nuclear Science Technology / A.S. General Engineering Technology,	
State Technical College	1990
Completed Boston University **Project Management Certificate Program**	2003

Continuing studies (through employer):
Employee relations, conflict management, safety, root-cause analysis, business presentation, goal-setting, and nuclear power-related training. Also Seven Habits of Highly Effective People and Imagine 21.

143

Marissa Whitney-Byrne

byrnewhit@adelphia.net

112 Brentwood Drive • Bloomfield Hills, MI 48302
Cell: 248 / 671.5776 • *Home:* 248 / 671.1061

Information Privacy / Risk Services Professional

Business privacy specialist with thorough knowledge and understanding of security methods and technical elements to protect corporate data. Experience implementing privacy and security programs, application security, and database technologies used to store enterprise information, directory services, and information systems. Strong command of technologies used to access, collect, and distribute data.

Qualifications in:

- Privacy Legislation Compliance
- Sarbanes-Oxley Act / SOA Compliance
- Information Risk Management Technology
- Business Solutions Integration
- Critical / Technical Security Measures
- Intellectual Property Management

- Data Collection / Usage / Disclosure Practices
- Business / Privacy Best Practices
- Consumer/Government/Media Inquiries/Complaints
- Disaster Recovery / Business Continuity
- Information Technology Strategies
- Asset Management / Business Priorities

Master of Science in Information Technology and Privacy Law

Business/Corporate Experience

FARMERS INSURANCE GROUP (1994-present); Troy, MI
IT Project Manager • 1994-present
Specialize in large-scale business information risk and legislative compliance initiatives. Provide information security services, including impact assessments, training, and business development. Responsible for end-to-end project management on development of the case, detailed project plans, tracking results, vendor management, coordination of IT, change management with users, and work process improvements.

Corporate Tax Accountant • 1994-96
Developed, prepared, and analyzed budgets, income statements, balance sheets, and other tax accounts; designed financial models, tools, and projections that responded to corporate forecasting needs. Tracked performance according to defined metrics, analyzed variances, and coordinated with other departments to ensure that financial assumptions were consistent across all departments.

WB VIDEO/PENCOM; West Bloomfield, MI
Owner • 1990-94
Full-service video franchise specializing in surveillance systems and equipment. Turned around from near bankruptcy to operating in the black the first year, with profitability increasing each successive year.

LAW OFFICES OF WHITNEY, CRANDALL & COBURN; Birmingham, MI
Tax Accountant • 1986-89
Represented corporate and individual clients in tax audits.

Project Management

- <u>Infrastructure</u>: technical infrastructure project management.
- <u>Legislative Compliance</u>: business compliance and legislative compliance projects.
- <u>Information Risk Management</u>: information privacy, confidentiality, integrity, information security, intellectual property management, and operational risks.
- <u>Data Mining</u>: multidimensional analysis, decision support, and predictive analysis.
- <u>Application Development</u>: new development and customization application development.
- <u>Redesign</u>: migration over multiple platforms. / <u>Research</u>: technical research projects.
- <u>Technical Strategy</u>: information technology alignment to business strategy.
- <u>Organizational Change/Reengineering</u>: planning, building, and deploying changes in the organization.

144

Education

SCHOOL OF LAW– NORTHWESTERN UNIVERSITY
Master of Science in Information Technology and Privacy Law *(with honors)* • June 2003

Legal topics/classes in • GLBA • HIPAA • Cybercrime • Electronic Contracting • Privacy Governance & Assurance • Intellectual Property • FCRA • FOIA • UCETA • EU Directive • eCommerce • High-Technology Litigation • Legal Research & Writing • Dispute Resolution Alternatives

UNIVERSITY OF MICHIGAN
Bachelor of Science / Minor in Accounting *(cum laude)* • January 1994

Technical/Legal/Business Seminars

Information Risk Management Best Practices for Financial Services – Enterprise Risk Management Research Study • 2002

Decision Models – Peter Senge / Risk Management – Carl Prichard • 2002

Legal Issues in IT Project Management, Data Warehouse Technical Primer – Recent trends in project management involving intellectual property management, contractual, and outsourcing issues • 2002

Bones, Clones, & Twilight Zones: The Digital Persona – Intellectual Property Management & Disputes • 2002

Information Security & Privacy in the Public Sector – Business Information Risk Management • 2001

IAPP International Association of Privacy Professionals – Information Privacy Exposition for Privacy Professionals • 2001

Data Warehousing Project Management – Data Warehousing Educational Series • 2001

Data Warehouse Technical Primer – Technical Data Structures of Operational Data Warehousing • 2000

Technical Experience
Languages / Platforms / Applications

MS Project, Lotus Notes, Knowledge Factory, JavaScript, HTML, COBOL, Basic, FORTRAN, SAS, SEER-SEM, SPSS, UNIX, Windows Operating System

---

Teaching/Public Relations

University of Michigan– **Teaching Assistant** for professor of Early American History as part of an honors program assignment

Ann Arbor Middle School – **Volunteer**, helped teacher with a class assignments and taught computer skills to children

Women's Protection Association – **Court Appointed Advocate for Women**

Professional Service Associations & Memberships

- The Michigan Bar Association
- Project Management Institute
- The Life Office Management Association
- Toastmasters International
- Data Warehousing - Project Management Leadership Series, Data Management Institute

- Intellectual Property Law Association of Detroit
- Central Michigan Chapter, PMI
- Life Management Institute
- CASA – Child Protection Network

Professional Designations/Honors & Awards

- University of Michigan Honors Society
- Women's Protection Assn., Citizen Award
- FLMI designation, Life Mgmt. Institute
- CLU – one more credit/class remaining to complete designation, Moorehead College

- ACS designation, Smythe Management Institute
- PMP designation, Project Management Professional
- Honors Status, Golden Key National Honors Society

1326 Stony Creekside Lane • Port Washington, WI 53011
Home: (262) 375-1938 • Mobile: (262) 333-8846

GENERAL MANAGEMENT PROFILE

Over seven years of mid- to senior-level management and consulting experience within global manufacturing and privately held businesses. Results-oriented with a solid accounting and information technology background. Demonstrated ability to develop and execute strategic and tactical operational plans; currently managing infrastructure systems for the $20 million North American arm of an international organization. Enrolled in Master of Business Administration degree program with triple undergraduate degrees in Accounting, Management Information Systems, and Marketing.

Recognized by Executive Management/Board of Directors for ability to identify/analyze operational issues, develop solutions, and implement best practices and process improvements that improve organizational bottom line in terms of profitability and improved sales.

Core competencies/areas of expertise include:

- Strategic and Tactical Business Planning
- Profit Improvements and Revenue Gains
- Budgeting, Planning, and Forecasting
- Process Design and Development

- General Ledger and Cost Accounting
- Full Lifecycle Project/Program Management
- Inventory, Supply Chain, and Logistics
- Customer Relationship Development

PROFESSIONAL EXPERIENCE

SIEVERS INCORPORATED – Milwaukee, WI   1990 to Present
North American subsidiary of Sievers Global providing engineering, manufacturing, and distribution of voltage transducers for industrial and traction applications.

INFRASTRUCTURE SYSTEMS MANAGER (2003 to Present)
INFORMATION SYSTEMS MANAGER, NORTH AMERICAN OPERATIONS (1996 to 2003)
ACCOUNTING MANAGER (1990 to 1996)

Recruited to develop business processes/procedures for accounting system and computer network. From 1990 to 2000, organization expanded to accommodate rapid business growth and sales volume: $5 million (1990) to $32 million (2004).

As Infrastructure Systems Manager, report to the U.S. General Manager and manage a team of 12 in support of a nationwide sales force. Direct accountability for quality customer service, order entry, purchasing, inventory planning, and logistics, with collateral accountability for network administration, computer systems, and accounting.

- Appointed in 2003 to a five-person executive management team charged with strategic business planning, budget development, and financial decision making for North American operations.
- Implemented improved sales forecasting procedures and developed an information database that rolls into production/ERP and budgeting systems. System is used throughout entire organization.
- Reduced inventory from $2.5 million to $1.5 million in 10 months. Implemented demand forecasting systems to maintain adequate inventory levels and improve on-time delivery.
- Improved logistics efficiencies and profitability through task automation, cost analysis, and re-negotiation of carrier contracts.
- Designed business software applications and databases for ISO 9000 documentation, customer relationship management, engineering change orders, and product technical information. Developed a global pricing database used throughout entire organization for raw material procurement.

146

PROFESSIONAL EXPERIENCE (continued)

SHORT-TERM CONTRACTS AND CONSULTING – Milwaukee, WI   Mar 1989 to Dec 1990

SOFTWARE CONSULTANT (6 months)
Marketed, sold, installed, and supported MAS90 accounting system software for local small business clientele. Performed system analysis to recommend best solutions. Migrated/converted client data to new system. Produced custom reports based on needs analysis. Educated clients to use full functionality of software.

ACCOUNTING MANAGER (6 months)
Managed and trained five employees. Restructured procedures and provided assistance with Accounts Payable, Accounts Receivable, Sales Order Entry, Credit, Inventory Management, and Purchasing functions. Researched and corrected negative stock issues; developed procedures to better track physical inventory. Developed reporting and macros to aid senior management with budgeting and financial analysis. Served as major player in accounting system conversion.

ACCOUNTING CONSULTANT (10 months)
Managed accounting, payroll, and job-costing functions for local manufacturing firms. Restructured job costing, accounts receivable, and order-entry procedures to improve efficiency, on-time delivery, and cost analysis. Developed management reporting to analyze labor and job profitability. Assisted with development of a complete business administration system: sales proposal through manufacturing/production and customer delivery.

EJ CONSTRUCTION COMPANY – Menomonee Falls, WI   Oct 1986 to Mar 1989
Privately held industrial and commercial construction firm with 100 employees.

OFFICE MANAGER
Position reported to the Controller and supervised a staff of four responsible for Accounts Payable, Accounts Receivable, Job Costing and Financial Analysis, General Ledger Reporting, Reconciliation/Month-End Close, Payroll, Tax Reporting, and Union Reporting. Administered computer system and Novell Network; performed hardware and software troubleshooting.

- Served as liaison between Accounting and Engineering Departments to improve processes and reduce job costs.
- Conducted full audit of previous seven years of accounting records; discovered more than $100,000 in missing revenue. Notified senior management who enlisted authorities to apprehend suspected employee. Developed and implemented complete accounting procedures with checks and balances to prevent future occurrences.
- Set up Purchasing and Equipment modules to the COINS System; developed reports using the Progress language.

EDUCATION

MBA PROGRAM   Expected Completion Fall 2006
Marquette University, Milwaukee, Wisconsin

BA (ACCOUNTING)   1993
Alverno College, Milwaukee, Wisconsin

BBA (MIS AND MARKETING – DOUBLE MAJOR COMPLETED IN THREE YEARS)   Aug 1986
University of Wisconsin, Madison, Wisconsin

Completed 12-month Internship with FIserv   June 1985 to May 1986

Harold Baker, CISM, CISSP, SSCP, CBCP

9720 Roosevelt Way
Seattle, Washington 98115

hbaker@earthlink.net

Home: (206) 528-8754
Cell: (206) 528-4744

Chief Information Security Officer / Senior Consultant / Director of Infrastructure

Certified Information Security Manager – Certified Information Systems Security Professional
Systems Security Certified Practitioner – Certified Business Continuity Professional

Business – Security – Business Continuity Planning (BCP) & Disaster Recovery (DR) – Network
Distributed Systems – Knowledge Management (KM) – Project Management (PM)

All Systems/Environments – Platforms – Technologies – Communication Protocols

Extensive Expertise in:

- Policy Framework, Documentation & Implementation
- System Threat & Vulnerability Analysis & Mitigation
- System & Environmental Audits
- Business Impact Analysis (BIA)
- Risk Assessment & Analysis
- Organizational Communication Plans
- Multi-Level Project Management

- System & Program Life Cycle Maturity
- Enterprise & Business Unit Infrastructure
- Total Cost of Ownership (TCO)
- Return on Investment (ROI) Strategies
- Audit Process, Execution, & Analysis
- Strategic Business & Tactical Visioning
- Business Consulting

PROFESSIONAL EXPERIENCE

Flextronics, Seattle, Washington   2002–Present
A global provider of electronics manufacturing and integrated supply chain services offering new product design materials management, high-tech manufacturing, and end-of-life support for high-tech electronics companies.

Senior IT Security & Business Continuity/Disaster Recovery Architect

Hired to build new security architecture for international enterprise with 32,000 end users in 131 locations worldwide.

As **Senior Architect**, lead projects and initiatives in the areas of Business, Security, Business Continuity Planning (BCP) and Disaster Recovery (DR), Network, Distributed Systems, Knowledge Management, and Project Management for Flextronics's organizations at both the enterprise and business unit level.

Provide **Business Consulting** through the identification, analysis, and documentation of business, security, and IT processes as well as business and IT technical needs and requirements as related to business mapping, business/IT strategy and alignment, BCP/DR strategies, plans and practices, tactical and strategic security planning and recommendations, and overall IT mapping.

Provide **Recommendations** through strategic and tactical visioning, written documentation, definition of policies and procedures, and oral and written communication plans and presentations for senior executives and board members as related to the business and IT environment.

Manage **Security, Wide Area Network/Local Area Network, BCP/DR, and Application** planning, analysis, design, development, implementation, documentation, and operations. Manage diverse functions including security architecture, design and implementation, WAN/LAN network projects, BCP/DR projects, network administration/implementation/management, and overall systems administration.

Lead the effort for **Enterprise-Wide Deployments** including IT risk assessments and DR plans; laptop encryption; host intrusion detection and network intrusion detection capability; security awareness; security risk assessment; security design and architecture; security policies and procedures; server and desktop hardware initiatives; VPN security; personal firewall, anti-virus, and management for all desktops.

Lead **Project Management** teams of up to 120 in collaborative efforts with overall project deliverables. Manage all aspects including planning, budget development/spend definition/administration, and project team development. Completed numerous projects on time and under budget. Currently leading:

AntiVirus and Firewall Project: $965K, 2-year, 3-phase enterprise-wide project
Anti-Spam Project: $210K anti-spam deployment to all email gateways (120 worldwide)
DR Project: $2 million initiative (first DR program in company's 30-year history)

148

Telecom E-Solutions, San Jose, California 1997–2002
Telecom's Consulting Group formed in 1997 specializing in Security Architecture. Group was spun off in 2002.

Business/Security/Network/BCP/DR Solutions Architect & Consultant

Led initiatives in the areas of Business, Security, BCP and DR, Network, and Distributed Systems for a diverse range of organizations including technology, telecommunications, insurance, financial, retail, oil, natural gas, utilities, and government.

Provided business consulting/recommendations and performed system, WAN/LAN, BCP/DR and applications planning, analysis, design, development, implementation, documentation, and operation. Conducted educational classes and seminars for peers and customers.

Representative Long-Term Assignments:

Security/Network/BCP/DR & Business Architect/Consultant – Diner Card Financial Services

Requested by Diner Card as Architect and Consultant in the areas of Security Planning, Design and Engineering, Network Planning and BCP/DR. Efforts included all areas of Security Architecture and Engineering, WAN/LAN Engineering, and BCP/DR.

Security/Network/BCP/DR & Business Architect/Consultant – Nortel Networks

Requested by Nortel Networks as Architect and Consultant in the areas of Security, Network Infrastructure, and general business direction. Managed projects related to Nortel's WAN/LAN; Extranet network for suppliers, vendors, manufacturers, and partners worldwide; Remote Office network for all engineering and sales offices worldwide; and Remote Access to Nortel's internal network.

IBM Global Services, Armonk, New York 1994–1997

Communications Design Engineer (1997)
FEP Planner/Engineer (1994–1997)
Communication Project Engineer (1993–1994)

Network Engineer Supervisor, IBM Account: Kimble Glass, Tampa, Florida
Network Service Analyst, IBM Account: Florida Eligibility, Tallahassee, Florida
Network Service Analyst, IBM Account: GM Assembly, Wilmington, Delaware

CERTIFICATIONS

Certified Information Security Manager (CISM), 2003
Certified Information Systems Security Professional (CISSP), 2002
Systems Security Certified Practitioner (SSCP), 2002
Certified Business Continuity Professional (CBCP), 2002
ISS Internet Scanner Certification, 2001
ISS Systems/Database Certification, 2001
Associate Business Continuity Planner (ABCP), 1999
Nortel Certified Network Associate (CCNA), 1999
Nortel Certified Design Associate (CCDA), 1999

EDUCATION / PROFESSIONAL DEVELOPMENT

MA, Computer Engineering Management – Clarkson University, Potsdam, New York

BBA, Business Administration – *Magna Cum Laude* – University of San Diego, California

IBM Global Services Telecommunications Professional Development (TPD), February 1992
IBM Global Services Network Communications Development (NCD), December 1989
IBM Global Services Management Internship Program, June 1989
IBM Global Services Operations Development (OPD), November 1985

AWARDS

Telecom Annual Excellence Contributor of the Year Award, 2001
Telecom Quarterly Excellence Award: Q4 2001 for consulting work at Discover Card
Telecom Quarterly Excellence Award: Q3 2000 for consulting work at Cisco Systems
Telecom E-Solutions 1999 Golden Wing Contributor of the Year Award
Telecom E-Solutions 1999 Golden Eagle Awards: (5) KDOT, OG&E, H&P, CCNA, CCDA

STANLEY GREGSON, PH.D.

700 West Drive, Montgomery, Alabama 36100

✉ sgregs@knology.net ☎ 334.569.3767 (Office) — 219.399.0960 (Cell)

WHAT I OFFER **JACOBS SVERDRUP** AS YOUR NEWEST **CHIEF TECHNOLOGIST**

Leadership to move IT development forward

Strategic mindset to help diverse, technical teams from the private and public sectors translate vision into results

Skill to build and maintain durable, **mutually beneficial relationships** within organizations and between organizations and customers

Persuasive, logically sound **communications abilities** that help people make contributions they didn't think possible

RELEVANT WORK HISTORY WITH EXAMPLES OF PROBLEMS SOLVED

More than 20 years in positions of increasing responsibility as a commissioned Air Force officer, including these relevant assignments:

Hired away by name to be the **Executive Vice President**, *endorsed by the Board of Visitors and promoted to* **Interim President**, Community College of the Air Force, Maxwell Air Force Base, Alabama, 03 – Present

CCAF is the largest technology-based, multi-campus community college in the world. We offer more than 2,200 courses, many of them technical, to 300,000 students at 121 locations.

Helped resolve a chronic problem that kept academia from providing high-quality space technicians to industry—our customers. Overcame resistance from private sector competitors and pulled together an educational consortium. *Outcome:* **In just one year**, National Science Foundation gave us **full funding** ($3M).

Selected over hundreds of tough competitors to pursue, at Air Force expense, a **Ph.D. in Aerospace Engineering** *at Penn State University, then served as* **Assistant Professor of Aerospace Engineering,** *and promoted to* **Deputy Department Head and Assistant Professor of Aerospace Engineering,** Air Force Institute of Technology, Wright Patterson Air Force Base, Ohio, 00 to 03

Went beyond traditional methods to build a truly high-speed algorithm for high-performance molecular simulations of rocket combustion processes. *Outcomes:* My method produced a **perfectly balanced, multi-processor algorithm** that ran 100 to **1,000 times faster**. Then showed our chemistry department that adding only a few lines of code would enable modeling they had sought for years.

Transformed a huge mass of simulation data into a 3-D, animated, full-color representation of supercritical evaporation using scientific first principles. Entire work done in only 90 days. *Outcomes:* **Customer saw the value at once.** My work helped us **win a major contract**.

More indicators of performance Jacobs Sverdrup can use

Stepped in smoothly when unexpected budget cuts threatened to shut down research efforts from combustion to thermodynamics, to heat transfer, to hypersonics, to space propulsion. Instructed dozens of students in all five areas. Also persuaded Wright-Patterson Laboratories and NASA Glenn Research Center to free up experts we needed. *Outcomes:* **Award-winning research** and qualified experts made available to our customers.

Designed, implemented, and **championed an unorthodox solution** to a lack of critically needed supercomputing power. **Partnered with local universities** to bring in $200K in scholarship funds—and the qualified people we needed to support our operations. *Outcomes:* **Customers very satisfied** with our work. **Enduring** professional **relationships** with academia cemented.

Instructor in Aeronautics, Air Force Academy, Colorado Springs, Colorado, 97 – 00

Chosen as the youngest faculty member ever to develop an advanced thermodynamics course. Without the benefit of overlap, produced this three-semester hour engineering course in a hurry. Then used my work to help senior engineering students. *Outcome:* **Passing rates** for EIT students **rose 20 percent** in the first year alone.

Assistant Professor of Aerospace Studies, University of Arizona, Tucson, Arizona, 94 – 97

Mastered new technology and customer needs to provide this organization with its **first technologically advanced instruction system**. *Outcome:* My system became **a model nationwide**.

Turbine Engine Research Engineer *promoted to* **Operations and Development Engineer**, NASA Lewis Research Center, Cleveland, Ohio, and Engine Test Facility, Arnold Engineering Development Center, Arnold Air Force Base, Tennessee, 90 – 94

Guided a collection of motivated contractors into a cooperative, closely knit group willing to commit to Center excellence. *Outcome:* Our **testing output rose dramatically**.

EDUCATION AND PROFESSIONAL DEVELOPMENT

Ph.D., **Aerospace Engineering**, Pennsylvania State University, 99 *Completed this ABET-accredited course early. My advisor, a full professor, said my **ratings** from my thesis review committee were the **highest he had ever seen**.*

M.S., **Mechanical Engineering**, University of Tennessee, 89 *Earned this degree while maintaining full-time employment at the Arnold Engineering Development Center and carrying a full academic load.*

B.S., **Mechanical Engineering**, Auburn University, 86 *Awarded a **full, four-year scholarship** by the Air Force. Only one of 30 mechanical engineers to graduate with **High Honors**. Inducted into the **national engineering honor society**. Worked 10 hours a week, but was still able to complete this program six months early.*

Relevant short courses including System Safety and Reliability Analysis, Astrodynamics, and Aerospace Propulsion, 90, 92, and 93

Related courses in Acquisition Planning and Analysis, 88 and 89

IT SKILLS

Expert in **parallel programming** (including MPI), FORTRAN, and UNIX

Proficient in **visualization** and **engineering simulation software**, Excel, Word, PowerPoint, Outlook, and LANtastic (a local area networking software)

Working knowledge of Fluent (a **fluid dynamics software** suite)

RELEVANT PUBLICATIONS AND PRESENTATIONS

"Technical Education in the Air Force," briefings to the Chief Scientist of the Air Force, CEO-equivalents in the Air Force education and training communities, and senior Air Force Headquarters executives, 00 – 02

"Qualifications for Space Technicians," briefings to senior NASA, corporate, and National Science Foundation executives, 02

Kaltz, T.L., Long, L.N., Micci, M.M., & Gregson, S.G., "Supercritical Vaporization of Liquid Oxygen Droplets Using Molecular Dynamics," _Combustion Science and Technology_, 136, pg. 279, 98

Gregson, S.G., "Parallel Molecular Dynamics using Truncated Octahedron Periodic Boundaries," Eighth SIAM Conference on Parallel Processing for Scientific Computing, 87

Little, J.K., "Simulation of Droplet Evaporation in Supercritical Environments using Parallel Molecular Dynamics," unpublished Ph.D. thesis, Pennsylvania State University, 96

Micci, M.M., Long, L.N., & Gregson, S.G., "Parallel Molecular Dynamics of Supercritical Evaporation," Proceedings of Parallel CFD, Capri, Italy, 96

Long, L.N., Micci, M.M., Kaltz, T.L., & Gregson, S.G., "Submicron Droplet Modeling using Molecular Dynamics," _AIAA 95-0412_, 95

Kaltz, T.L., Gregson, S.G., Wong, B., Micci, M.M., & Long, L.N., "Supercritical Droplet Evaporation Modeled using Molecular Dynamics of Parallel Processors," Proceedings of Euromech Colloquium 324, The Combustion of Drops, Sprays, and Aerosols, Marseilles, France, 94

Gregson, S.G., Allen, G.P., McDonald, G. E., & Hendricks, R.C., "Ribbon-Burner Simulation of the T-700 Turbine Shroud Section for Ceramic-Lined Seals Research," NASA Technical Memorandum 86940, NASA Lewis Research Center, 85

Biesiandny, T.J., McDonald, G.E., Hendricks, J.K., Gregson, S.G., Robinson, R.A., Klann, G.A., & Lassow, E., "Experimental and Analytical Study of Ceramic-Coated Turbine-Tip Shroud Seal for Small Turbine Engines," NASA Technical Memorandum 86881, NASA Lewis Research Center, 85

Biesiandny, T.J., Klann, G.A., & Gregson, S.G., "Response of a Small-Turboshaft-Engine Compression System to Inlet Temperature Distortion, NASA Technical Memorandum 83765, NASA Lewis Research Center, 84

PROFESSIONAL AFFILIATIONS

American Society of Engineering Education, since 92

American Institute of Aeronautics and Astronautics, since 98

SECURITY CLEARANCE

Top Secret

Available for relocation to the Santa Barbara area

MARY CARLSON

2020 Nautical Road	843.295.3111 (Office)
Charleston, South Carolina 29401 mcarlson034@msn.com	843.866.9065 (Home)

WHAT I CAN OFFER THE MONARCH CORPORATION AS YOUR NEWEST CHIEF KNOWLEDGE OFFICER

Proven skill at inspiring people to harvest and share knowledge that **boosts productivity and profits**—faster than your competition.

Solid experience in using KM to **maximize ROI** on *all* your investments while limiting liabilities across the board.

Tested leadership transforms isolated groups of "subject matter experts" into a **synergistic community** that thrives on the rewards cooperation brings.

Practiced communication skills to find who has **knowledge we all need**, which questions I should ask, and what the answers should look like.

Honed intellect that separates the urgent from the important, spots important trends on sight, and **translates data into vital information.**

RECENT WORK HISTORY WITH EXAMPLES OF PROBLEMS SOLVED

Hired away by a director to be **Senior Internal Auditor,** *then promoted over 20, more experienced professionals to be* **Control Design Analyst;** *then sought out by IT management to be promoted over 200 competitors to be* **Lead Analyst,** *later promoted from four eligibles to be* **Business Systems Consultant.**
Timberland Corporation, Charleston, South Carolina   Jun 99 to Present

Timberland builds upon its 75-year history to be the industry leader in building products, household, and industry paper products. Annual sales approach $26B.

Serve as indirect reporting official for a team of 25 from lead analysts to systems analysts to programmer analysts to business analysts. Build and **defend all KM budgets** ($500K) with direct impact on operations valued at $1.5M.

Helped every level below senior management see clearly—for the first time—how their reporting efforts kept our company competitive. What managers once saw as "busy work" is now viewed as cooperative tools to remove roadblocks and save time. *Payoffs:* Centers of excellence working together as never before. **Now people *want* to be accountable.**

Guided teams to replace our growing expensive, numerous, and incompatible databases that drove everything from accounts receivable to priceless customer information. Got just the wisdom I needed from a metadata expert. Used new approach to deploy an **improved information tool.** *Payoffs:* Better **management info available 30 times faster.** Support costs cut by double digits. Thousands of manhours redirected more profitably.

Broke the cycle of frustrated customers and the harried programs that supported them. Captured key knowledge and critical nodes to design a quick reaction guide to troubleshoot customized software. *Payoffs:* In 90 days, **training times declined steeply**. Customer complaints fell to low levels. Recruiting **costs amortized twice as fast**.

Applied KM when our only expert in bad debt left with no warning. Went beyond just capturing his expertise to make certain his wisdom became a part of our company from now on. *Payoffs:* Bad debt **collections done four times faster** and **$100K in labor costs saved** — all in 60 days without spending an extra dime.

Led a parochial, closed array of software development groups to become a smoothly running team. Worked steadily to show each team member how participation would enhance, not threaten, his or her status as an expert. *Payoffs:* Expensive trial and error a thing of the past. **People competing to share expertise** jealously guarded in the past.

Recruited by a partner to serve as an **Experienced Senior Consultant in Computer Risk Management**, Arthur Andersen & Co., Chicago, Illinois   Jun 97 to Jun 99

Served as direct reporting official for eight project management teams. Managed budgets ranging from $250K to $500K.

Mastered plant security, in a hurry, to help a client swamped with data. Used KM to uncover process relationships. Designed, built, and validated a tool that manages by exception. *Payoffs:* Client **dropped 90 full-time equivalent** employees. Despite a 10% budget cut, brought this project in **a week early**. My work helped **capture** other **contracts in the $500K range**.

Information Systems Associate, Coopers & Lybrand, Chicago, Illinois   Aug 95 to Jun 97

RECOGNITION IN MY FIELD:

Led my staff group to top 16 tough competitors as the **first** organization **of its kind** to win two corporate-wide competitions in three years   04 and 05

CONTRIBUTIONS TO KNOWLEDGE MANAGEMENT COMMUNITY

Presentations before industry leaders

"Using Knowledge Harvesting to Capture the Best." Sought out at the vice-presidential level at Lucent Technologies to be the **visionary keynote speaker** at a symposium of 200 KM professionals with an audience of several thousand more on line, Sep 03

"Building Innovative and Creative Technology Teams." Invited to speak to 2,000 IT professionals at the Timberland IT Managers Summit, Sep 01 (Summit was cancelled after Sep 11)

"Harvesting E-Business Knowhow." Asked by senior leadership of the Delphi Group to address 60 KM professionals in two sessions, May 02

Publications for professionals

With Charles W. Worth, "Gathering Knowledge When It's Ready," *Knowledge Management Magazine*, April 2003, Volume 9, Number 2

EDUCATION AND PROFESSIONAL DEVELOPMENT

B.S., **Accounting** (with concentration in **Computer Science**), University of Kentucky, Lexington, Kentucky   92

With distinction. Paid my own way by working 32 hours a week while carrying a full academic load. One of only two (from more than 1,000 eligibles) chosen as an Outstanding Accounting Student. Selected from the top 5% for induction into two honorary societies: one for business; the other for accounting. Faculty chose me from 5,000 eligibles to be one of two recipients of an education grant; Dean selected me as to be one of five recipients of an additional grant.

B.S. (with concentration in **Business and Administration**), University of Illinois, Champaign, Illinois   88

Worked nights to help put myself through school.

"Best Practices in Knowledge Management," Institute for International Research, three days   01

"Integrating Business and Technology Strategies," MetaGroup, four days   00

"Knowledge Harvesting," Knowledge Harvesting, Inc., three days   99

"How to Determine ROI in Economic Value Added," Stern, Stewart & Company   97

"Implementing Change," Ernst & Young, one week   96

CAPABILITIES THAT LEVERAGE THE POWER OF IT

Expert in PowerPoint, Excel, Word, Outlook, QuickPlace, SameTime (KM software suites), SharePoint Portal Server, NetMeeting (teleconferencing software)

Proficient in SAP, Infinium accounting software, FrontPage, eGain (knowledge and solution compilation software suite)

Working knowledge of C, BASIC, PASCAL, assembler language, HTML, JavaScript

CHAPTER 8

Best Resumes for Transitioning Into Training and Education Careers

Building the Foundation

Transferability of skills is the foundation upon which every effective career transition resume is written. Your challenge, therefore, is to identify the skills, qualifications, experiences, and competencies you have that will be of value in your new job, career, or industry. Those skills then become the key points in your resume around which everything else is written.

To help you get started with identifying your transferable skills, review the brief listing below of *some* of the skills, qualifications, and competencies that companies and recruiters look for in candidates seeking positions in training, education, or related career tracks. *(Note that this is only a partial listing of the countless different skills that companies look for in qualified candidates.)*

Carefully review the keywords and keyword phrases to identify those that accurately reflect skills you possess and which are transferable into your new position. Then, be sure to incorporate those words into your resume, your cover letters, and any other career marketing documents that you create. They will capture a prospective employer's interest and open the door to interviews and opportunities.

Adult Learning Theory
Certification & Credentialing Programs
Classroom Management
Curriculum Design & Development
E-Learning & E-Instruction
Education Administration
Grant Writing & Administration
Instructional Materials
Learner Motivation
Learning Needs & Objectives

Organizational Needs Assessment
Program Design & Development
Public Speaking & Presentations
Resource Allocation & Management
Special Education
Staff Training & Development
Student Advocacy
Student Placement
Testing & Evaluation
Train the Trainer

Sample Career Transition Resumes

Following are five sample resumes for individuals transitioning into training, education, or related career tracks. Each of these resumes was written by a professional resume writer with extensive experience working with, writing for, and positioning individuals in career transition. Full contact information for each of these writers is in the Appendix. To understand why these resumes were written and designed the way that they were, it is critical that you read the following information that explains the specific objective of each of these job seekers and the particular strategy that was used to prepare their resume.

Resume: Laura Evans (page 159)
Writer: Cindy Kraft
Objective: To transition from a successful career in technology into a technology training and development position as an adjunct professor in a college setting.
Strategy: Focused resume on her various training roles and the subjects she is qualified to teach. Effective use of two-column resume format, using left column exclusively to highlight related training skills and competencies. Professional experience section brief with primary emphasis on training, certification, and curriculum development.

Resume: Anne-Marie Souza (pages 160-161)
Writer: Kirsten Dixson
Objective: To transition from the classroom into an educational technology consultant position.
Strategy: Crafted functional summary section for all of page one to highlight related technology skills, competencies, and achievements, along with relevant teaching experience and credentials. Focused job descriptions on technology-related projects and information, with little detail about general classroom functions.

Resume: Nancy A. Monroe (page 162)
Writer: Louise Garver
Objective: To transition from an education services customer support position into a management-level, education services delivery position with a larger company.
Strategy: Created one-page resume that emphasized only her prior education service roles and accomplishments, bringing them to the forefront. Integrated college degrees into summary to save space. Only listed titles and dates of her other, non-relevant positions.

Resume: David C. Benier (pages 163-164)
Writer: Joyce Fortier

Objective: To transition from executive management in several successful corporations into a senior-level management role directing a private educational institution.

Strategy: Clearly demonstrated cross-functional set of executive-level skills easily transferable into education management with strong summary and clear headline of objective. Utilized job descriptions to communicate overall scope of executive responsibility, most notable achievements, and track record of performance.

Resume: Josiah H. Amberly (pages 165-172)

Writer: Don Orlando

Objective: To transition from the "trenches" of education as a professor/administrator and secure a position as a college president.

Strategy: Merged the formats of executive resumes and CVs to create a modified presentation that highlighted his academic credentials along with his lengthy track record of performance as a "manager" of educational programs, activities, processes, and more that are representative of a college president's accountabilities. Completed resume with highlights of his administrative management experience and academic contributions, along with all of the traditional CV components including extensive listings of training, presentations, publications, and more.

LAURA EVANS

205–222–6677 ▪ levans@email.com

1999 Eclipse Drive ▪ Birmingham ▪ AL ▪ 35204

TRAINER …
INSTRUCTOR

More than 15 years' experience teaching, training, and mentoring students, employees, and clients. Developed effective internal and external training programs for technical staff that led to the department being named internal "subject matter experts" for health care and information technology.

EXPERTISE

Math/Science … Chemistry, Physics, Biology

Computer … XLM, Microsoft Suites, UNIX, and Applications

Information Technology … Integration, Networking, Hardware, and Software

Software Development

Performance Management

Change Management/ Project Management

Process Improvement … CMM, Six Sigma, ISO9000

Quality Assurance and Quality Control

Business Management

PROFESSIONAL EXPERIENCE

COMPUTER CONSULTANTS, Birmingham, Alabama
(Leading supplier of Best-of-Breed Clinical Information Systems (CIS) in the nation with 800 employees worldwide)

Manager of Process Improvement – since 1999
Challenged to build the internal training program to grow consultants and develop employees. Key contributor to the organizational growth that dominated market share and drove revenue increases of 48% within two years.
- Developed certification programs for online training.
- Created Personal Development Plans (PDP) and conducted one–on–one training.
- Led monthly, quarterly, and annual classroom training sessions.

HEALTHCARE SERVICES, INC., Baltimore, Maryland
(A nonprofit, integrated network of health care services that includes hospitals, home health agencies, nursing centers, and other health care services; 7,000 employees serving 200,000+ patients annually)

Regional Manager of Laboratory Services – 1997 to 1999
Outreach & Marketing Manager – 1994 to 1997
Hematology Laboratory Manager – 1993 to 1994
Championed the process/performance improvement mechanism that improved training and performance management of health care providers.
- Pioneered the "Train the Trainer" concept to empower employees to accept and implement technology changes, leading to better decision–making and increased efficiency and productivity.
- Adjunct professor at Hampton University, teaching 4th year Medical Technology Program students.

HEALTH CARE CONSULTANT, Ada, Alabama
Provided consulting and training to health care professionals and organizations to ensure regulatory compliance.
- Upgraded policies, procedure, training, and curriculum to comply with CLIA 88 Regulations. Trained front–end staff (office managers, physicians, and support staff) and back–end staff (technicians and technologists).

EDUCATION

Master of Science in Health Administration
University of Alabama, Birmingham, Alabama

Bachelor of Science in Medical Technology, Minor in Chemistry
University of North Carolina, Chapel Hill, North Carolina

159

Anne-Marie Souza

132 Janet Lane
Kingston, NH 03848

souza132@comcast.net
(603) 686-6344

Education Consultant & Technology Curriculum Integration Specialist

- 15 years' experience as a Middle School Educator—ten in the classroom and four as a Special Education Teacher—facilitating students' discovery of the learning process

- Experience teaching multiple grade levels and subjects in both self-contained and team-teaching environments

- Recognized by Compaq and NASA for innovating use of technology in the classroom State of New Hampshire Teacher Certification, 1990–2005

- Member, National Education Association, Association for Curriculum and Supervision, and New England League of Middle Schools

- Visionary educator who excels at conceiving and building programs from the ground up through demonstrated competencies in:

Grant Writing	**Teacher Training**
Teaching	**Special Education**
Technology Support & Integration	**Creative Thinking & Problem-Solving**

Career Highlights

Technology Training & Implementation

- Selected as one of 53 teachers, from among 2700 applicants nationwide, to participate in the NASA Classroom of the Future Program. Contributed to the development of educational software and programs to integrate Mars exploration, space shuttle simulations, and computer technology into the classroom.

- Designated Technology Integration Lead Teacher for Compaq's Teaching with Computer Technology Grant Program. Wrote article, *Simulations Then, Now, and Tomorrow,* for Compaq's website and incorporated SIMCITY into social studies mapping.

- Developed and delivered a teacher workshop, *Design and Implementation of a Successful Technology Program,* for the New England League of Middle Schools Conference.

- Awarded Technology Literacy Grant and held weekly classes for community members in basic computer literacy, use of Internet, and e-mail. Also, developed and ran a Summer Teacher Training Technology Institute.

- Earned New Hampshire Highly Qualified Teacher Certification for Technology.

- Integrated Critical Thinking Skills into teacher training and the curriculum utilizing online WebQuest, Microsoft FrontPage, PowerPoint, and Hyper Studio.

Grant Writing and Program Development

- Awarded grant to create Homework Helpspace, an after-school, call-in homework program for middle school students.

- Awarded grant to develop a career awareness program for eighth grade students, "Let's Start Thinking About Tomorrow."

160

Education

Master of Education, Instructional Technology (with honors)   2001
University of New Hampshire, Durham, NH

Earned 14 Graduate Credits, NASA Educational Training   Summers 1997–1998
Wheeling Jesuit University, Wheeling, WV

Bachelor of Arts, Elementary Education (Psychology concentration)   1989
Bachelor of Science, Special Education
Boston College, Boston, MA

Ongoing Professional Development
- Highly Qualified Teacher Certification for Math, Social Studies, and Language Arts   Present
- Compaq Computer Technology Integration Leader Certificate   1999
- Microsoft Certification Courses for Windows 98   1999
- Critical Skills Teacher Certification   1998
- Studied at University of Galway to compare European and North American approaches to Special Education. Discovered that the European curriculum was more community-oriented and subsequently established ways to integrate community happenings into the classroom.

Professional Experience

Classroom Teacher   1994–Present
SAU 16 Cooperative Middle School, Stratham, NH

Taught Math, Science, Social Studies, and Language Arts in grades 4 and 5. Created a technology-rich classroom environment that encourages familiarity with computers, software programs, and the Internet.

Computer Integration Specialist (part-time)   1995–2002
SAU 16 Cooperative Middle School, Stratham, NH

Concurrently managed all computer technology for Mountain View Middle School with teaching responsibilities. Served on the District Technology Committee. Accountable for troubleshooting, technology curriculum integration, teacher training, grant writing, and budget planning. Contributed to district receipt of numerous technology grants, including Microsoft Certification Training Center funds and State of New Hampshire Technology Literacy Funds.

Special Educator   1989–1994
SAU 16 Cooperative Middle School, Stratham, NH

Taught special education population in grades 5 and 6. Collaborated with teachers to modify classroom for learning needs.

Nancy A. Monroe

670 E. Higgins Road • Naperville, IL 60563

630.983.7544
namonroe@hotmail.com

VALUE OFFERED AS DIRECTOR OF EDUCATION DELIVERY

Demonstrated track record of improving and directing global education services programs that maximize instructor realization, curriculum quality, revenue growth, and profitability at technology organizations.

- **Provide the vision, innovation, and leadership to improve internal processes in Education Services** with a talent for identifying and resolving operational challenges to enhance revenues/profits.
- **Effective in assessing and driving instructor skill set development, budget and resource management,** as well as partnering with internal departments to meet education needs for a diverse customer base.
- **Experienced in the design and delivery of curriculum programs** that support and achieve business objectives.
- **Repeatedly built and empowered cohesive teams that achieved high standards** of quality and productivity in competitive markets.
- **M.B.A. and B.S. in Education,** Springfield College, Springfield, MA.

PROFESSIONAL EXPERIENCE

SIMTECH CORPORATION, CHICAGO, IL   1996 to present
Promoted through series of high-profile management positions in global Education Services and Customer Support: Global Support Programs Manager (2003 to 2005), Best Practices Manager (2000 to 2003), and Education Services Manager (1996 to 2000).

▶ **As Education Services Manager, repositioned, upgraded, and transformed Education Services department from an under-performing training function to a profit-generating global organization. P&L management accountability for 12 global Customer Education Centers, team of 17 instructors, curriculum design, facilities management/leasing negotiations, and budget growth to $4MM.**

- Introduced and educated team on concepts of adult learning theory to better serve students. Turned around team morale from a low of 2 to an average high of 4 as indicated by survey results.
- Determined core product offering, set revenue mix and gross profit margin, and developed knowledge transfer process in collaboration with Product Management and Customer Support departments.
- Established a consistent learning environment for all students globally that eliminated revenue delays and led unit's revenue growth from $4MM to $10MM in billable customer education during 12-month tenure.
- Implemented ASP model for online registration and payment. Produced $600K in additional revenue in first 3 months; achieved double annual quota in first 6 months; doubled revenues in 6 months.
- Succeeded in creating additional revenue stream with multimillion-dollar potential where previous team failed after acquiring $250K of software that could not be implemented.
- Created multi-level certification programs with validation protocol for customers, partners, and employees using ASP model for less than $50K. The certification program revenue potential is millions of dollars annually.
- Took charge of and delivered new education class for applications product line in just 3 months despite failure of consulting team to produce program after 9 months of effort.
- Enhanced company's ability to launch new product lines by designing and ensuring curriculum availability on all product lines by the rollout date. Created incremental education product updates for existing customers.

WORLDWIDE SOLUTIONS, NEW YORK, NY   1995 to 1996

▶ **As Operations Manager of Education Services, provided strategic planning and leadership effectiveness that drove Education Services revenue growth by 150% ($5MM to $7MM). Directed 12 instructors globally. Supervised curriculum development with team in Germany.**

- Managed the training channel, created certification program, conducted Partner Certification programs, and ensured accreditation of internal resources and third party delivery resources (partners and subcontractors).
- Automated Education Services function and enrollment process using Access database, turning around employee morale and reducing customer calls from 500 a week down to just 25 while improving customer satisfaction.

162

DAVID C. BENIER

791 Oak Tree Lane ~ Northville, MI 48160
Home: 248.444.1666 ~ david_benier@hotmail.com ~ Cell: 248.333.4848

HEAD ADMINISTRATOR
Private Education Institutions

Twenty-year management career leading, building, revitalizing and/or improving organizational infrastructures, technologies, processes, measurement systems and sales/marketing strategies to optimize results. Strong leadership, communication, negotiation, finance, creative and analytical skills. Decisive, solutions-focused and results-oriented. Appointed to Board positions at several companies.

- **Provides strategic and tactical planning**, giving direction, leadership and day-to-day management to organizations.
- **Sets standards and goals to attain results**, establishing policies and procedures to meet/exceed expectations.
- **Develops programs and monitors progress**, training and motivating staff to carry out programs.
- **Maintains records and prepares budgets** in accordance with allotted funds and state regulations.
- **Cultivates school/business partnerships** with organizations in the community to enhance programs and offerings.
- **Establishes resources** to address crime, drug and alcohol abuse .
- **Remains sensitive to the needs of non-English** speaking and culturally diverse students.
- **Writes grants** and oversees **contract negotiations.**
- **Served on area school board and worked with various youth organizations** such as Big Brothers and the YMCA.

PROFESSIONAL EXPERIENCE

INNOVATIVE TECHNOLOGIES, INC., Westland, MI   2002 — 2004
A $15 million start-up company that supplies leather to the auto industry, delivering its product to Mexico.
CEO / PRESIDENT

Recruited to turn company around and oversee all aspects of the business. Held full P&L, strategic planning, financial, operating, marketing, technology and administrative leadership responsibility for organization (five direct reports and 60 employees). Reported to an absentee owner.
- Increased revenues by $2 million, despite no cash, by raising product prices and increasing market share.
- Reduced cost of operations by improving quality and productivity and controlling costs, including headcount reduction.
- Worked with principal in selling company assets to new owner.

EFFECTIVE PLASTICS, Wixom, MI   1995 — 2001
A tier-one plastics supplier to the automotive industry with 34 plants in the United States, Canada, Mexico and Europe and annual revenue of $550 million.
CHIEF EXECUTIVE OFFICER

Promoted to CEO to continue to guide company through a high-growth period. Held full strategic planning, operating and P&L responsibility for the organization. Accountable for business planning and development, sales/marketing, administration, finance, accounting, MIS and human resources. Reported to the Board of Directors; three direct reports and 6,000 employees.
- Expanded company from two domestic locations and 500 employees to 34 global locations and 6,000 employees during 16 years of employment with the company. Obtained funding in order to support the rapid growth of the company, constantly evaluating loan cost sources and negotiating financial arrangements.

163

CEO, continued......

- Grew business from $250 million to $550 million, soliciting new growth opportunities and acquisitions, eventually developing 34 operating locations throughout the US, Canada, Mexico and Europe.
- Interacted with and built relationships with major corporate customers such as General Motors, Ford and Daimler-Chrysler, in addition to tier-one suppliers.
- Motivated the management team after filing for Chapter 11 and then exited Chapter 11 a year later by selling company to a new equity sponsor.
- Appointed to the Board of Directors.

EXECUTIVE VICE PRESIDENT   1986 — 1995

Took over all financial, human resources and business issues for this new division that was a spin-off of Key International. Reported to company President and was one of three Board Members.
- Authored strategic business, financial and marketing plans to develop the company into one of the largest plastic suppliers of interior component parts in the world. 50% of growth came from acquisitions and 50% was internal growth.
- Built seven plants from the ground up, two in Mexico and the rest in the United States.
- Negotiated all financing and acquisitions, orchestrating an aggressive acquisition program to fund expansion and capital improvement. Developed compensation and stock option plans.
- Recruited a top-notch management team, training and mentoring them to reach and exceed company objectives.
- Financed the new company and distributed $50 million to shareholders within the first five years. Grew business from $40 million to $250 million during tenure as EVP

SEMANS INTERNATIONAL, Southfield, MI   1981 — 1986
A conglomerate company in the fastener, scrap metal, plastic and real estate businesses. Company was primarily in Detroit and New York City and had $110 million in annual sales.
CHIEF FINANCIAL OFFICER

Responsible for the strategic planning, development and leadership of the financial operations of the company. Scope of responsibility was diverse and included financial analysis/reporting, tax planning, cash management, corporate banking, budgeting and audit management. Had five direct reports.
- Set up four distinct businesses, made possible by orchestrating one of the first leveraged buyouts, borrowing $90 million with $5 million in equity.
- Negotiated refinancing for company debt and, working with President, did four separate leverage buy-outs in 1986.
- Handled the finances of a large real estate project in NYC, bringing the project under control and completing it. Dealt with lawsuits, tenants and others to bring the project to a conclusion.

Previous employment: **DIRECTOR OF INTERNATIONAL FINANCE / CONTROLLER** for MANUFACTURING DATA SYSTEMS, INC., Ann Arbor, MI; **ASSISTANT TO THE CONTROLLER** for R. P. SCHERER CORPORATION, Detroit, MI; and **SENIOR ANALYST** for ARTHUR ANDERSON, Detroit, MI.

Elected to a local school board, serving in various capacities. Set district policy and participated in the searches for a new superintendent. Attended regular meetings of the Michigan School Board Association.

Served as a Board Member of CTM, Inc. between 1996 and 2001; Board Member of Reid Plastics, Inc. from 1990 to 1995.

EDUCATION

MBA, WAYNE STATE UNIVERSITY, Detroit, MI ~ **BA**, *Economics*, ALBION COLLEGE, Albion, MI

Curriculum vitæ

JOSIAH H. AMBERLY, PH. D.

1440 Cedar Ridge Road	Troy, Alabama 36000	[334] 772-1919

EDUCATION:

Ph. D., **Special Education Administration**, Georgia State University, Valdosta, Georgia, 1985 *Paid my own way to earn this degree at night while working full time.*

Ed. S., **School Psychology**, Georgia Southern College, Statesboro, Georgia, 1980 *Drove more than 600 miles a week to earn this degree despite a full teaching and administrative load.*

M. Ed., **Special Education**, Valdosta State University, Valdosta, Georgia, 1978 *Earned this degree at night, working during the day.*

B. S., **Social Studies Education**, Florida State University, Tallahassee, Florida, 1977

A. A., General Studies, St. Johns River Junior College, Palataka, Florida, 1975

SELECTED EXAMPLES OF QUALIFICATIONS IN ACTION:

Developing and maintaining programs to meet the educational needs in our service area: Soon after I became Director of Clinical Experiences, I improved how we serve principals, teachers, and nearly 300 undergraduates in our teacher education program. My goal was to make this culminating educational experience as educationally sound as our limited budget would allow.

First, I visited or spoke with all 25 principals and central offices in our service area. They liked our commitment to match our interns with their special needs. They also liked my pledge of no more than one student teacher in each classroom. My next challenge was to make the system work with very little money.

Travel had strained the budget for years. I placed students at schools closer to campus and so their full-time teaching responsibility rose by 75%. My plan encouraged our faculty to spend more time with students in classrooms. As a side benefit, our teaching staff kept current about everyday problems in schools. We delivered more education for each dollar spent.

The results were gratifying. Once principal said, "Because of your commitment to our needs, and since no other college treats us as well, we will only consider your students for practica." Students liked it because they spent more time teaching and felt much better prepared. Our staff liked it because they could use my newly designed evaluation forms to tailor instruction to student needs.

Keeping constituencies informed: The faculty I joined had nearly 10 times my teaching experience. Their former leader had 20 years in the field. He encouraged unstructured academic experiences. It was a comfortable culture. It also contained a "hidden," but growing threat.

Our professors prepare placement files describing student performance. Schools used these folders to decide on teacher assignments and tenure. The unstructured comments in these forms lowered our credibility and raised our liability.

These points persuaded my skeptical colleagues to use a more focused evaluation system. The students liked the new form because it closely resembled those they would see on the job.

Meeting mission goals and academic ideals with academic credentials: Troy State asked me to design an undergraduate program for teachers of the learning disabled. This new curriculum had to do well with no additional resources. Even the vacancy in our department would have to remain unfilled.

I built our program from scratch, integrating 45 new hours into 90 hours of core curriculum. The Curriculum, Faculty, General Studies, Executive, and Administrative Council Committees made virtually no changes and gave unanimous approval. The Alabama State Department of Education granted licensure and our work met accreditation standards. The new curriculum needed no new faculty, no classrooms, materials, or library collections. The entire effort was done in just two months, three times faster than usual.

Translating strategies into effective actions: Our graduate program in teacher education was outdated. Principals and superintendents were forced to use teachers in areas for which we hadn't prepared them. Even in primary areas, our graduates felt unready.

Our faculty was proud of the syllabi they had used for nearly 15 years. It was comprehensive, but narrowly focused. I helped them see how to translate their individual expertise into a synergistic family of offerings. Together, we replaced four outdated courses with three new ones and matched scheduling preferences with class times. The students reinforced our perceptions. The new offerings were much more effective, even though we hadn't spent an additional dollar.

A proven commitment to diversity: Our campus encompasses diversity on a broad scale. Nearly 22% of our students are racial, ethnic, or economic minorities. Helping these students get the most from their education required my visible, practical, personal efforts.

I am particularly sensitive to those whose intelligence outstrips their ability to read and write. These students respond well to my offers to spend out-of-class time with them. Their confidence—and their grades—are improving. Moreover, I am able to do authentic assessments.

Being a visible advocate for students: For me, student advocacy means helping students solve problems. I stand up for them to resolve academic issues. Often I find students fall behind for reasons other than academic. Sometimes they lack an advisor. Sometimes they are pressured to follow a major with which they are uncomfortable. Whatever the reason, students seek me out for help.

We formulate a comprehensive plan for their success. Often, we prepare a flexible, tailor-made "contract" approved by the student, the faculty, and the dean. This new approach pays off. Students we might have otherwise lost leave us prepared to contribute to society.

Budgeting fiscal resources: As the new Director of Clinical Experience, I had no budget. I knew I could improve our programs without more money, but I wanted the chance to allocate dollars against requirements. It was a tough sell—there had been no such "new" budgets in years.

I would never have convinced the Dean, the Vice President for Financial Affairs, and the Provost, without doing my homework. I successfully defended a $200,000 annual budget line by line. Under this new fiscal plan, we could do more. By controlling costs carefully, I could offer small honoraria to guest speakers for the first time. For two years we hadn't been able to attract a single speaker. Our new plan brought in two major experts in its first year. We even saved enough money to equip our offices with our first computers.

Building strong ties with the local community: With my wife, started our first effort to support the Salvation Army's Christmas Program. Persuaded skeptical members and the administrative board to endorse this effort. We raised $1,000 in the first year. Nearly 40% of our congregation participated. We also built a Family Life Program from scratch. Guided our members to expand their knowledge over a wide range of personal and family subjects. More than 100 attended, a large turnout for a program that had to be conducted at night.

Budgeting and managing fiscal resources: Voluntarily took on the advisorship of Greek society, a task normally discharged by two or three faculty advisors. When I arrived, this chapter of 60 active members had been heavily in debt for years. Using the tools I gave them, the chapter was debt free in just two years.

Advancing student advocacy: Helped the membership of a fraternity reach and maintain academic standards. Our society was the academic runner-up among six organizations twice in six years.

CONTINUING PROFESSIONAL DEVELOPMENT IN SCHOOL ADMINISTRATION AND STUDENT GUIDANCE:

Carlton State University, via the Internet, 1998
    Staff Development for Distance Education

At Valdosta State University, Valdosta, Georgia, 1977 – 1984

    Supervising and Administering School Personnel

    School Finance

    School Law

    Administering Special Education Programs

At Georgia Southern University, Statesboro, Georgia, 1981 - 1982

Supervision in Special Education Programs

Advanced Administration of Special Education

TEACHING EXPERIENCE:

Associate Professor, Department of Curriculum and Teaching,   1987 – Present
Carlton State University, Troy, Alabama

Courses taught:

Learning Disabilities	Diagnostic and Prescriptive Teaching
Curriculum for Exceptional Learners	History of Education
Classroom Management	Cultural Foundations in Education
Speech and Language Development for Exceptional Learners	Practicum and Internships for Graduate and Undergraduate Students

Adjunct Professor, University College, Guantanamo Bay, Cuba, Key   August 1990 and
West Naval Air Station, Florida, and the Naval Training Center,   August 1991
Orlando, Florida

Courses taught:

Psychological Foundations of Education

Methods and Materials of Educational Evaluation

Administering School Personnel

Part-time Instructor, Special Education and Psychology, Guidance and   1978 – 1987
Counseling Departments, Valdosta State College, Valdosta, Georgia

Courses taught:

Core curriculum courses for majors in Special Education	Introduction to Educating Exceptional Children
Methods and Materials for Teaching Children with Behavior Disorders	Classroom Management of Exceptional Children
The Nature of Behavior Disorders	Psychology of Early Childhood
Psychology of Early Childhood	Assessment of Exceptional Children

Inservice Instructor, Valdosta Public School System, Valdosta, Georgia   1975 – 1976

Courses taught:

Elementary through high school core curriculum courses for behavior-disordered students, the learning disabled, and those with severe behavior and emotional problems.

ADMINISTRATIVE EXPERIENCE:

At Carlton State University, Troy, Alabama, 1981 – 1998

Director of Clinical Experiences, Certification, and Admissions, 1989 – 1998

Certification Officer, College of Education, 1989 – 1998

Director of Admissions for the Undergraduate Teacher Education and the College of Education's Alternative Master's in Science in Education Programs, 1985 - 1989

For the Comprehensive Psychoeducational Service of South Georgia, Valdosta, Georgia, 1981 – 1988

School Psychologist responsible for evaluating students, from one to 21 years old, with emotional and learning difficulties. Provided group and individual counseling, and met regularly with parents. Served on the Eligibility and Placement Committees.

Program Evaluator responsible for evaluating how well our program met the needs of parents, teachers, and principals. Tracked every aspect of this program on a monthly, quarterly, and annual basis and used this information to build reports for state educational agencies. Helped the Program Director solve due process problems.

Assistant Director of Special Education, 1979 – 1981

I served as the single point of contact to certain students who graduated from our teacher education programs and met all the requirements for licensure in Alabama. Students from other institutions (in and out of state) sent me their transcripts so I could guide them to get licenses in Alabama.

At the Valdosta Public School System, Valdosta, Georgia, 1976 – 1978

School Psychologist providing initial and continuing evaluations of gifted children in intellectual, academic, processing, and visual-motor skills. Tailored the core curriculum for these students, helped teachers design and evaluate behavioral change programs, and conducted frequent parent-teacher conferences. Sat on the Placement Committee. Developed and taught the Behavior Disorders Program

At the Sanford Street Elementary School, Eufaula, Alabama, 1988

Consultant for classroom organization and management.

At the Pike County Schools, Alabama, 1989 – Present

Consultant for Special Education Programs.

Josiah H. Amberly

SELECTED CONTRIBUTIONS TO ACADEMIA AND EDUCATIONAL COMMUNITIES:

Certified Evaluator and Trainer, Teacher Evaluation Program, Alabama State Department of Education, 1996

Developed and presented these inservice training programs:

For general and special education teachers and classroom aides employed by public schools in the Wiregrass Area, 1991 – 1993:

Learning Strategies for Disabled Learners

Teaching Methods for Teaching Science and Mathematics to Learning Disabled Students

Attention Deficient Disorder and the General Classroom

For the Valdosta Public Schools and Comprehensive Psychoeducational Services of South Georgia, 1985 – 1986:

Due Process

Individualized Education Plan Development

Writing Eligibility Reports

For Coastal Plains Regional Educational Services, 1984 – 1985:

Teaching Exceptional Students

Classroom Management for Classroom Aides

ADVISORSHIPS:

Alabama Association of Teacher Educators, 1990 – Present
College of Education, Carlton State University representative

Advisor to Lambda Chi Alpha Fraternity, Carlton State University, Troy, Alabama 1989 – 1995

Honors Program Project on Leadership, Carlton State University, 1995

Student Council for Exceptional Children, Carlton State University, 1988 – 1990

Advisory Board, Department of Psychology, Guidance, and Counseling, Valdosta State College, 1985 – 1988

ACADEMIC COMMITTEE ASSIGNMENTS (CARLTON STATE UNIVERSITY):

Chair, Advisory Committee for Clinical Experience, 1989 – 1998

College of Education Executive Committee, 1989 – 1998

College of Education Curriculum Committee, 1989 – 1998

All University Council on Teacher Education, 1989 – 1998

Chair, Committee for the Development of a Master of Science Degree in Educational Leadership for off-campus programs, 1995

Admission to Professional Education Program Committee, 1991 - 1997

Educational Program Committee, self-study for the Southern Association of Schools and Colleges, 1994 – 1995

School of Education Research and Faculty Development Committee, 1994 - 1995

University Student Retention and Advisement Committee, 1994 – 1995

Who's Who Committee, 1990 – 1992

Chair, Interdepartmental Committee for the Development of a Teacher Education Program in Environmental Education, Spring and Summer, 1991

COMPUTER LITERACY:

Proficient: WordPerfect (Corel 8), and WordPerfect 6.1 for Windows.

Working knowledge: Corel WordPerfect Presentation, QuattroPro, Internet search protocols.

PUBLICATIONS:

With Liu, Jane. "Teachers' Attitude Toward and Perceived Professional Need for an Inclusive Classroom," submitted for publication November 1998, Journal of Teacher Education and Special Education

"Student Perception of Social Science Education Program Effectiveness," Unpublished manuscript, 1993

Internship Handbook, Revision, Troy, Alabama: TSU Publications, 1992

Professional Laboratory Experiences Handbook (Revision), Troy, Alabama: TSU Publications, 1991

"Non-Traditional Fifty-Year Course of Study for Area of Learning Disabilities," May, 1998. Approved by the State of Alabama Board of Education, September, 1989

"Undergraduate Course of Study for Area of Learning Disabilities," June, 1988. Approved by the State of Alabama Board of Education, October, 1988

"The Revised Behavior Problem Checklist Measuring the Severity Level of Emotional Behavior Disturbances," Dissertation Abstracts International, 1986, 47/02A, p. 502

"Regional Education Service Area Information Guide or Georgia TCT," School Psychology, 1986, Coastal Plains RESA, Georgia Department of Education

"The WISC-Résumé Subtest Profile of a Sample of Severely Emotionally Disturbed Children, Psychological Report, Volume 45, pp. 317 –325, 1979

Josiah H. Amberly

PRESENTATIONS:

Review Results to the Teacher Education Division, State Standards Review Team:

Jacksonville State University, Auburn University, 1995 –1996

University of Alabama, Stillman College (team chair), 1993

Auburn University-Montgomery, Alabama State University, 1988 – 1990

"First-Year Teacher Workshop," College of Education, Carlton State University, 1990 – 1996 *Organized and conducted this annual workshop from its inception.*

Regional Inservice Education Program, Special Education Conference, Carlton State University, 1990 – 1991

Mainstreaming for Special Education Students, Troy City Schools, Troy, Alabama, 1990

Students for Action for Education (an organization of Alabama high school students to promote education), District IX, Fall Quarters, Carlton State University, 1989 – 1990

Alabama Psychological Association Research Papers, School of Education, Carlton State University, Fall, Winter, and Spring Quarters, 1988 – 1989

Report to the Teacher Education Division, Special Education Standards Revision Committee, Alabama State Department of Education, Montgomery, 1989

"Management of Children with Behavior or Emotional Problems at Home," Turner County Department of Family and Children Services, 1987

MEMBERSHIP IN PROFESSIONAL ORGANIZATONS:

Alabama Association of Teacher Educators (ALACTE), 1991 – Present

Vice President, 1992 – 1993; President, 1993 – 1994

Attended the National Conference in 1990 and 1997

American Association of Colleges of Teacher Education (AACTE), 1990 – 1998

Secretary/Treasurer, 1991 – 1992

Attended Education Workshops in the Fall, 1990; Winter, Spring, and Summer, 1991

Council for Exceptional Children, 1980 – Present

Alabama Association of Colleges for Teacher Education

College of Education Representative, 1989 – 1998

Certification Officers and Personnel in Education (COPE), 1989 – 1998

HONORS:

Distinguished Alumni Award, St. Johns River Community College, Palataka, Florida, 1995 *This annual award is given to the individual who has shown the value of a community college education through his professional accomplishments.*

Membership Award, Alabama Association of Teacher Educators, 1989 – 1990 *For recruiting more members than 15 other universities.*

Outstanding Young Men of America, 1979

CHAPTER 9

Best Resumes for Transitioning Into Health Care Careers

Building the Foundation

Transferability of skills is the foundation upon which every effective career transition resume is written. Your challenge, therefore, is to identify the skills, qualifications, experiences, and competencies you have that will be of value in your new job, career, or industry. Those skills then become the key points in your resume around which everything else is written.

To help you get started with identifying your transferable skills, review the brief listing below of *some* of the skills, qualifications, and competencies that companies and recruiters look for in candidates seeking positions in health care and related career tracks. *(Note that this is only a partial listing of the countless different skills that companies look for in qualified candidates.)*

Carefully review the keywords and keyword phrases to identify those that accurately reflect skills you possess and which are transferable into your new position. Then, be sure to incorporate those words into your resume, your cover letters, and any other career marketing documents that you create. They will capture a prospective employer's interest and open the door to interviews and opportunities.

Acute Care	Instrumentation & Calibration
Biotechnology	Managed Care
Chronic Care	Multidisciplinary Care Team
Cost Containment	Nursing Care & Management
Crisis Intervention	Patient Relations
Disease Management	Preferred Provider Organizations
Emergency Care & Response	Program Management
Foundations & Grants	Provider Relations
Health Care Administration	Public Health
Health Care Delivery	Third-Party Insurance

Sample Career Transition Resumes

Following are five sample resumes for individuals transitioning into health care and related careers. Each of these resumes was written by a professional resume writer with extensive experience working with, writing for, and positioning individuals in career transition. Full contact information for each of these writers is in the Appendix. To understand why these resumes were written and designed the way that they were, it is critical that you read the following information that explains the specific objective of each of these job seekers and the particular strategy that was used to prepare their resume.

Resume:	Michael W. Taylor (pages 176)
Writer:	Cindy Kraft
Objective:	To transition from career as a paramedic and into an outside sales position in the medical device/equipment industry.
Strategy:	Focused resume on his top-notch people, persuasion, training, and communication skills, along with his extensive medical experience, including his knowledge of specific medical equipment, devices, and instrumentation. Positioned him as a prime candidate for medical sales/account management.

Resume:	Lydia N. Jackson (pages 177-178)
Writer:	Diane Burns
Objective:	To transition from retail management/franchise management career in nutritional products into a career in pharmaceutical sales and marketing.
Strategy:	Extensive focus on sales, sales training, and sales management qualifications, along with mention of her communication and charismatic people-to-people skills. Emphasis on business management, staff management, organizational, and financial skills to further support her candidacy.

Resume:	Alyssa Martin (pages 179)
Writer:	Cindy Kraft
Objective:	To transition from 20-year clinical nursing career into a career as a legal nurse consultant.
Strategy:	Utilized one-page, hard-hitting resume to highlight her licenses and certifications, areas of expertise, and years of experience within the industry. Dual-column resume format provides a quick and easy read with clear demonstration of her qualifications for new career track.

Resume:	Olivia L. Tyler (pages 180-181)
Writer:	Marcy Johnson
Objective:	To transition out of a scientific career in academia into a position in health care practice marketing and management.
Strategy:	Created a strong summary section with notable (and related) career achievements and a comprehensive listing of her core competencies. Followed with brief, yet prominent, mention of educational credentials. Professional experi-

ence section uses headings to highlight skills and performance most supportive of current career objective.

Resume: Barry D. Kaplan (pages 182-183)

Writer: Jean Cummings

Objective: To transition from career as a physician in "traditional" health care settings
into a new career path leading international reproductive health projects.

Strategy: Leveraged his past international health care projects and his academic training on page one to firmly position himself as a qualified candidate. Clearly
communicated his professional goals with all supporting documentation. Page
two was brief, only providing a short listing of his clinical experience and
hospital appointments, as they are not directly relevant to career transition.

MICHAEL W. TAYLOR

703–228–4444
mtaylor@email.com
1437 Princeton Road, Vienna, VA 22181

SALES PROFESSIONAL
Medical Devices • Medical Equipment

CLINICAL EXPERIENCE & KNOWLEDGE

- Adult, Pediatric, and Neonate Intravenous Cannulation
- Subclavian and Internal Jugular Vein Cut Down and Cannulation
- Chest Decompression via Chest Tube and Angiocath Placement
- Intracardiac Injection
- Intraosseous Cannulation Medication
- Transcutaneous Pacemaker
- Synchronized Cardioversion
- Defibrillation
- End Tidal CO2 Waveform Interpretation and Secondary Treatment
- Childbirth
- CPAP
- Ez-Pap
- Nebulized Medication
- IV Medication
- IM and SQ Medication
- Episiotomy

SPECIALIZED TRAINING

University of Virginia,
- Advanced 12-Lead EKG Interpretation
- Prehospital Trauma Life Support
- Emergency Medical Hazmat Providers
- Pediatric Advanced Life Support – Basic and Instructor
- Advanced Cardiac Life Support – Basic and Instructor

VALUE OFFERED

Artful negotiator. Effectively negotiated with the county for EMPACCT members to receive an additional paid day off every 3 weeks with a 14.75% pay increase.

Problem solver. Collaborated with the county, fire department, physicians, and non–emergency personnel to finalize an agreement to use private ambulance companies for non–emergency transports, freeing up emergency rescue units for true emergencies.

Excellence. Named Paramedic of the Year in 2001.

Knowledge base. Understand the efficacy, pharmacokinetics, and pharmacodynamics of a broad range of drugs, with extensive knowledge of medical devices and equipment.

Trainer. Selected by Vienna Community College as its Primary Physician/Registered Nurse Advanced Cardiac Life Support Instructor.

Expert witness. Routinely solicited by physicians to testify in paramedical malpractice lawsuits.

PROFESSIONAL EXPERIENCE

EMERGENCY MEDICAL PERSONNEL & CRITICAL CARE TECHNICIANS (EMPACCT), Vienna, Virginia
President – since 1998
Recruited to negotiate contracts, review annual business plans, analyze and evaluate employee health plans, and represent union members during grievances and arbitrations.

ST. JOHN'S HOSPITAL, Vienna, Virginia
Paramedic – 2000 to 2003
Key member of the trauma team handling airway management, responding to cardiac arrests, writing reports, and dispensing medication.

FAIRFAX COUNTY FIRE RESCUE, Vienna, Virginia
Field Training Officer – 2000
Lieutenant – 1998 to 2000
Senior Paramedic – 1996 to 1998
Paramedic – 1994 to 1996
Fast–track promotions gaining experience in managing medications and equipment, training staff, and evaluating regulated documentation. Key contributor to the quality improvement team.

EDUCATION

Associate in Science – EMS Education – 1994
Fairfax Community College, Vienna, Virginia

LYDIA N. JACKSON

2786 Meadow Creek Lane * Yorba Linda, CA 92807
714-998-0359 (h) * 714-775-9523 (c) * lydianjack@comcast.net

CAREER FOCUS

PHARMACEUTICAL SALES & MARKETING

PROFILE

- Seven years' entrepreneurial experience in operations management, sales, and marketing strategies. Strong record of accomplishments for building businesses, creating sales, forming talented teams, and providing knowledge transfer.

- Managed fiscal requirements to build solvency. Organized various simultaneous activities and operations. Multi-task oriented. Overachiever.

- Extremely detail-oriented with superior organizational skills. Quickly review processes, identify deficiencies, and make recommendations to change operations, improve productivity, and increase bottom-line profits.

- Offer superior customer service. Established rapport with customers to build a strong customer base and loyal clientele. Strong presentation and communication skills.

Professional and Personal Value Offered:

· **Retail Sales**	· **Business Development**
· **Work Independently**	· **Operations Management**
· **Mentor, Coach, Advisor**	· **"Customer-Service-First" Philosophy**
· **Trainer & Motivator**	· **Strong Business Acumen**
· **Account Management**	· **Negotiation & Closing Skills**
· **Troubleshooter & Problem Solver**	· **Organizational Efficiency Expert**

PROFESSIONAL EXPERIENCE

BASIC NUTRITION CENTERS, CALIFORNIA   1995 – present

Basic Nutrition Centers is an internationally recognized franchise operation offering nutritional and dietary supplement solutions for healthy living.

Regional Manager, Southern California   11/2002 – present

- Rotate between 12 retail stores to provide guidance and organizational efficiency advice to various staffs. Manage daily operations including opening and closing stores, receipt of inventory, stocking and displays, employee training (including sales and product knowledge), accounting, and account management.

- Designed a computerized Excel daily register report and successfully converted 12 stores from a manual sales reporting system.

Continued...

- ❑ Requested to analyze in-place processes and organizational deficiencies. Note organizational deficiencies and make recommendations to improve processes, increase productivity, and boost profits. Apply product knowledge to achieve sales goals.

- ❑ Guide customers in locating appropriate nutritional supplements according to their physician's recommendation to supplement prescription medication. Direct customers to the automated in-store computer touch screen to look up their medical condition and attain recommended supplements.

- ❑ Clientele seeking dietary supplements to complement traditional medicine may be undergoing treatment for cancer and chemotherapy sessions, prostate conditions, diabetes, incontinence, urinary tract infections, migraines, arthritis, depression, pregnancy, digestive upsets, heart problems, sports injuries, or other conditions. Advise customers in the appropriate use of dietary supplement products.

Operations Manager/Owner, Yorba Linda, CA   05/1999 – present
Operations Manager/Owner, Anaheim Hills, CA   02/1995 – present

- ❑ Purchased, launched, and manage two franchise stores simultaneously with annual gross sales volume of $1.7 million. Purchased capital equipment and implemented a business plan. Recruited, interviewed, hired, trained, and staffed a team of 10 between the two locations. Developed a strong customer base.

- ❑ Manage all retail and store operations: sales, marketing and promotions, personnel administration, training, inventory, cash flow, and fiscal decisions and financials. Monitor P&L. Monitor stock and inventory levels. Order and purchase stock from various vendors, distributors, and warehouses.

- ❑ Direct and position the sales program to ensure quality customer service and use of promotional campaigns. Develop product displays.

- ❑ Implement organizational and operational efficiencies to improve sales, responsiveness, and performance, reduce overhead, and streamline business operations. Established solid management principles and fiscal responsibility.

- ❑ Established community contacts and built solid customer relationships. Managed customer complaints and diffused problems with customers or employees.

- ❑ Manage accounting functions, prepare full monthly financial reports, and work with a tax accountant. Used Word, Quicken, Excel, and the Internet to develop financial reports and draft correspondence. Conduct extensive research.

- ❑ Received numerous awards for "Best Store Operator" and "Best Store Presentation."

- ❑ Promoted to Regional Manager with salary and perks, in addition to managing/owning two stores.

EDUCATION

- · **Bachelor of Science in Accounting**, University of Irvine, California, 1996

ALYSSA MARTIN
RN, BS, CLC, LHRM, CPHA(A)

713-222-1234
nurseexpert@email .com
148 W. 16th Avenue, Houston, TX 77006

CERTIFIED LEGAL NURSE CONSULTANT

LICENSES

Licensed Healthcare Risk
Manager (LHRM)

State of Texas: Board of Nursing,
Registered Nurse (RN)

CERTIFICATIONS

Certified Legal Consultant (CLC)

Certified Professional Healthcare
Administrator (Advanced)
CPHA(A)

Advanced Cardiac Life Support
(ACLS)

RELEVANT TRAINING

- Medical Malpractice
- Risk Management
- Case Management &
  Reimbursement
- Legal and Ethical Implications
  of Documentation
- OSHA
- AIDS
- Domestic Violence

EDUCATION

**Bachelor of Science in Health
Care Administration**
University of Texas
Dallas, Texas

Licensed HCRM
TX Risk Management Institute
Houston, Texas

MEDICAL EXPERTISE

Labor & Delivery ... High–risk pregnancies and deliveries, antepartum fetal testing, surgery scrubbing, circulating

Gynecology Oncology ... Chemotherapy, antiemetics, outpatient care

Facial Plastic Surgery ... Charting, Botox and collagen injections, microdermabrasion & intense pulse light treatments, laser surgery, facelifts, rhinoplasties, blepharoplasties, chin & cheek implants, brow lift devices, glycolic and blue peels, wound care and suture removal, pre– and post–op education

Hospice ... All aspects of life–limiting illnesses, wound and bedsore care, home health care

PROFESSIONAL EXPERIENCE

Clinical Director – 1999 to 2005
STEVEN MYERS, M.D., Houston, TX
FACIAL PLASTIC & COSMETIC SURGERY CENTER
Direct a 7-person staff in daily operations. Provide compassionate patient care and education; conduct telephone consultations; and assist surgeon. Interview and train medical and non-professional staff. Oversee hazardous materials compliance with OSHA regulations. Attained and maintained all accreditation compliance standards; internal risk manager.

Primary Care Nurse – 1994 to 1999
HOSPICE OF GREATER HOUSTON, Houston, TX
Nurse Preceptor for a team providing palliative and supportive care to patient and family units. Personally managed a 12–18 patient and family caseload. Trained medical students and new nurses. Oversaw Medicaid and Medicare recordkeeping.

Clinical Office Nurse/Private Scrub Nurse – 1993 to 1994
STEVEN MYERS, M.D., Houston, TX
Functioned as scrub nurse at hospitals and in office surgeries. Conducted patient teaching, scheduled surgeries, and oversaw pre- and post-operative care. Taught medical students and residents.

Clinical Nurse (Gynecologic Oncology)
HOUSTON CANCER CENTER, Houston, TX

Clinical Research Nurse (Drug Studies/Research Projects)
UT, DEPARTMENT OF OBSTETRICS & GYNECOLOGY, Houston, TX

Clinical Nurse/Manager (Antepartum Fetal Testing)
WOMEN'S HOSPITAL - LABOR & DELIVERY, Houston, TX

Clinical Nurse/Charge Nurse (High- & Low-Risk Deliveries)
MEMORIAL MEDICAL CENTER - LABOR & DELIVERY, Houston, TX

Olivia L. Tyler

11805 East Devoe Street
Iowa City, Iowa 50266

oliviatyler@earthlink.net

Home: 712-946-9595
Cell: 712-294-4393

CAREER GOAL: HEALTH CARE PRACTICE MARKETING & MANAGEMENT

Results-driven professional leveraging a microbiology degree with extensive experience maximizing change for internal and external customers of a statewide organization. Known as a pioneering implementer successful at fusing the best of science, education, and information. A thirst for scientific knowledge complemented by a history reacting immediately to fulfill client needs and promoting services that "make a difference."

Notable Accomplishments

▶ Retained 95% of internal customers after implementing a fee-based, change-management initiative.

▶ Increased customer service productivity by 126+% over 10 years by problem solving via sample, phone, and email.

▶ Earned secondary teaching endorsement for biology, chemistry, general science, and physical science.

▶ Implemented beginning stages of Homeland Security diagnostic and reporting system to ensure plant safety.

▶ Selected as member of first-ever Iowa "Experience Leadership" extension staff development program.

Core Competencies

Analytical Methods ▲ Product Knowledge ▲ Client Presentations ▲ Program Development ▲ Budgeting Documentation ▲ Relationship Management ▲ Analytical Instrumentation Troubleshooting ▲ Training Guides Client/Vendor Interface ▲ Protocols ▲ Clinical Data Management ▲ Database Development ▲ Disease Management Quality Assurance ▲ Biotechnology ▲ Relationship Management ▲ Technology Implementation ▲ Team Building

EDUCATION

Master of Science, University of Nebraska, Lincoln, Nebraska 1989
Major: Plant Pathology, GPA: 3.9

Bachelor of Science, The University of Iowa, Iowa City, Iowa 1987
Major: Microbiology, GPA: 3.9

CAREER PATH

THE UNIVERSITY OF IOWA, Iowa City, Iowa   **1989 to Present**

Director, University Plant Disease Clinic

Manage expense budget and supervise a three-person team while directing day-to-day activities of the university's Plant Disease Clinic. Forge collaborative relationships with commercial growers, general public, and Extension leaders in all 99 Iowa counties. Negotiate with vendors to acquire cost-effective products and services.

Diagnose plant health problems and recommend management strategies to inside and outside clients spanning the state of Iowa. Address timely disease issues by authoring bulletins, newsletters, newspaper, and magazine articles. Create and present weekly and monthly radio, video, and live uplink segments on plant health issues.

CUSTOMER RELATIONSHIP MANAGEMENT

▶ Revitalized plant disease clinic, turning a former volunteer effort into a highly respected organization known as a valuable resource for the citizens of Iowa. Determined responsibilities at the county, university, and student level, balancing fast-paced priorities to meet needs of diverse clientele.

▶ Formed long-term professional relationships throughout the industry, employing a proactive and investigative approach to problem solving and customer situation management.

— Continued —

CAREER PATH (continued)

CUTTING-EDGE DIAGNOSTIC TOOLS

▶ Implemented inaugural stages of agricultural national security initiative for the state of Iowa as part of Homeland Security diagnostic laboratory team.

▶ Researched and implemented cutting-edge diagnostic technologies (within limited budget) to offer strategic solutions for constantly evolving plant issues throughout the Midwest.

DATA AND SAFETY MANAGEMENT

▶ Teamed up to develop an Access database and correspondence tracking system, recording details of over 5,000 plant samples, soil samples, telephone inquiries, and email inquiries each year. Manage all incoming hard- and soft-copy communications for annual report.

▶ Ensured implementation of technology upgrades to comply with national USDA guidelines in accordance with Homeland Security requirements.

▶ Trained student employees to comply with safety regulations related to chemical use.

PRESENTATION & TEACHING SKILLS

▶ Revamped a weak undergraduate course into a creative, capstone senior-level class. Incorporated "real-world" clinic problems, allowing students to resolve tangible diagnostic issues.

▶ Employ proactive education, using multi-tasking skills to assess an organization's need and prepare information for current and potential problems. A respected speaker in high demand by colleagues and external groups.

▶ Assumed responsibilities for teaching three undergraduate Plant Health and Protection courses in addition to clinic leadership role. Rated 4.62-5.00 of a possible 5.00 in Plant Pathology course evaluations, Spring 2003.

PROFESSIONAL TRAINING AND AWARDS

Additional Training:
Secondary Education Teaching Certificate, The University of Iowa ▲ 1999
Endorsements: Biology, Chemistry, General Science, and Physical Science

Computer Skills:
Microsoft Word, Excel, Access; Netscape

Awards:
Meritorious Service Award, The University of Iowa Extension ▲ 2002

Professional and Scientific Award for Achievement and Service,
The University of Iowa College of Agriculture Award ▲ 2001

PROFESSIONAL / HONORARY MEMBERSHIPS AND LEADERSHIP

American Phytopathological Society ▲ Phi Beta Kappa ▲ Phi Kappa Phi

Project Storybook
Iowa Correctional Institution for Women, Lutheran Social Services
(Assist inmates in reading and recording books to send to their children.)

Mentor Iowa
(Mentor abused, neglected, and delinquent children under the jurisdiction of the Juvenile Court.)

BARRY D. KAPLAN, M.D.

FACOG
Diplomat, American Board of Obstetrics and Gynecology

642 Braddock Park
Boston, MA 02116
(617) 349-9785
BarryKaplan45@hotmail.com

CAREER PROFILE

Career Objective: ⇒ **Program Manager: International Reproductive Health**

Medical Area of Specialty: ⇒ **Obstetrician/Gynecologist with Board Certification in Maternal-Fetal Medicine**

Extensive medical experience that includes working in two private practices, serving on hospital staffs, teaching at several universities and advancing the state of professional knowledge in the field of perinatal medicine. **Master of Public Health degree from Harvard University**. Conversational Spanish. US citizen.

Recent field experience in Kosovo as a clinician and consultant working for an American NGO and two U.N. agencies. Knowledgeable about the international donor community. Excellent communicator skilled at making large presentations to both medical and non-medical audiences. Well-developed abilities in negotiation, conflict analysis/management, and staff security. Experience working with U.N.-supported police force.

EDUCATION

Doctor of Medicine, TUFTS UNIVERSITY SCHOOL OF MEDICINE, Boston, MA (1981)

Bachelor of Science, HARVARD UNIVERSITY, Cambridge, MA (1978)

Master of Public Health, HARVARD SCHOOL OF PUBLIC HEALTH, Boston, MA (2002)

PROFESSIONAL EXPERIENCE

CLINICAL AND CONSULTING EXPERIENCE — INTERNATIONAL REPRODUCTIVE HEALTH

UNITED NATIONS POPULATION FUND, Mission to Kosovo, Pristina, Kosovo (2004)
Perinatal Technical Consultant

- Organized, managed, and conducted a comprehensive, Kosovo-wide survey of the maternity services and equipment needs in 20 regional hospitals and health houses.
- Ensured appropriate allocation of $600,000 in medical equipment.
- Analyzed and interpreted Kosovo-wide perinatal health data collected by WHO, Pristina office.
- Convened a Kosovo-wide meeting for representatives of aid agencies to discuss findings and make recommendations for modified or new reproductive and perinatal health strategies and policies.

WORLD HEALTH ORGANIZATION, Mother and Child Health Unit, Pristina, Kosovo (2002 to 2003)
Perinatal Technical Advisor/Medical Officer

- Contributed to the monitoring, analysis, and interpretation of Kosovo-wide perinatal data for WHO.
- Participated in adapting and implementing Kosovo-wide training-of-trainers interventions specifically directed at improving obstetric care practices using WHO's Essential Obstetric Care (EOC) educational intervention.
- Made connections within the NGO reproductive health community in the interests of ensuring efficient deployment of resources.

182

DOCTORS INTERNATIONAL, Pristina, Kosovo (2000)
Clinician — USAID-Funded Maternal and Infant Health Project

- Provided perinatal technical assistance to the Maternal and Infant Health Project at tertiary and regional hospitals.
- Provided medical monitoring of pregnancy-related health outcomes of a minority Roma population in Kosovo.
- Contributed to the reformulation of project goals, objectives, and priorities after assessing the clinical services and perinatal and neonatal health indicators.
- Acquired knowledge of and experience with the policies and procedures of a wide range of international humanitarian assistance and reproductive health programs including USAID.
- Analyzed/interpreted Kosovo maternal and neonatal data and presented findings at an international conference.

CLINICAL EXPERIENCE — PERINATAL MEDICINE

VIA CHRISTI HEALTH SYSTEM, KS (2000 to 2004)
Medical Director, Maternal-Fetal Medicine

PERINATAL & PEDIATRIC SPECIALISTS MEDICAL GROUP, INC., Sacramento, CA (1998 to 2000)
Associate — Private practice in maternal-fetal medicine and perinatal genetics

MISSOURI DIABETES & PREGNANCY PROGRAM, St. Louis, MO (1996 to 1998)
Regional Medical Director

WASHINGTON PRENATAL DIAGNOSIS CENTER, St. Louis, MO (1995 to 1996)
Co-Director

WASHINGTON HOSPITAL, St. Louis, MO (1996 to 1998)
Medical Director, Pregnancy Program

Hospital Appointments

Laduc Regional Medical Center, St. Francis and St. Joseph Hospitals, St. Louis, MO (1998 to 2004)
Professional Staff

Washington Community Hospitals of St. Louis, MO (1996 to 2000)
Professional Staff

Medical College of New York Hospitals, Department of Obstetrics and Gynecology, New York, NY (1994 to 1995)
Attending Physician

St. John Municipal Hospital Center, New York, NY (1990 to 1992)
Attending Physician

BOARD CERTIFICATION AND LICENSURE

Diplomat, American Board of Obstetrics and Gynecology
Certified by the American Board of Obstetrics and Gynecology in Maternal-Fetal Medicine
American Board of Obstetrics and Gynecology
Certification of Special Competence in Maternal-Fetal Medicine
Licensed in MO and NY

PROFESSIONAL AFFILIATIONS (SELECTED)

Fellow, American College of Obstetrics and Gynecology
Regular Member, Society of Maternal-Fetal Medicine
General Member, American Institute of Ultrasound in Medicine
Member, American Society of Human Genetics

CHAPTER 10

Best Resumes for Transitioning Into Nonprofit, Government, and Association Careers

Building the Foundation

Transferability of skills is the foundation upon which every effective career transition resume is written. Your challenge, therefore, is to identify the skills, qualifications, experiences, and competencies you have that will be of value in your new job, career, or industry. Those skills then become the key points in your resume around which everything else is written.

To help you get started with identifying your transferable skills, review the brief listing below of *some* of the skills, qualifications and competencies that companies and recruiters look for in candidates seeking positions in the nonprofit, government, or association sectors. *(Note that this is only a partial listing of countless different skills that companies look for in qualified candidates.)*

Carefully review the keywords and keyword phrases to identify those that accurately reflect skills you possess and which are transferable into your new position. Then, be sure to incorporate those words into your resume, your cover letters, and any other career marketing documents that you create. They will capture a prospective employer's interest and open the door to interviews and opportunities.

Administration	Organizational Leadership
Budgeting & Fiscal Management	Policies & Procedures
Community Outreach	Public Affairs & Public Relations
Economic Development	Public/Private Sector Alliances
Fundraising	Regulatory Affairs & Compliance
Government Relations	Services Delivery
Grant Writing & Administration	Special Events Planning & Management
Legislative Advocacy	Statutory Compliance & Reporting
Media Affairs & Press Relations	Strategic Planning & Direction
Member Development & Retention	Training & Development

Sample Career Transition Resumes

Following are seven sample resumes for individuals transitioning into the nonprofit, government, or association markets. Each of these resumes was written by a professional resume writer with extensive experience working with, writing for, and positioning individuals in career transition. Full contact information for each of these writers is in the Appendix. To understand why these resumes were written and designed the way that they were, it is critical that you read the following information that explains the specific objective of each of these job seekers and the particular strategy that was used to prepare their resume.

Resume:	David Marshall (pages 187-188)
Writer:	Louise Garver
Objective:	To transition from successful sales career into a position as a city manager.
Strategy:	Focused resume on 12-year career as a selectman and all of the associated responsibilities, projects, and achievements. Used page two to highlight management and marketing skills from his sales career that are directly relevant to new career transition goal.

Resume:	Elizabeth Roberts (pages 189-190)
Writer:	Kirsten Dixson
Objective:	To transition from customer service/client relations career at major corporations into a position in community relations.
Strategy:	Created combination resume putting her professional experience on page two to minimize the fact that she is not currently employed in community relations. Started with a prominent headline on page one and then showcased her transferable skills, supported by a detailed listing of relevant achievements. Developed special section to emphasize relevant community leadership experience.

Resume:	Mary Ann Lainer (pages 191-192)
Writer:	Diane Burns
Objective:	To transition from career as owner/director of a mortuary into an operational management position for a nonprofit organization or government agency.
Strategy:	Created a resume that instantly highlighted her objective, record of performance in sales, operations and management, educational credentials, and commitment to the community. Used page two to list actual work experience and attempt to downplay the negative connotation of a mortuary. Focused job descriptions on superior performance results.

Resume:	Keith F. Green (pages 193-194)
Writer:	Michele Haffner
Objective:	To transition out of 20-year career in airline management into a city manager or government agency manager position.

Strategy: Focused resume on bottom-line achievements transferable into new career track with particular emphasis on management, leadership, emergency response, people, and organizational skills. Demonstrated a wealth of transferable skills within each job description, focusing whenever possible on government, regulatory, and related functions and achievements.

Resume: Rowena A. Willemson (pages 195-196)
Writer: Marcy Johnson
Objective: To transition out of careers in both economic development and HR into new career track in association leadership.
Strategy: Designed one-page resume to clearly and succinctly communicate her wealth of talents for an association leadership position. Focused on transferable skills, areas of management effectiveness, track record of performance, and notable professional recognition. Included only a very brief listing of actual work experience.

Resume: Abigail W. Ash (pages 197-198)
Writer: Bill Kinser
Objective: To transition out of association marketing and into a special events planning/management position with a for-profit corporation.
Strategy: Dedicated all of page one to the context and extent of her work in planning one large annual conference in combination with her bottom-line financial achievements to the association. Utilized graphic representation to visualize scope and breadth of conference. Page two is a more traditional format with work history and other relevant qualifications.

Resume: Gloria J. Adak (pages 199-200)
Writer: Don Orlando
Objective: To transition out of the mortgage banking industry and into a leadership position with a nonprofit organization.
Strategy: Unique format immediately demonstrates value to the hiring organization, then follows with a unique presentation of professional experience and results that are directly relevant to new career goal. Used bold to highlight numbers and notable results in "soft skills" that are vitally important to a nonprofit.

David Marshall

562 Greentree Road • Enfield, CT 06082 • (860) 741–5544 • dmarshall@aol.com

CITY MANAGER

Over 12 years of leadership experience in town government as an elected chief administrative and fiscal officer. Key contributor impacting operational, budgetary, staffing, and resource needs throughout the municipality.

Extensive human resources and public speaking background. Effective communicator and team builder with planning, organizational, and negotiation strengths as well as the ability to lead, reach consensus, establish goals, and attain results. Additional business management experience in the private sector. Competencies include:

- **Management/Administration**
- **Fiscal Management/Budgeting**
- **Project/Program Management**
- **Public/Private Sector Alliances**
- **Economic Development**
- **Staff Development/Empowerment**

PROFESSIONAL QUALIFICATIONS

TOWN OF ENFIELD, Enfield, CT   1993 to Present
SELECTMAN

Administration/Management – Proactive executive providing strategic planning and leadership direction to diverse municipal departments as one of 3 elected board members governing the Town of Enfield. As board member, direct multiple open town meetings, develop and oversee $10 million budget, and administer various projects. Experience includes chairing Board of Selectmen for 6 years.

Human Resources – Oversee recruitment, promotion, and supervision of town administrator, 10 department heads with up to 214 full- and part-time staff, as well as Department of Public Works and Police Department. Personnel functions also encompass recruitment, contract negotiations, benefits administration, employee relations, and policy development and implementation.

Economic Development – Support strong public/private partnership toward diversified growth and prosperity. Source and negotiate with businesses as well as secure agreements to retain and attract new businesses. Develop financial vehicles for public improvements.

Regulatory Affairs – Develop and manage relationships, as well as advocate for municipal affairs, with federal and state regulatory agencies, local business executives, congressional members, and other legislators.

Public/Community Relations – Instrumental in the enhancement of town's image and building consensus with all boards. Active participant in numerous annual community events; act as spokesperson with the media.

Achievements

- **Turned around employee morale and productivity,** instituted training and employee recognition programs, and fostered interdepartmental cooperation, creating a positive work environment while restoring accountability and confidence in the administration. Town of Enfield is recognized by the state municipal association for having the "most responsive and best managed administration statewide."

- **Orchestrated multiple town revitalization projects,** following failed attempts by prior boards:
  - $2.9 million renovations to Town Hall and $5 million public safety complex.
  - $1.3 million public library project with state library grant offsets of $200,000.
  - $15 million sewer project with over $5 million secured in federal grant funding.

- **Effectively negotiated with company CEOs to relocate their businesses back to Enfield.** Results led to construction of new plants for 4 companies employing 2,550 people combined and an agreement to expand employee base.

- **Instrumental in attracting and retaining businesses** in the community by personally negotiating Tax Incentive Financing Agreements.

- **Spearheaded search for new providers and negotiated improved employee benefits** program while avoiding any rate increase.

BUSINESS MANAGEMENT EXPERIENCE

SANDERSOLL CORPORATION, New York, NY   1993 to present
  Regional Manager (2002 to present)
  District Manager (1997 to 2002)
  Account Manager (1993 to 1997)

Promoted to manage $23 million region that extends from the Northeast to Florida at a multi-billion-dollar food processing manufacturer. Lead and motivate the direct sales team of 35 plus 5 broker organizations. Develop and execute sales and marketing programs. Manage $2.5 million annual marketing/advertising budget.

Achievements

- **Created sales and marketing initiatives that turned around the region's ranking from #6 to #1** out of 8 regions nationwide. Consistently exceeded annual sales plan despite a declining industry.

- **Led the region's successful transition from a direct sales force to a productive food-broker network;** efforts charted an entirely new direction in the company, and the new business model was adopted in all regions.

- **Drove expansion of existing account base while capturing 5 key accounts that generated $10.5 million** in annual business volume for the district.

- **Elected to the Leadership Club in 1997, 1996, 1995, and 1994** for consistently ranking among the top 10% of account managers in overall sales performance throughout company.

- **Renegotiated marketing programs with major customers that increased sales and profits** while achieving acceptable dollar spends.

EDUCATION/PROFESSIONAL DEVELOPMENT

WESTERN NEW ENGLAND COLLEGE, Springfield, MA
M.B.A., Finance, 2001
B.S., Business Administration, 1995

Additional: Municipal Administration seminars

COMMUNITY AFFILIATIONS/LEADERSHIP

Connecticut Municipal Association
Vice President, Enfield Rotary Club
Chair, Connecticut Conservation Commission

ELIZABETH ROBERTS

249 Peachtree Lane
Decatur, GA 30030

404-373-4497
eroberts@yahoo.com

COMMUNITY RELATIONS DIRECTOR

- 15+ years of progressive management experience with proven leadership of strategic and tactical implementations and demonstrated passion for world-class customer and community service.

- Recognized for employment of people, process, and project management capabilities to exceed business objectives while concurrently fostering a productive work environment.

- Well-honed communication skills to tailor messaging to diverse audiences.

- Commitment to professional development and management by example.

- Positively influenced organizational growth, retention, and service through demonstrated competencies in:

Relationship Building	**Talent Acquisition & Development**
Community Development	**Oral & Written Communications**
Change Management	**Strategic Planning**
Project Management	**Problem Solving** .
Computer Technology	**Resource Allocation**

RELEVANT ACHIEVEMENTS

Management

- Achieved lowest attrition rate and best customer service scores—out of the five teams in the state—for a team of 200 that managed at Blue Cross-Blue Shield.

- Led project for Blue Cross-Blue Shield to transfer 5,000 customer accounts from the New York office to the New Hampshire office and divide them among five customer service teams.

- Improved efficiency rate 20% by directing team to create a training lab for newly hired Blue Cross customer service representatives.

- Enhanced performance management by instituting a telephone tracking system for the software licensing department, providing data on call volume and overall talk times.

- Reinvented HP application packagers as subject-matter experts, following offshoring, for knowledge transfer to other businesses, which jumpstarted other projects and effectively reallocated existing talent.

Communication

- Secured $2 million in new business for North American start-up of a European Microsoft business by cultivating relationships with prospective clients.

- Invited as keynote speaker on "Effective Leadership" at a Blue Cross-Blue Shield all-employee communication forum.

- Created a management tool for staff to report monthly on progress, goals, and required support that facilitated performance reviews and allowed for early identification of issues.

- Encouraged active communication by initiating brown-bag lunch sessions and monthly employee roundtables that improved employee satisfaction.

- Initiated Microsoft donation of computer equipment to Atlanta public schools and managed communications and approval process.

Customer Service

- Overcame severe backlog in Blue Cross-Blue Shield medical claims department by cross-training customer service representatives to process less complex claims during off-peak hours. Within three weeks, decreased call volume 50% and improved customer satisfaction.

- Successfully transitioned and retained 100 customer accounts during an acquisition.

- Recruited highly skilled talent that improved Software Service capabilities.

- Persuaded colleagues to re-distribute territories to equalize volume which enhanced service.

PROFESSIONAL EXPERIENCE

Business Development/Client Manager, Microsoft Corporation, Atlanta, GA   1999–Present
Global technology company with 45,000 employees and an 11th place ranking on the Fortune 500

Served as Client Manager for Software Licensing team, working with large global enterprise customers with Windows 2000/XP deployments, creating service contracts, and managing the implementation of a new, worldwide database for Software Licensing. Recruited, after 18 months, as Business Development Manager for Software Services. Launched North American division and managed accounts for this European business with three direct reports (technical consultants) and a $13 million sales revenue goal. Responded to RFPs, negotiated pricing, and presented at customer sites.

Customer Service Manager, Blue Cross-Blue Shield, Atlanta, GA   1994–1999
Healthcare insurance company with 3000 employee and more than 1.5 million members

Managed Customer Service/Call Center team of 200 customer service representatives and 6-8 Team Leaders. Held complete authority for budgets, staffing, and training to achieve a service level of 95%. Identified service problems and devised cost-effective solutions.

Customer Service Supervisor, Consolidated Group Claims, Decatur, GA   1989–1994
Accountable for training and development of medical customer service staff. Troubleshot customer issues that escalated.

COMMUNITY LEADERSHIP

Big Sister Volunteer, Big Brothers Big Sisters	2003–Present
Microsoft Liaison for Local Public Schools	2004–Present
Volunteer, Home Health and Hospice	2002–Present
Executive Board Member, Atlanta Youth Council	1997–2000
Board Member, Georgia State Quality Council	1997–1999
Steering Committee Member, Leadership Greater Atlanta	1998–1999

EDUCATION AND TRAINING

MBA, Georgia State University, School of Management, Atlanta, GA   expected 2006

Bachelor of Science, Organizational Management, Emory University, Atlanta, GA   1999
Earned degree with high honors while working full-time.

Ongoing Professional Development
Leadership/Management: Simmons College Women's Leadership Conference, Atlanta Chamber of Commerce's Leadership Program, Dr. Demings Leadership and Quality Training Program, Leadership Essentials, Franklin Time Management, Human Resources Training, Personalysis Training, Project Management (American Management Association and Skillpath)

Customer Service: Kaset International Customer Service Training Program, QPC Service Excellence Training, Tom Peters Pursuit of WOW Training, Granite State Quality Conference, Coping with Difficult Customers

Communication: Presentation Skills for Women, Zenger-Miller Facilitating for Results Program

MARY ANN LAINER

4598 Carlinda Street * Anaheim, CA 92807
714-998-8745 (h) * 714.446.8451 (c) * marylainer@yahoo.com

CAREER FOCUS

EXECUTIVE-LEVEL / NOT-FOR-PROFIT / GOVERNMENT RELATIONS
OPERATIONS MANAGEMENT · BUSINESS MANAGEMENT · SALES AND MARKETING

PROFILE

▪ Diversified experience in operations management, business turnarounds, and sales and marketing strategies. Strong record of accomplishments for building successful businesses, creating high-volume sales, forming talented teams, and teaching the next generation of American youth.

▪ Manage fiscal requirements and build solvency. Organize various simultaneous activities and operations. Multi-task oriented. Supervise and coordinate large groups of individuals. Strong leader and motivator.

Professional and Personal Value Offered:

· Community Leadership	· Business Development
· Liaison	· Project Management
· Event & Activity Coordination	· Operations Management
· Human Relations	· Outside Sales
· Interpersonal Skills & Engaging Personality	· Negotiation & Closing Skills
· Excellent Communicator	· Account Management
· Instructor, Mentor, Coach, & Advisor	· Problem Solving
· Trainer & Motivator	· "Customer-Service-First" Philosophy/Client
· Student & Leadership Development	Relations

EDUCATION

· **M.A., Government and Politics, University of Fullerton, CA, 2003**
· **30 hours post-graduate work in Sociology and Local/State Government**
· **B.S. in Business, Irvine College, CA, 1979**

COMMITMENT TO COMMUNITY

· Ten years' experience as a community activist founding organizations and building consensus to educate and inform the public on important issues.
· Elected Chairperson for the Orange County Human Rights Commission. Implemented newly enacted human rights legislation.
· Appointed by the Orange County Executive, as Chairman, Education Task Force. Investigated disciplinary and suspension policies within the Orange County Schools.
· Co-founder of organization established for young people to become involved in the fair housing process.

91

PROFESSIONAL EXPERIENCE

GENERAL MANAGER/PRESIDENT/TREASURER/SALES MANAGER
Lincolnton Memorial Park Corporation, Fullerton, CA   1995 — Present
* Lincolnton County Memorial Park is a family-owned and operated cemetery specializing in pre-need funeral arrangements, offering a full range of services. The site averages over 400 burials annually with sales over $1.6 million.

- Inherited the business with delinquent taxes and lagging sales. Took charge and turned around the operation, paying off all tax liabilities and dramatically improving sales, business operations, responsiveness, and performance. Implemented solid management principles and fiscal responsibility to re-ignite the business and create a profit margin.
- Manage operations, sales and marketing, HR, payroll, administration, and fiscal decisions and financials. Supervise a staff of 14.
- Direct and position the sales program, which includes meeting with families in their homes. Schedule appointments. Create print ads in collaboration with graphic artists.
- Boosted personal sales volume since January 1995, totaling nearly $1.6 million in pre- and at-need sales annually. Built the business to a referral operation with nearly 82% of sales coming from referrals.

REAL ESTATE AGENT
Hiban Realty, Irvine, CA   1990 — 1995

- Million Dollar Real Estate Sales Agent for five years, working part-time.
- Provided superior customer service. Remained very sensitive and responsive to customer needs. Honest and engaging personality boosted sales.
- Listed and sold residential real estate. Coordinated appointments, managed financial and closing paperwork, and communicated with financial inspectors, loan officers, assessors, housing inspectors, and attorneys.

TEACHER
FOREIGN EXCHANGE PROGRAM COORDINATOR
SPORTS COACH
Board of Education of Orange County, CA   1980 — 1990

- Taught students at four different Orange County high schools in history and social issues. Managed and supervised the teaching and grades for nearly 180 students per quarter. Maintained classroom order. Instructed and mentored students. Coordinated activities and events. Developed curriculum, wrote tests, and maintained grade books.
- Coordinated and led successful international foreign exchange programs. Orchestrated a home-stay exchange program with a school in Kiev (Ukraine) and one in Italy.
- Successful record as a high school basketball coach for 10 years. Selected as Orange County Coach of the Year by the *Orange County Sun* and the Orange County Coaches Association.

KEITH F. GREEN

W59 N456 Capitol Road
Brookfield, WI 53216

Residence: (262) 376-8954
E-mail: kfgreen@juno.com

EXECUTIVE PROFILE

▶ *City airline operations manager with more than 20 years of experience and a track record of bottom-line achievements through new business initiatives, process improvements, and cost containment efforts transitioning into state-level governmental administration.*

▶ Background includes military airfield management and emergency preparedness/risk management.

▶ Recognized by superiors, staff, and peers for effective communications skills and the ability to relate successfully to individuals at all levels within and outside of the organization.

CORE COMPETENCIES INCLUDE

- Strategic/Tactical Organizational Planning
- Team Coaching, Mentoring, & Performance Improvement
- Labor Relations & Arbitration

- Continuous Quality Improvement
- Profit & Loss Management
- Performance-Based Contracting
- Sales, Marketing, & Public Relations

PROFESSIONAL EXPERIENCE

MIDWEST AIRLINES – Milwaukee, WI   1983 to Present
Publicly traded (NYSE:MWA); in the top ten of U.S. airlines with 2003 sales of $2 billion.

CITY MANAGER, Glendale, CA / Portland, OR / Milwaukee, WI (1990 to Present)
Promoted and re-located to facilitate operation startups in three cities. Served two years in Glendale, CA (1990 to 1992), moved to Portland, OR for eight months, and received long-term assignment in 1993.

Direct a staff of 35 with two supervisors accountable for ticketing, passenger service, ground operations, and fleet services for daily inbound and outbound flights. Track, analyze, and report key performance measurements relative to operation plan with full P&L responsibility for annual revenues of $3.8 million and operating/capital budgets of $2.5 million. Manage personnel development and labor relations; ensure staff compliance with corporate policy and operational safety guidelines. *Serve on the Milwaukee Country Airline Managers' Council and function as Co-Chair of the Airport Security Sub-Committee.*

- *Achieved rankings in the top 25% of 15 cities for on-time service, baggage handling, customer service, and safety.*
- Negotiated and administered a six-year, co-share contract (1997 through July 2003) with National Airlines to provide complete customer service and fleet services for 12 daily flights (in addition to Midwest's three regular flights). Recruited, trained, and directed a total staff of 80 with four supervisors.
- Secured contract with Local Trans Airways (LTA) to provide fleet services for eight daily flights and replace revenue from discontinued co-shared National Airlines contract. Improved profit margin by 20% through process improvements and significant expense reductions. Generated six additional service contracts adding over $1 million in annual revenues.
- Wrote and established corporate manpower guidelines. Served as Co-Chair of the Divisional Headcount Committee; evaluated staffing requests for potential co-share/synergy opportunities. Analyzed procedural differences to gain operational efficiencies.
- As co-chair of Airport Security Sub-Committee, successfully resolved water runoff, snow removal, and emergency/security issues with Milwaukee County. Developed strategies to foster teamwork between airport agencies and improve overall airport safety.

CUSTOMER SERVICE AND GROUND OPERATIONS MANAGER, Kansas City, KS (1987 to 1990)
Promoted to assist City Manager with personnel administration, cost accounting, regulatory compliance, and safety.

- Ensured adequate manpower during peak business hours; prepared schedules for more than 200 full-time and part-time employees.
- Compiled and maintained a cost-effective budget for the entire city operation.
- Wrote procedural guidelines for a safe and effective operation; ensured compliance with all directives.

CUSTOMER SERVICE AND OPERATIONS SUPERVISOR, Kansas City, KS (1986 to 1987)
Managed and trained a staff of 200 Customer Service Representatives and Operations Agents. Established the HUB Operations Department for the organization's second busiest airport location with 100 daily flights. Implemented procedures to obtain inbound/outbound flight statistics.

CUSTOMER SERVICE/OPERATIONS AGENT, Milwaukee, WI (1983 to 1986)

CONSULTING EXPERIENCE

KFG AVIATION CONSULTING – Milwaukee, Wisconsin   1996 to Present

AVIATION CONSULTANT
Assist aviation-related businesses and governmental entities with the development of emergency policy and procedural manuals. Provide specialized training and administration assistance.

MILITARY EXPERIENCE

McCHORD AIR FORCE BASE – Tacoma, Washington   1980 to 1984

AIRFIELD MANAGEMENT SPECIALIST
Coordinated all activities involving aircraft movement, in-flight emergencies, and runway inspections. Edited flight plans, monitored weather, and handled classified documents.

EDUCATION & CERTIFICATIONS

AIRLINE/TRAVEL DIPLOMA, International Air Academy – Vancouver, Washington   1983 to 1984

CERTIFICATIONS
Ground Security Coordinator, Airport Operations

SPECIALIZED TRAINING (PARTIAL LISTING)
Organizational Behavior, Substance Abuse Recognition, Management Development, Critical Command, Central Command

PROFESSIONAL AFFILIATIONS

Wyoming Sports, Incorporated – Member, Board of Directors   1998 to Present
Midwest Machining Services, Incorporated – Member, Board of Directors   1997 to 2000

194

ROWENA A. WILLEMSEN

rowenawillemsen@earthlink.net
11805 U.S. Hwy 69 • Des Moines, Iowa 50201
515-388-5252 (h) • 515-291-4487 (c)

MULTI-DISCIPLINED ASSOCIATION MANAGER

Administration • Human Resources • Finance • Economic Development • Public Relations

Accomplished senior-level leader with interpersonal and organizational skills to envision and actualize complex programs for associations, city government, or business enterprises. Detail oriented; able to work effectively within board/manager relationships. Dynamic experience working with elected officials at all levels.

Core Competencies:

- ▸ Key Relationship Management
- ▸ High-Platform Communication and Presentation Skills
- ▸ Team Building, Leadership, and Mentoring
- ▸ Area Leadership Program Facilitation
- ▸ Personnel Administration

- ▸ Multimillion-dollar Budget Management
- ▸ Legislative Advocacy
- ▸ Public Financial Management
- ▸ Local Government Operations
- ▸ New Business Development

Management Effectiveness:

- Formed and managed civic alliances and successfully promoted economic growth for 2 communities.
- Initiated first intergovernmental strategic planning session to address overlapping community issues.
- Established HR processes for business startup, meeting staffing needs during 53% growth in first year.
- Facilitated area leadership program developing emerging leaders for advanced service opportunities.
- Oversaw audit requirements, as economic development treasurer, for assets that increased by $3.9M.

CAREER SYNOPSIS

Crowner Envelope, Inc., Des Moines, Iowa • 2003 to 2005
Office Manager / Human Resource Officer (Iowa Facility)

Madison Chamber & Area Development (MCAD), Madison, Wisconsin • 2002 to 2003
Executive Director

City of Knoxville, Knoxville, Iowa • 1986 to 2001
Fiscal & Administrative Services Director

CERTIFICATIONS AND PROFESSIONAL RECOGNITION

Third Sustaining Membership (46th individual internationally to advance to top status) • 1996 to Present
Senior Professional in Human Resources (SPHR) Certification • 1993 to Present
International Institute of Municipal Clerks (IIMC) Designations • 1983
Chamber of Commerce Professional Woman of the Year • 1997

CAREER PATH

CROWNER ENVELOPE, INC., Des Moines, Iowa   2003 to 2005

Office Manager / Human Resource Officer (Iowa Facility) — Hired to establish and oversee administrative functions for start-up of 40,000 sq. ft. Iowa facility adding machine capacity and new options for envelope production. Coordinated human resource functions including recruitment and benefit administration.

- Used background in marketing, purchasing, AR/AP, vendor negotiations, safety, and personnel administration to set up office policies and procedures.

- Determined training needs, administered 206E funding program, and scheduled training programs based on company production processes for staff that grew from 17 to 23 employees in less than one year.

MADISON CHAMBER & AREA DEVELOPMENT (MCAD), Madison, Wisconsin   2002 to 2003

Executive Director – Served as Chief Operating Officer managing economic development efforts for the Madison Chamber & Area Development Board under leadership of board of directors. As chamber ambassador, coordinated development function with resources in the community and other relevant funding sources. Directed 2 paid staff members and approximately 50 community volunteers.

- Assertively promoted economic growth through new commercial, service, and industrial recruitment, existing industry expansion, and business growth.

CITY OF KNOXVILLE, Knoxville, Iowa   1986 to 2001

Fiscal & Administrative Services Director – As chief appointed official, acted as city's representative forming and managing alliances between county, schools, business community, and Knoxville Economic Development Council (KEDC). Supervised preparation and administration of municipal operating budget of $3M+ and capital improvement budget over $10M. Experienced in bonding, debt management, property tax issues, financial forecasting, cash-flow projection, and project management skills.

- Initiated first intergovernmental strategic planning sessions uniting diverse community groups to discuss overlapping debt and revitalization issues.

- Reactivated Knoxville Economic Development Council.

- Played key role in implementing leveraging tools and incentives including Tax Increment Financing (TIF), Tax Abatement, and Local Option Sales Tax.

- Procured and administered final multimillion-dollar EPA grant for wastewater treatment, positioning community for growth in strategic areas.

- Served as treasurer of KEDC, providing appropriate internal control and oversight of audit requirements of assets that grew from $95,000 to almost $4M.

LEADERSHIP AND COMMUNITY INVOLVEMENT

Active Kiwanis Member • 2003 to Present

School to Work Advisory Board • 1996 to Present

Leadership Knoxville Advisory Board • 1994 to 2004

Facilitator, Leadership Knoxville Program • 1996 to 2003

Chair, Knoxville Chamber of Commerce Legislative Committee • 1995 to 2001

Character Madison Board of Directors • 2001

Professional Affiliations & Training Addendum Provided On Request

Abigail W. Ash

301 Inner Harbor Way, Baltimore, MD 21201
Telephone: (410) 719-5501, E-mail: awash@mailbox.com

QUALIFICATIONS SUMMARY

Customer-centric professional with nearly 10 years of **event planning experience** for a national association. Demonstrated history of success in working with internal stakeholders, constituents/customers, and hospitality industry vendors to coordinate all aspects of national conferences. Hold an **event management certification** from George Washington University (GWU).

Areas of Strength:

- Vendor Negotiations
- Marketing Activities

- Event Planning
- Cost Reductions/Avoidance
- Budget Execution

- Project Management
- Liaison Roles
- Strategic Planning

PROFESSIONAL EXPERIENCE

NATIONAL ASSOCIATION OF ENVIRONMENTAL LEADERS (NAEL), Baltimore, MD 1996–Present
Director of Communications & Constituency Outreach (2001–Present)

Key Event Planning Achievements:	
Event:	Annual Conference of Environmental Leaders Council (ELC)
Meetings Planned:	Albuquerque, NM, 2001 ● Boston, MA, 2002 ● Santa Barbara, CA, 2003 Jacksonville, FL, 2004 ● Chicago, IL, 2005 (planning in process) (Assisted in the planning of previous annual conferences, 1996–2000.
Attendance:	150+ members of the constituency-wide ELC attend the week-long conference.
Budget:	Leveraged a lean, $22,000 annual budget to **reengineer a historically unprofitable conference to one generating consistent profits** since 2002, as follows.

- Secured $8,500+ in corporate sponsorships by innovating sponsorship opportunities so that vendors could sponsor conference events, which represented far more value than the historically requested $500 donation.
- Saved $1,500+ by shipping the Association's LCD projector and laptop to meeting locations for use by all speakers, in lieu of paying premium rates to rent the equipment on site.
- Optimized use of travel dollars by selecting local speakers to reduce travel and lodging costs.
- Slashed the conference catering bill by transitioning from a final night dinner and reception to a beverage-only (beer and wine) reception with a cash bar available.

Event Responsibilities:

- Collaborate with the ELC Steering Committee (18 volunteer members) as the lead staff person for this group of environmental conservationists from across the United States.
- Lead the ELC Steering Committee in planning all aspects of the meetings, which include coordinating the agenda and after-hours activities, obtaining approximately five speakers, and securing 15 sponsors.
- Research vendors to select potential team-building activities for conferences and present the options for the Steering Committee's approval, subsequently contracting with the chosen vendor.
- Work closely with the Association's meeting planner in evaluating and selecting conference sites.
- Plan two receptions per meeting, which includes coordinating the opening/welcome reception.
- Oversee the creation of all collaterals such as name tags, registration lists, hotel information, and other handouts for arriving participants.
- Brainstorm with the ELC Chairman to prepare written remarks and to anticipate potential issues.
- Work closely with hotels' conference services managers to plan all menus and food for catered functions.
- Serve as the lead contact during the meeting with signatory authority for all banquet event orders (BEOs).

Continued

NATIONAL ASSOCIATION OF ENVIRONMENTAL LEADERS (NAEL)
(Continued)

Publications Coordinator (1998–2001)
Retain the following responsibilities as the ***Director of Communications & Constituency Outreach.***

- Serve as the Managing Editor in producing *Environmental Awareness* magazine, a bi-weekly, four-color magazine of 80–100 pages. Managed publication of 40+ issues from 1998 to date.
- Eliminated $15,000 in publication distribution costs by converting the Association's bi-weekly newsletter to HTML for online viewing and e-mail distribution to 6,000 subscribers.
- Work closely with the staff, publisher, editor, and advertising team to meet multiple deadlines.
- Partner with the executive team to plan the Association's publications for the year.
- Serve as the Association's point of contact (POC) with the publishing vendor, integrating content developed in-house with the vendor's responsibilities of selling ads, designing the layout, and printing.
- Create a yearly editorial calendar and identify current industry topics as themes for each publication.
- Collect all editorial material and content, in collaboration with all Association departments.
- Author articles and conceive ideas for freelance writers' use in developing articles.
- Coordinate accomplishment of all tasks within deadlines for pre-production, review, and editing of the entire magazine, and approval of printing of the edited publication.

Assistant, Marketing & Communications Division (1996–1998)

- Provided administrative support to the Vice President of Marketing & Communications and participated in most aspects of convention/meeting preparation.

WASHINGTON HOSPITAL CENTER, Washington, DC   1995–1996
Staff Assistant, Marketing Department

- Worked with the Director of Marketing to create a marketing campaign for a new managed care organization (MCO) for low-income patients.
- Collaborated with an ad agency to roll out a $4 million media (print/radio/TV) campaign.
- Tracked a $3+ million advertising budget.

EDUCATION

Event Management Certificate, George Washington University (GWU), Washington, DC   2004
Web Site Design I, II, III; Photoshop; and PageMaker; Computer Savvy Trainers, Columbia, MD   2001
BS, Business Administration & Marketing, Strayer University, Baltimore, MD   1995

COMPUTER SKILLS

Proficient in the following in a Windows environment:
Microsoft (MS) Office Suite, HTML, Adobe Acrobat, and **Pagemaker.**

GLORIA J. ADAK
2550 Indian School Road
Phoenix, Arizona 85001

glahd@aol.com

602.555.1234 (Office)
602.555.4321 (Residence)

WHAT I CAN BRING TO THE ARIZONA MULTIFAMILY LOAN CONSORTIUM AS YOUR NONPROFIT EXECUTIVE DIRECTOR

The **leadership** to help people focus on the mission alone,

The **ability** to translate corporate vision into profits, and

The **intelligence** to find and fix the right problems the first time.

RECENT PROFESSIONAL EXPERIENCE WITH SELECTED CONTRIBUTIONS

Sought out by the President to serve as **Senior Vice President**, Panella Mortgage Company, Mesa, Arizona, April 99 – Present

My Product Support Division assists some 125 professionals nationwide. Panella services about 190,000 loans in a $15B portfolio and originated up to $3B in new loans. Three vice presidents, two assistant vice presidents, and a clerical staff report directly to me.

Overhauled an accounts payable system that frustrated senior executives, vendors, and employees for years. President approved my plan virtually unchanged. **Outcomes: Gained one full day** of **productivity a week**, late payments to vendors stopped, managers enthusiastically on board—all in just 90 days.

Chosen to bring us to Y2K compliance. Our team found thousands of needs from hundreds of sources. Guided our selection of a software vendor to fix the problem—a critical decision. **Outcomes:** Gently **overcame** widespread **resistance to change**. Met the Federal Reserve's deadline with **flawless operations**.

Hired away by the Chairman and CEO to be **Senior Vice President**, Saguaro Mortgage, Inc., Montgomery, Alabama, August 94 – March 99

Seventy-five people—from vice presidents to clerical specialists—reported to me from across the Southwest. Our organization serviced some $9B in loans with new loan originations of up to $1B.

One of five members of our **Executive Team** that provided continuous strategic, corporate guidance and policy.

Helped a senior manager overcome her lack of trust in others, after others had tried and failed to make her a team player. Rejected conventional wisdom by giving her more responsibility while still protecting our productivity. **Outcomes:** Her **contributions soared**, I had a stronger manager on my team, **our employees happier**.

Designed and managed a "retreat" to help refocus and draft part of our strategic plan. Inspired managers to contribute creative ideas in every area. **Outcomes:** Employees felt more ownership than ever before. **Teamwork enhanced**.

Asked to guide the "**securitzation**" of our parent's **$400M loan portfolio** in a hurry. Quickly recruited a team, then helped them gather a mass of information from an unairconditioned warehouse—in July. **Outcomes:** Inspired **great loyalty**. Did **three months work in 30 days**. People saw me ready to do anything I asked of them. **Leverage** and **earnings rose** and stayed high.

More indicators of performance ☞

199

Professional Experience (continued)

Hired away by the President and CEO to be **Senior Vice President for Secondary Marketing** *and later* **Regional Manager, Wholesale Production Division**, Sunshine Mortgage Corporation, Tucson, Arizona, March 86 – August 94

> Thrust into senior leadership role when our "hands-on" President fell ill with no warning. Handled different, often conflicting, responsibilities with two others who had much more experience. *Outcome:* Our **minute-by-minute decisions made** the company **money** for the year it took to restore the presidency.

> Asked to fix a policy manual our customers needed, but complained about chronically. Coordinated across the company so we could **speak to our customers with one voice**. Validated the new instructions with largest customer. *Outcomes:* **Alliances** with accounts got **much stronger**. Our employees **much better** able to **help** corporate customers.

Mortgage Finance Specialist, Prudential-Bache Securities, Atlanta, Georgia, November 84 – March 86

> Hired to **guide** this company in its **first effort to broker financial packages**. Started with no staff, no support, no budget, no well-defined mission, no customers, and no name recognition. Later, fought off corporate efforts to disband us. *Outcomes:* Brought in **rising sales** through persuasive "cold calling."

Secondary Market Account Executive, Mortgage Guaranty Insurance Corporation, Atlanta, Georgia, April 82 – November 84

> Made the time to find, and fill, all the needs of many major customers. Used solid logic to guide their businesses toward us. *Outcome:* **Negotiated our largest sale in five years**.

Assistant Vice President, Collateral Investment Company (now Collateral Mortgage, Ltd.), Birmingham, Alabama, November 78 – April 82

> **Sold more than $350M** of our products and met tough delivery dates every month.

Management Assistant *promoted to* Assistant Department Manager *promoted to* Manager (Consumer Credit and Commercial Loans), *later* **Bank Officer** and **Trust Department Officer**, First National Bank of Charlotte, Charlotte, North Carolina, June 72 – October 78

> Selected to help our Commercial Loan Conversion Team computerize thousands of loans in our main office and 32 branches.

EDUCATION

B. S., **Marketing**, University of Alabama, Tuscaloosa, Alabama 72 *Earned this degree while working up to 20 hours a week at night and on weekends.*

COMPUTER CAPABILITIES

Working knowledge of LoanQuest (loan origination software), Outlook, Word, Internet search protocols.

Page two

CHAPTER 11

Best Resumes for Transitioning Into Consulting Careers

Building the Foundation

Transferability of skills is the foundation upon which every effective career transition resume is written. Your challenge, therefore, is to identify the skills, qualifications, experiences, and competencies you have that will be of value in your new job, career, or industry. Those skills then become the key points in your resume around which everything else is written.

To help you get started with identifying your transferable skills, review the brief listing below of *some* of the skills, qualifications, and competencies that companies and recruiters look for in candidates seeking positions in consulting. *(Note that this is only a partial listing of the countless different skills that companies look for in qualified candidates.)*

Carefully review the keywords and keyword phrases to identify those that accurately reflect skills you possess and which are transferable into your new position. Then, be sure to incorporate those words into your resume, your cover letters, and any other career marketing documents that you create. They will capture a prospective employer's interest and open the door to interviews and opportunities.

Account Relationship Management
Business Transformation
Change Management
Client Acquisition & Retention
Client Engagement Management
Executive Coaching
Leadership Development
Negotiations
New Business Development
Organizational Design & Development

Project Planning & Delivery
Project Management & Administration
Proposal Development
Reengineering & Revitalization
Services Delivery
Solutions Delivery
Team Building & Leadership
Sample Career Transition Resumes
Process Redesign & Optimization
Professional Services Organization

Sample Career Transition Resumes

Following are four sample resumes for individuals transitioning into consulting careers. Each of these resumes was written by a professional resume writer with extensive experience working with, writing for, and positioning individuals in career transition. Full contact information for each of these writers is in the Appendix. To understand why these resumes were written and designed the way that they were, it is critical that you read the following information that explains the specific objective of each of these job seekers and the particular strategy that was used to prepare their resume.

Resume: Frances B. Carlin (pages 204)
Writer: Bill Kinser
Objective: To transition from career as a senior-level, supervisory economist with the federal government into a career in management consulting, either on a freelance or contract basis, or with a large consulting firm.
Strategy: Created strategic, one-page abbreviated resume focusing on her value to entrepreneurs by helping them develop efficient, cost-effective, and reliable business systems and processes. Followed with information on two current, informal consulting engagements; then details about her federal career. Concluded with brief presentation of education, honors, and awards.

Resume: Anita Murphy (pages 205-206)
Writer: Roberta Gamza
Objective: To transition from impressive career with IBM into a consulting position with emphasis on cross-cultural communications, cross-cultural relations, and international business partnerships.
Strategy: Used extensive professional summary section to highlight all relevant skills and qualifications, along with areas of expertise and profile of "who" she is. Professional experience centered on career highlights that positioned her as an expert in the field, rather than quantified her corporate accomplishments.

Resume: Timothy R. Becker (pages 207-208)
Writer: Janet Beckstrom
Objective: To transition from a retired police officer into a new career consulting in security and law enforcement.
Strategy: Wrote strong profile section to clearly communicate "who" he is and value he brings to an organization. Focused resume on three primary facets of his experience: administrative/management, law enforcement, and communications. Page two includes succinct summary of work experience and notable education, training, and honors to round out presentation.

Resume: Rachel N. Rollins (pages 209-210)
Writer: Bill Kinser

Objective: To transition out of 15-year banking industry career into a senior business consultant position with an international retail food chain.

Strategy: Crafted resume to focus on her achievements within the core functional areas that relate most to her target consulting position – strategic planning, operating management, leadership, team building, coaching, problem solving and more. Utilized functional format to include specific information and accomplishments relevant to each of these performance areas. Simultaneously, downplayed extensive banking career with one- to two-sentence job descriptions.

FRANCES B. CARLIN

1425 Rhode Island Ave., NW, #1230, Washington, DC 20001
Cell: (202) 273-1044, E-mail: fran_carlin@isp.com

MANAGEMENT CONSULTANT

Management consultant experienced as a public sector, international economist. Pursuing an **MBA degree with concentrations in entrepreneurship and business strategy;** hold a **BA degree in economics, complemented by international economic studies** completed abroad. Skilled at advising entrepreneurs, among diverse industries, in positioning their ventures for long-term systemization and profitability. Fluent in Russian.

Areas of Strength:

• Change Management	• Technology Solutions	• Market Segmentation
• Business Planning	• Contract Negotiations	• Proposal Development
	• Research & Analysis	• Project Administration

PROFESSIONAL EXPERIENCE

Management Consultant, Washington, DC   2003–Present

- Advise *an emerging media design firm* on contract negotiations, bid proposal development, and project estimates.
- Advise *a web-based business* in conducting market research, developing product offerings, identifying customer segmentations, and evaluating contracts.

Supervisory Economist, United States Department of Agriculture (USDA), Washington, DC   2000–Present

Monitor agricultural economics and statistics throughout the U.S. and among various developed countries. Serve on the 10-member, international food sources team working in close collaboration to develop comprehensive, unilateral data that is comparable among countries.

Key Achievements:

- Reduced report production time by 25% by working with an organizational database development team.
- Appointed to supervise five economists in developing and publishing news releases.
- Selected to provide software/macro installation and troubleshooting support for the entire division.
- Initiated recruitment efforts for the division by establishing partnerships with other USDA divisions to increase the number of colleges and universities visited.
- Received two performance awards within the first 18 months of service.

Founder/President, Exponential Potential Investment Club, Washington, DC   2000–Present
Intern, Montgomery County, MD, Office of Economic Development, Rockville, MD   1999

EDUCATION

Candidate, **MBA,** Kogod School of Business, American University, Washington, DC   2004–Present
- *Concentrations in Entrepreneurship and Business Strategy,* Cumulative GPA: 3.75

BA, Economics *(Business Concentration),* American University, Washington, DC   2000
- Magna Cum Laude Graduate (3.90 GPA), Academic Scholarship, Dean's List

International Economics Studies, University of Economics in London, London, England   Fall 1999

HONORS AND AWARDS

- **Recipient of a 2004 USDA Award for Excellence** for co-authoring the article *"International Agricultural Resources for the 21st Century,"* Agricultural Industry Insider, June 2003, Vol. 152, No. 6.

- **Two-Time Recipient of the USDA Foundation Scholarship.**

204

Anita Murphy

CROSS-CULTURAL FACILITATOR

FACILITATING SUCCESSFUL INTERNATIONAL BUSINESS PARTNERSHIPS IN LATIN AMERICA
OVERCOMING CULTURAL BARRIERS / ACHIEVING BUSINESS OBJECTIVES

PROFESSIONAL SUMMARY

Consulting:	International Business and Cultural Integration
Corporate Management:	Latin American Business Development Manager
Qualifications:	Teaching English as Foreign Language (TEFL), 2004 Six Sigma Certification, 2002 Emotional Intelligence at Work, 2001 Understanding the Human Element at Work, 2000
Specialization Area:	Cross-Cultural Barriers Organizational Behavior Modification Cross-Cultural Relationship Building Teamwork Promotion Business Goals and Objective Achievement
Business Focus:	Importing/Exporting

AREAS OF EXPERTISE

- Cultural Knowledge Transfer
- Business and Social Etiquette
- Negotiations and Diplomacy
- Meeting Planning & Facilitation
- Project Management & Leadership
- Language Instruction (English and Spanish)

- Interpretation (English and Spanish)
- International Travel Safety
- Business Trip Planning
- Traveling Tips (Dining, Entertainment, Sightseeing Activities, Transportation, Shopping, and Souvenir Hunting)

PROFILE

A highly skilled and accomplished international business and cultural consultant, Anita Murphy enjoyed a successful corporate career in international business ventures. She has bridged the gap between cultures, facilitating revenue growth, increasing profit margins, realizing revenues previously considered lost, and strengthening business relationships for future partnerships.

Anita has earned a reputation for accomplishing goals and getting results. Her passion for quality and excellence drives her to find the root cause of a problem. Her deep insights, intellectual curiosity, business acumen, and cultural understanding guide her to develop optimum cross-cultural solutions that get to the heart of the problem and put businesses back on the right track. She applies this same insight to each and every client, whether they are just embarking on a new international venture and need guidance to avoid pitfalls, or have an ongoing international business venture that has stalled despite the best efforts of all parties.

Anita works well with established teams. She can assume a leadership role to educate team members on cultural barriers and facilitate organizational behavior changes necessary to achieve established objectives.

2345 South Ithaca Street ▪ Denver, CO 80236 ▪ 303.555.4567 ▪ animurph@msn.net

Anita Murphy

PROFILE CONTINUED

In her corporate roles, Anita was highly regarded by her management team and was often selected to manage the most challenging accounts or take over projects in crisis. She has a history of turning dissatisfied customers into highly satisfied, loyal clients, and recovered revenues from severely past due accounts.

Creativity and innovation are the hallmarks of Anita's work. She ardently seeks to understand and exceed expectations. Anita takes the time to know her clients and their requirements as well as the business scenario/drivers to ensure she provides the most valuable solutions possible.

CORPORATE CAREER HIGHLIGHTS

✓ Applied knowledge of U.S. and Latin cultures to first build a foundational relationship, the necessary groundwork for successful business relationships within Latin America. With the relationship established, created common business goals and integrated business policies and procedures. Eliminated confusion and diffused conflict, resulting in higher profit margins.

✓ Recognized the lack of a foundational relationship was responsible for high delinquency rates with agents (third-party agent distributors) throughout Latin America. Built and strengthened relationships to facilitate the collections process, yielding $6M from past-due accounts. Documented this repeatable relationship-based collection process for wider implementation.

✓ Recovered $1M in withheld taxes previously written off as a loss. Customers in Latin America withheld 30% of the invoice amount as tax payment. Company was entitled to a refund, but had no process to recover the money. After a thorough investigation, developed and implemented a repeatable process and recovered $1M in the first year of implementation.

✓ Launched the first sales and telemarketing teams in Mexico City for an international telecommunications company offering long-distance service from foreign countries to the U.S. Developed and implemented innovative sales strategies and tactics resulting in $1M in revenue in the first year.

CAREER HISTORY

Founder & Principal Consultant, Cultural Advances, Denver, CO June 2004 – Present

IBM Network Solutions, Niwot, CO, 1997 – 2002
    Manager, Latin America Operations, 2002
    Project Manager, Americas Services Team (2001 – 2002)
    Latin America Coordinator 1997 – 2000

Latin America Business Development Manager, World Communications, Denver, CO 1993 – 1997

Timothy R. Becker

4431 Oakwood Drive   303-239-1486
Westminster, CO 80031   cmdrbecker@isp.com   *(unlisted)*

PROFILE

- Accomplished career officer earning consistent promotions to positions of increasing authority.
- Track record of building cohesive teams, mentoring and fostering growth among constantly changing team members.
- An effective communicator and negotiator; able to build a consensus among those with diverse agendas.
- Decisive—demonstrated ability to make immediate, difficult decisions in crisis situations.
- Strong leadership and administrative skills; one who leads by example.
- Highly dedicated to duty, performance and promotion of law enforcement goals and principles.

HIGHLIGHTS OF EXPERIENCE

Administrative/Management

- Developed and monitored $2.5+ million budget with reporting responsibilities to represented jurisdictions and state officials.
- Ensured task force operations adhered to established goals, objectives and policies.
- Managed administrative functions including employee supervision, vehicle fleet, and equipment and facility maintenance.
- Collaborated with Executive Board to perform and implement strategic planning.
- Compiled statistics and generated reports to assess effectiveness of operations.
- Identified sources for and prepared grant applications including a $625,000 request for narcotics investigations which was subsequently funded.
- Approved all unit expenditures including overtime, spending of grant monies, and funds required for investigations; performed regular accounting of expenditures.
- Maintained record keeping and accountability for evidence; ensured proper forfeiture sharing among respective jurisdictions.

Law Enforcement and Tactical

- Established investigative priorities based on crime trends, reports from jurisdictions, and feedback from street teams. Developed specific investigative plans and assigned appropriate teams.
- Led investigations of personal and property crimes.
- Coordinated training on relevant topics to facilitate knowledge and safety of team members.
- Served on Emergency Support Team (similar to SWAT) for 14 years. Completed extensive physical and tactical training. Responded to crisis situations across the state. Conducted hostage negotiations. Provided protection for dignitaries and high-profile events.

Communications

- Oversaw interagency relations with federal, state, county and local units (including FBI, DEA, ATF, Secret Service, U.S. Customs and U.S. Postal Service).
- Acted as liaison and maintained open lines of communication with officials from agencies represented on multi-jurisdictional teams.
- Forged relationships and interacted effectively with administrators and political leaders.
- Developed and maintained external associations and public relations.

Timothy R. Becker   303-239-1486
                                                                  (unlisted)

PROFESSIONAL HISTORY

COLORADO STATE PATROL - Various posts and assignments   1978-2005
**Detective First Lieutenant / Commander of Denver Area Narcotics Team (DANT) and
Northwestern Unit for Narcotics (NUN)**
> Served as Commanding Officer of multi-jurisdictional narcotics cooperative forces. (Initially
> assigned only to DANT; subsequently was given additional responsibility for NUN.) Managed all
> facets of task force comprising 45+ law enforcement officers assigned on a rotating basis
> representing state, county and local agencies.

Previous positions and ranks:
Team Leader – Colorado State Patrol Emergency Support Team
Detective Lieutenant & Street Team Administrator/Supervisor – Down State Narcotics Team
Administrative Sergeant – Oversaw property, forfeitures and finances
Sergeant Shift Supervisor – Colorado Springs post
Undercover Officer – Northwestern Unit for Narcotics
Temporary Instructor – Colorado State Patrol Training Academy
Patrol Officer

EDUCATION & TRAINING

Police Academy Graduate • Colorado State Patrol   CPR and First Aid Certified
Associate Degree, Criminal Justice • Aims College   Hazardous Materials Certified

Selected specialized training:
- Emergency Support Team   - Sexual Harassment
- Terrorism & Domestic Preparedness   - Law Enforcement & Youth
- Basic & Advanced Narcotics   - Leadership Training
- Advanced Accident Investigation   - Supervisory Skills Development

---

HONORS

Professional Excellence Commendations (2)   Distinguished Expert (marksmanship)
Lifesaving   Gold Badge (physical training)

COMMUNITY INVOLVEMENT

Boulder Athletic Association - Served as President, Vice President, and Director
Pikes Peak Conservation Club – Member

References available on request

Rachel N. Rollins

12345 Sky Harbor Way, Apt. 450 ● Seattle, WA 98101
Cell: 206-448-0103 ● E-mail: rachnroll@isp.net

PROFESSIONAL PROFILE

Results-oriented manager with proven experience in **strategic planning, communications, organizational change, and performance improvement.** Adept at developing, planning, and implementing corporate visions, strategies, and initiatives. Skilled in building consensus internally and externally, and in motivating staffs to achieve desired results. Active in coaching and developing staff with a proven ability to transfer job knowledge and skills to individuals at all levels. Experienced liaison accustomed to collaborating effectively with staff and management.

Core Strengths

- Strategic Planning
- Operating Improvement
- Facilitating and Coaching

- Communications
- Change Management
- Business Plan Development

SELECTED ACCOMPLISHMENTS

Strategic Planning and Operating Improvement

- Reengineered N&W National Bank's strategic planning process, successfully implementing an approach that increased revenues and reduced expenses.
  - ➢ Served as a facilitator for the senior management team in developing an organizational vision and supporting business strategies.
  - ➢ Created a comprehensive business planning guide to provide uniform guidance to staff members throughout the organization.
  - ➢ Launched business metrics for tracking progress in meeting organizational goals and objectives.
  - ➢ Led an expense efficiency team which identified opportunities to recapture approximately $6 million in lost revenue.
- Created and deployed a performance management culture at the Office of Thrift Supervision (OTS).
  - ➢ Supervised a five-member team and collaborated with staff across the agency to develop the first OTS strategic plan and annual performance report encompassing all operating units.
  - ➢ Received recognition when the OTS planning process was cited as "a best practice government-wide" by the General Services Administration (GSA).

Leadership, Team Building, Coaching, and Consulting

- Facilitated a cross-functional workgroup to provide user input in developing the structure for the OTS strategic planning and performance-based reporting process.
  - ➢ Involved senior and mid-level staff from all business units as well as information technology (IT) and financial advisors.
- Advised OTS management from various business units on maintaining morale and easing the challenges of organizational change following two reductions-in-force (RIFs) within a short period of time.
- Trained OTS staff in effective business planning methods and techniques.
- Coached and counseled employees and customers of failed savings and loan institutions as to the ramifications of the institutions' liquidations.

Continued

SELECTED ACCOMPLISHMENTS (continued)

Analysis and Problem-Solving

- Increased effectiveness of N&W National Bank's organizational communications through the development and launch of a strategic planning intranet site.
  - ➤ Improved the operational correlation between business strategy, IT functions, and financial planning.
- Reengineered N&W's planning process, reducing the amount of time required for the process by 35%.
  - ➤ Developed and implemented a structured process for identifying, prioritizing, and funding investment opportunities.

Communications

- Prepared and delivered presentations and recommendations to N&W's senior and mid-level managers.
- Served as a liaison between OTS and potential acquirers of failed savings and loan institutions.
- Developed Congressional testimony for the Chairman of the OTS, addressing the agency's strategic plan and key performance results.
- Acted as the OTS liaison to the Senate Banking Committee and the Federal Reserve on progress in meeting various performance-based, governmental mandates.

PROFESSIONAL EXPERIENCE

N&W NATIONAL BANCORP, Seattle, WA   2000–2005

- Reengineered the bank's strategic planning process and advised management and staff across the organization on business planning and performance improvement.

Vice President & Corporate Strategist

OFFICE OF THRIFT SUPERVISION (OTS), Washington, DC   1990–2000

- Rapid promotion through increasingly responsible positions with this federal regulatory agency, overseeing the safety and soundness of savings and loan institutions.
  - ➤ Selected as one of the first employees to participate in the government-wide "Executive Development Program," which prepares high-potential employees for management positions.

Division Director, Agency Planning Division, 1996–2000
Senior Program Analyst, 1994–1996
Special Assistant to the Chief Financial Officer (CFO), 1992–1994
Operations Specialist, 1990–1992

EDUCATION

Georgetown University, Washington, DC
MBA, Finance, 1990
BS, Finance, 1987

CHAPTER 12

Best Resumes for Transitioning Out of Consulting and Entrepreneurial Careers

Building the Foundation

Transferability of skills is the foundation upon which every effective career transition resume is written. Your challenge, therefore, is to identify the skills, qualifications, experiences, and competencies you have that will be of value in your new job, career, or industry. Those skills then become the key points in your resume around which everything else is written.

To help you get started with identifying your transferable skills, review the brief listing below of *some* of the skills, qualifications, and competencies that companies and recruiters look for in candidates seeking to transition out of consulting or entrepreneurial careers and into corporate careers. *(Note that this is only a partial listing of the countless different skills that companies look for in qualified candidates.)*

Carefully review the keywords and keyword phrases to identify those that accurately reflect skills you possess and which are transferable into your new position. Then, be sure to incorporate those words into your resume, your cover letters, and any other career marketing documents that you create. They will capture a prospective employer's interest and open the door to interviews and opportunities.

Board of Directors Affairs	Infrastructure Development
Corporate Administration	Operating Management
Corporate Finance	Organizational Development
Corporate Reporting	Performance Improvement & Management
Corporate Risk Management	Policy & Procedure Development
Corporate Strategy	Quality Assurance & Improvement
Customer-Centric Operations	Productivity Improvement
Executive Presentations	Regulatory Reporting
General Management	Teamwork & Teambuilding
Global Business Management	Transformational Leadership

Sample Career Transition Resumes

Following are seven sample resumes for individuals transitioning out of consulting or entrepreneurial careers and into corporate careers. Each of these resumes was written by a professional resume writer with extensive experience working with, writing for, and positioning individuals in career transition. Full contact information for each of these writers is in
the Appendix. To understand why these resumes were written and designed the way that
they were, it is critical that you read the following information, which explains the specific
objective of each of these job seekers and the particular strategy that was used to prepare
their resume.

Resume: Stephen Johnson (page 214)
Writer: Louise Garver
Objective: To transition from entrepreneurial career as company owner/president into
                 a career in corporate sales and/or territory management.
Strategy: Created one-page chronological resume with a focused profile on his sales
                 strengths, followed by only his sales accomplishments in the career achieve-
                 ments section of each of his two positions. Note there is no mention that he
                 owned his most recent employer - just that he was the manager.

Resume: Susan Stewart (pages 215-216)
Writer: Joyce Fortier
Objective: To transition out of restaurant ownership and into a career in senior citizen
                 tour and event planning.
Strategy: Started with headline format to clearly communicate objective, followed by
                 paragraph highlighting relevant skills. Next section of qualifications outlines
                 all of her transferable skills important to new career path. Job descriptions
                 focus on scope of responsibility and achievements; volunteer and commu-
                 nity service communicates that she's visible and well-connected.

Resume: Walter Scott (pages 217-219)
Writer: Annemarie Cross
Objective: To transition out of 30-year career in family-owned business into a high-
                 profile, high-paying position in agricultural sales.
Strategy: Began resume with headline to communicate "who" he is and followed with
                 an extensive summary of qualifications directly related to career goal. Em-
                 phasized size and scope of sales operations he managed in current position,
                 using bold headings within the job description to highlight vast array of pro-
                 fessional talents. Professional awards prominently displayed along with rel-
                 evant education and affiliation.

Resume: Margaret P. Coleman (pages 220-221)
Writer: Janet Beckstrom

Objective: To transition out of family-owned business and into a fresh management career with strong growth opportunities.

Strategy: Designed resume to minimize connection to family-owned business by highlighting broad range of skills and competencies reflective of any competent general management professional. Demonstrated diversity of skills in management, technology, and finance. Dedicated page two to very brief listing of work experience with no detail that would detract from overall presentation.

Resume: George Powell (pages 222-225)
Writer: Deborah Wile Dib
Objective: To return to a senior-level corporate management position after years of management consulting experience.

Strategy: Launched resume with a testimonial as to his corporate performance and clearly demonstrated his abilities in the corporate world by referencing his past successes within a corporate environment. Positioned his consulting experience as a value add to his body of work by showing high-value contributions; focused on project scope, budgeting, staffing, and P&L. Included addendum to showcase best-in-class contributions and used quotes to develop chemistry that would deliver a sense of his passion and promise.

Resume: Jonathan Buchanan (pages 226-229)
Writer: Deborah Wile Dib
Objective: To leave his current consulting career behind and return to an executive-level management position within the corporate real estate industry.

Strategy: Proved Jonathan's abilities in the corporate world by highlighting his past successes within corporate environments with a unique and high-profile resume presentation, particularly the format selected for page one. Positioned his consulting experience as a valuable addition by highlighted key clients, massive projects, budgeting and P&L responsibilities, team leadership responsibility, and more. Comprehensive corporate job descriptions from past work experience further strengthen this resume.

Resume: Gerald F. Hewlitt (230-232)
Writer: Deborah Wile Dib
Objective: To transition from an extensive career as a restaurant owner and entrepreneur into a new career track as a senior manager with a major hotel chain or other leading hospitality company.

Strategy: Began resume with a strong, high-level, executive profile and summary of qualifications to demonstrate his cross-functional leadership and operating management talents. Demonstrated his innovative thinking and management style, then translated that into bottom-line results by showing how his ideas cut costs, improve quality, reduce turnover and achieve profitability within a volatile business market. Powerful executive format with tangible results sections clearly demonstrates his capabilities and value.

Stephen Johnson

E-mail: sjohnson@cox.net

732.239.8113
177 Washington Avenue • Edison, NJ 08818

Sales/Territory Management Professional

Delivering consistent and sustainable revenue gains, profit growth and market-share increases through strategic sales leadership of multi-site branches. Valued offered:

✓ Driver of innovative programs that provide a competitive edge and establish company as a full-service market leader.
✓ Proactive, creative problem solver who develops solutions that save time, cut costs, and ensure consistent product quality.
✓ Empowering leader who recruits, develops, coaches, motivates, and inspires sales teams to top performance.
✓ Innovative in developing and implementing win-win solutions to maximize account expansion, retention, and satisfaction.

Selected Career Achievements

RANFORD COMPANY • Edison, NJ   1990 to 2005

As Branch Manager/Principal, reinvigorated the sales organization, growing company sales from $9MM to $11MM, expanding account base from 450 to 680 and increasing market share 15%. Established new performance benchmark and trained sales force on implementing sales-building customer inventory rationalization programs.

- **Revitalized and restored profitability of 2 underperforming territories** by coaching and developing territory reps.

- **Penetrated 2 new markets and** secured a lucrative market niche in abrasive products. Staffed, opened, and managed the 2 branch locations in New Jersey—one of which alone produced $3MM+ over 3 years.

- **Initiated and advanced the skills of sales force to effectively promote and sell increasingly technical product lines** in response to changing market demands.

Increased profit margins and dollar volume through product mix diversification and expansion. Created product catalogs and marketing literature.

- **Ensured that the company maintained its competitive edge in the marketplace** by adding several cross-functional product lines.

- **Led highly profitable new product introduction with a 40% profit margin** that produced $100K annually in new business.

BERLIN COMPANY • Trenton, NJ   1985 to 1990

As Account Executive, rejuvenated sales performance of a stagnant territory. Turned around customer perception by cultivating exceptional relationships through solutions-based selling and delivering value-added service. Recognized as a peak performer company-wide who consistently ranked #1 in sales and #1 in profits.

- **Positioned and established company as a full-service supplier** to drive sales revenues by translating customer needs to product solutions.

- **More than doubled territory sales from $700K to $1.6MM** during tenure and grew account base from 80 to 125 through new market penetration. **Landed and managed 3 of company's 6 largest accounts** and grew remaining 3.

- **Captured a lucrative account and drove annual sales from $100K in the first year to $400K in 3 years**—outperforming the competition without any price-cutting.

- **Mentored new and existing territory reps** on customer relationship management, solutions-selling strategies, advanced product knowledge and customer programs.

Education

BS in Business Management—Rhode Island University, Providence, RI

SUSAN STEWART

16 Main Street ~ Albion, MI 49224 ~ cell: 517.222.3827 ~ work: 517.999.0442
sstewart16@hotmail.com

TOUR DIRECTOR - EVENT PLANNER
Marketing ▪ Sales ▪ Senior Citizens

Self-motivated professional with superior communication and interpersonal skills. Over 15 years' experience in hospitality, nonprofit, recruiting, volunteer management and entrepreneurial ventures. Enthusiastic, self-directed, highly effective communicator with demonstrated ability to satisfy client needs through troubleshooting, research, and problem resolution. Experienced in impacting bottom-line results.

SUMMARY OF QUALIFICATIONS

- **Plans, organizes, and conducts** travel expeditions, remaining totally client-focused, to meet individual/group objectives.
- **Creative thinker and idea generator** with excellent analytical skills, able to break down a project into its essential parts and develop effective solutions.
- **General business manager,** who works well under pressure and meets all deadlines.
- Adept at **creating and facilitating informative presentations.**
- **Demonstrates high level of skill in planning, coordinating, and organizing**, with the ability to manage several tasks simultaneously.
- **Displays high degree of problem-solving skills,** maintaining poise and composure during emergencies.
- **Coordinates effective teams**, guiding them in their projects and facilitating their effectiveness.
- **Successfully manages contract negotiations** and independent contractor relations, including monitoring service performance.
- **Cultivates and maintains a great network of resources, considering cost and quality,** in order to meet client needs and expectations.
- **Strong interpersonal skills;** effective in both independent and collaborative settings.
- Specific experience in **booking practices, event budgeting and finance, customer service, administration, and operations.**

PROFESSIONAL EXPERIENCE

THE GOLDEN GOOSE RESTAURANT, Grayling, MI   1999 — 2005
OWNER

Purchased and renovated an old house that was situated on a beautiful private lake, converting it into a fine-dining restaurant that could accommodate up to 50 diners and had a staff of 8-10. Responsible for every aspect of the business.
- Created an ambiance of fine dining for customers, providing the atmosphere and service that created customer loyalty and brought repeat business.
- Arranged for private parties and weddings, accommodating up to 100 people, overseeing all aspects in order to meet customer wants and expectations.
- Acted as General Contractor during the renovation stage, ensuring all work met codes. Handled design and decorating, and complied with all requirements to obtain a liquor license.

215

ALBION COLLEGE, Albion, MI   1990 — 1999
ASSISTANT DIRECTOR OF ADMISSIONS

Managed a geographic territory (Northern Michigan, Wisconsin, Minnesota, and the West Coast) with responsibility for the alumni volunteer program for admissions/recruitment. Worked with prospective students and parents from recruitment through enrollment and recruited alumni to interact with prospective students. Responsibilities included group presentations, event planning, written and verbal communication, generation of new ideas, and ongoing consultation with the Alumni Board of Directors.

- Planned, arranged for, and accompanied students on yearly trips abroad in Europe and South America, taking as many as 50 on the various trips.
- Created and presented presentations to the school board, educating them on the importance of expanding the students' education with the opportunity to study abroad.
- Formed relationships with students and parents considering Albion College, working with them to determine if the institution was the type of college experience they desired.
- Put a system into place to communicate more effectively with the volunteer staff, in order to keep them up-to-date on college news and activities.
- Developed opportunities for college alumni to work with the college staff in the recruiting process, getting them to volunteer at the College for admissions and to act as goodwill ambassadors.
- Doubled assigned quota the second year there.

VOLUNTEER SERVICES AND COMMUNITY ACTIVITIES

Elected to the Gaylord School Board for 18 years — President for nine years
- Set policy as a member of a seven-person board for school district. Led two superintendent searches incorporating community and faculty support. Recognized nationally for the bond campaign, design, and utilization of new community high school. Served on Michigan School Board Association Legislative Committee, attending regular meetings in the state capitol with lobbyists and elected leaders on important issues/agendas for education.

Appointed Member — Otsego Memorial Hospital Foundation Board — President for five years
- Guided the board through a reorganization process as the hospital retooled to meet changing health care environment. Restructuring the board resulted in a positive working relationship between the foundation and the hospital trustees, creating increased opportunities for fund-raising and general goodwill.

Appointed Member — United Way Board of Trustees for 12 years
- Campaign chairperson two years, instituted a more systematic tracking of donors and new publication sequence during campaign months, resulting in doubling the previous years' donations.
- Participated in annual allocation process, evaluating grant proposals and program results.

EDUCATION

BA, *Economics*, ALBION COLLEGE, Albion, MI — studied in Europe for one year

WALTER SCOTT

975 Braddock Street, Athens, Ohio 45701 • 740.593.1389 • 740.593.7895
wscott@hotmail.com

SENIOR SALES EXECUTIVE

Agricultural Machinery / Agricultural Commodities / Farming Equipment

QUALIFICATIONS PROFILE

Performance-driven, commercially astute Senior Executive with 20+ years delivering outstanding returns within the agricultural industry. Combine the incisive ability to strategize and execute forward-thinking revenue-generating solutions with excellent product knowledge. Specialize in evolving markets with outstanding track record in the development of appropriate industry and customer approaches to drive rapid customer acquisition and retention. Possess keen focus on revenue growth, setting and achieving aggressive targets, and rapid action to synchronize with rapidly changing market conditions. Cross-functional team leadership and management, facilitating large-scale operational change and advancement within a highly competitive industry. Proven expertise within:

- Organization Restructure & Process Redesign
- Policy/Procedure Development & Review
- Negotiations, Presentations & Consultations
- Key Alliance & Relationship Management
- Financial & Contract Negotiations
- Sales Training & Team Empowerment
- Performance & Productivity Improvement
- Communication & Interpersonal Excellence

- Business Development & Turnaround
- Strategic Planning & Vision
- Competitive Market Positioning
- Innovative Promotions & Advertising
- Budget Forecasting & Achievement
- Acquisition Negotiation & Integration
- Recruitment, Selection & Training
- Analytical & Conceptual Problem Solving

WORK EXPERIENCE

WILTONS FARM SUPPLIES PTY LTD   1974 to Present

Worked in the family business originally established in 1957, specializing in sales/service of John Deere products including 70HP-450HP tractors, combine harvesters, and seeding equipment. Growing operations from 1 to 4 highly profitable branches and a staff of 60+, servicing a broad client base covering a combined area of approximately 60% of Ohio.

Dealer Principal (1990 to Present)**/*Director*** (1992 to Present)

Pivotal leadership role influencing growth and optimization across all areas of operations positioning company for a decade of rapid expansion into grain trading, transportation, chemical, and traditional farm machinery sales. Instrumental in transforming a single outlet machinery dealership with approximately 25% market share and $5M annual sales to a four-branch enterprise and market leader with 75.2% John Deere product share and a combined income of $106M per annum.

Steer and optimize operational efficiency and profitability; ensure performance targets are achieved and adequate finances are available to underpin continued business expansion. Train, supervise, and motivate staff; empower and infuse confidence in all department heads to take ownership of the business; and, encourage a collaborative and supportive culture throughout the organization. Foster strong customer relationships to maximize client satisfaction and repeat business.

- Redeveloped underperforming grain trading business in 1982, propelling market share by 66%, sales by 75%, bottom-line profitability by 88%, and storage from 5,000 to 30,000 tons per annum, becoming a substantial earner for the company. Business later sold to finance Ohio dealership expansion strategy.

- Championed development of a highly successful general and bulk freight transportation business in 1983 with annual revenues of $5.6M. Later sold for a lucrative profit to allow expansion into core business of machinery sales.

Continued…

- Pitched and won buy-in of key stakeholders to sell grain and transportation businesses and refine marketing thrust to specialize in farm machinery sales, following recognition of potential growth within this area in 2000. Researched, strategized business plan, and consummated deal within 2 months.
- Ranked Number 1 dealership for John Deere products sold for the past two consecutive years.

Business Redevelopment & Specialization

- Consolidated company within farm equipment sales, exploiting economies of scale, purchasing power, and spreading risks over varying geographical areas (weather and different modes of primary production).
- Captured steady and sustainable market share growth, reflecting 25%-2000; 30%-2001; 35%-2002; 49%-2003; 58%-2004, boosting annual sales from $5m to $45M over the past 10 years.

Dealership Setup & Expansion

- Launched Dallas dealership from ground up in 2001. Solely arranged takeover pre-work, recruited manager, and initiated strategies that have built the business into a $15M operation with steady growth in whole goods sales, parts, and services.
- Co-founded JD dealership in Texas in 1996. Sourced suitable premises and located talented staff, successfully developing a strong dealership within a crucial food-growing area of Houston.
- Contributed industry and business operations prowess to the newly established Ohio dealership in 2003.

Valuation & Appraisal

- Harnessed exceptional appraisal/valuation talent to reap lucrative profits on the purchase of used farming equipment both privately and at auction nationwide.
- Renowned expert within the industry requested to value and appraise machinery during partnership dissolutions and farm auctions.

Marketing & Customer Relations

- Developed numerous market-penetrating and revenue-boosting TV, print, and website marketing and advertising campaigns that secured 89% return on investment.
- Fostered strong customer relationships by orchestrating customer group special events, social functions, and IT training seminars, building a solid client base of repeat and referring customers.

Product Launch, Market Penetration, & Profitability Growth

- Amplified revenues and profit margins by 66% through launching new product/company lines including CRT, Honda, Kohler, Flexicoil, Sakundiak, Hardie, and Horwood Bagshaw. Remained abreast of industry innovations and new product releases throughout the United States, Australia, Europe, and Canada through regular business trips.
- Steered company through devastating market plunges caused by droughts and low commodity prices by slashing operational expenditures through temporarily repositioning staff to other branches and bringing outstanding annual leave liabilities up-to-date.
- Exploited quiet periods by utilizing staff to perform plant/building maintenance, and minimized loss of key people by staying focused on forthcoming season upturns.

Operations & Staffing

- Recaptured department managers' focus and commitment through initiating annually reviewed, clearly written goals/targets and key performance indicators.
- Revitalized and maintained staffing efficiency, and performance by introducing management bonuses, open book policies, World Class Dealership program, and an active social club.
- Overcame challenges of differing dealership policies/procedures and arising communication difficulties inherent in business advancement by helping to orchestrate Branch Business Managers to concentrate on sales, new opportunities, and other crucial business operations.

Continued…

- Enhanced efficiency organization-wide by deploying streamlined uniform procedures and forms.
- Instrumental in implementing cutting-edge fully integrated 24/7 online accounting and stock control system, professionalizing entire financial/inventory management and monitoring process.

SCOTT HOLDINGS PTY LTD, Sea Lake   1996 to Present

Sole United States Wholesaler/Importer of Sakundiak grain augers, ranked as one of the premium grain augers within Canada and worldwide.

Managing Director

Negotiated, secured, and grew importing business into a $2.5M annual revenue operation with continuing execution of market and sales initiatives set to underpin continued growth and profitability across the agricultural marketplace on a national level.

Forecast and set annual sales targets; procure suitable stock levels 6 months prior to selling seasons in March/April and September/October; outsource manufacture of standard drive belt guards and fitment; and supervise team of 6 in the loading/unloading of approximately 75 augers per year.

- Influenced up-selling by expanding product offerings and subsequent revenues with complementary grain auger lines, including Hawes Auger Mover — an OHS initiative that reduces operator strain by eliminating manual lifting/positioning, and Reverse Gearbox — allowing easy access for equipment cleaning.
- Sourced, set up, nurtured, and continue to expand 3 profitable retail distributors capturing market share within Nashville, Madison, and Cheyenne territories.

AWARDS AND SPECIAL RECOGNITION

John Deere Credit Award — *within the top 10 for writing finance contracts*

Top Dealer Award in the group for market share (2004)

Top Dealer Award in the group for market share (2003)

- *John Deere World Class Dealer* — *Pilot Program* (2000)
  - One of seven people handpicked from throughout the United States to participate in a pilot program positioned to boost dealership standards nationwide by teaching skills and techniques to develop best-in-class standards.
- *John Deere Dealer Quality Control Council* (2000 to 2003)
  - Key advisor to John Deere Inc., on issues impacting dealers around the globe.

EDUCATION

Certificate IV in Business (Frontline Management) — 2004 ◆ Boyle Consulting

Safe Handling & Sales of Chemicals — 1996 ◆ AgSafe

Bachelor's Degree ◆ St. John's University

Countless hours of courses through John Deere Training School, including:

*Techniques of Professional Sales * Selling Management Product * Knowledge Accounting * Sales Systems * Business Management*

PROFESSIONAL ASSOCIATION

Farm Machinery Dealers Association

TECHNICAL INVENTORY

Computer Fiscal Services (CFS) Accounting Software * John Deere Pricing Configurator * Microsoft Word * Microsoft Excel * SAP (Wholegoods/Spareparts Inventory Systems) * QATS (John Deere Finance Quoting System) * Internet * Email

Margaret P. Coleman

246 Grove Street
Orlando, FL 32835

321-525-8249
simmsjp@aol.com

Profile

➤ Highly knowledgeable and experienced in all facets of business operations management.

➤ Expertise in business development, customer service, staff development, employee relations, and funds management.

➤ Maintain vision and big-picture perspective while successfully managing the details.

➤ Ability to make and implement decisions which consistently and positively impact bottom-line.

➤ Strong interpersonal skills and friendly demeanor with ability to communicate effectively with customers, employees, and suppliers.

➤ Detail-oriented and analytical . . . a proven problem-solver . . . excellent organizational skills.

Summary of Experience

MANAGEMENT
- Serve as Secretary/Treasurer on Board of Directors of two related yet distinct enterprises.
- Advise Principal/Owner on all issues; participate in strategic planning.
- Attend industry markets; evaluate and select products, and negotiate prices; ensure adequate inventory to meet fluctuating demand.
- Ensure consistent level of customer service reflecting tradition of 38-year old business.
- Lead, manage, and motivate 60+ employees in two locations.
- Perform troubleshooting in all operational areas.
- Routinely communicate with legal advisors regarding various issues.
- Provide sales assistance to customers; mentor and motivate sales teams; develop incentives.
- Monitor and evaluate health and safety issues.
- Instituted drug screening for applicants and employees.
- *Earned designation as one of FTDs 2001 Red Ribbon winners.*

COMPUTER OPERATIONS
- Act as system administrator; troubleshoot problems and act as resource person for employees; act as liaison with vendors as needed.
- Supervise ongoing computer training for employees; ensure their continued competency.
- Maintain personal competency in:
  - Windows
  - Lotus Notes
  - Microsoft Word
  - Spreadsheet applications
  - Industry-specific software
  - Finance/payment calculation software
- Coordinate businesses' presence on Internet; ensure adherence to corporate guidelines.
- Oversaw update of antiquated computer system; collaborated with vendor to design system, coordinated its installation, and facilitated employee training.

FINANCIAL OPERATIONS
- Monitor account balances and verify funds availability; adjust lines of credit accordingly.
- Manage corporate funds; act as liaison with financial representatives.
- Initiated an investment program (in collaboration with financial advisor) for corporate funds, resulting in 38% ROI in less than one year.
- Verify credit worthiness and approve lines of credit for commercial customer accounts.

Margaret P. Coleman   321-525-8249

Professional Experience

Operations Manager of two distinct businesses
ACCENT ON EVENTS! • Orlando, Florida   1997-Present
BONNIE'S BLOOMS • Kissimmee, Florida   1991-Present

Education

FLORIDA STATE UNIVERSITY • Tallahassee, Florida
Bachelor of Business Administration   1994
Dual Major: Business Management, Marketing
Associate of Arts in Advertising   1991

Selected Specialized Training

- ➤ FTD Management Academy
- ➤ Zig Ziglar's Assuring Customer Loyalty
- ➤ Customer Satisfaction Management
- ➤ Selling Satisfaction
- ➤ Management Excellence
- ➤ Computer Administration

References available on request

E-mail: GeorgePow@yahoo.com
Website: www.GPowell.info
2859 Albany Avenue, Littletown, PA 22222
Home: 812-483-2873 • Cell: 519-322-9090

GEORGE POWELL

SENIOR EXECUTIVE • STRATEGY • MARKETING • LEADERSHIP

EXECUTIVE PROFILE

"I quickly see what will and won't work and form an optimal strategy and execution plan. I am pragmatic and have a clear history of actionable recommendations. I am a strong leader and a team builder who can excite and motivate a staff to success. **In short, I move the organization forward.***"*

- Fifteen+ years executive domestic and international operations, marketing, and consulting experience with Fortune 500, 100, and 50 companies including Intel, IBM, Lucent, Verizon, Sprint PCS, Motorola, and others.

- Delivered consistent 40+% year-over-year revenue growth while boosting margins of key product / service offerings for start-up and growth phases of well-regarded professional services organizations. 100% of personal client base initiated new business.

- Garner buy-in and generate excitement behind major programs while building credibility and delivering customer confidence. Seen as the subject matter expert and the person who knows what has to be done and how to get it through.

- Mentor and instruct staff, keeping them motivated, fresh, and focused while improving job satisfaction and retention, especially on high-profile, high-stress engagements. Seen as the manager for whom everyone wants to work.

- Create and clearly deliver corporate officer-level presentations, often the primary deliverable for clients. Make information understandable and compelling so that clients can effectively use the work and sign for repeat engagements.

EXPERTISE

- Business & Thought Leadership
- P&L Management & Improvement
- Budgeting—Forecasting, Analysis, & Control
- Pricing Strategies & Structures
- Team Building & Leadership
- Internal & External Customer Relations
- New Business Development & Growth

- Strategic & Tactical Marketing
- Multichannel Marketing & Distribution
- Market Research—Qualitative & Quantitative
- Statistical Analysis & Segmentation
- Competitive Analysis & Positioning
- Brand Development & Management
- Product/Service Development & Rollout

PROFESSIONAL EXPERIENCE

PAL Associates, Inc., Highland, OH   **1997 to 2004**

PRESIDENT & MANAGING DIRECTOR

Primary driving force behind start-up and growth of this boutique consulting firm specializing in strategy, market research, focus group/expert panel moderation, and related consulting services targeted to corporate clients in the communications, technology, and manufacturing/distribution industries. Held full P&L accountability.

Managed all aspects of internal operations—new business development, sales and marketing, IT, financial planning/reporting, operating/capital budgeting, customer relations—and provided technical and managerial oversight to large ($100K+), complex client engagements.

Clients included Lucent, Telcordia, IBM, Sprint PCS, Motorola, Comverse, SBC (Ameritech and PacTel), Qwest (US West).

Business Leadership & Operations Management

- Authored and executed business plan, built organizational structure, and contributed vision and thought leadership during start-up and growth phases. Grew business to over 10 Fortune 500 clients averaging $100,000+ per client.

- Assembled team of consultants with direct experience in marketing, branding, and product management with industry expertise in high-tech telecom, software, and IT industries.

- Served as primary source for strategy; client advisory; recommendations and solutions; big-picture perspective; quantitative market research; and SME in data communications, RF communications, wireless communications, voice services, security, enterprise solutions, and multi-channel distribution.

- Delivered 43% CAGR over six years despite downturn in the economy and the technology sector.

PROFESSIONAL EXPERIENCE / PAL Associates, Inc., continued

New Business Development & Marketing

- Captured immediate customer-perceived value and enabled sales-on-value vs. price by creating an "actionable" service delivery model.

- Distinguished company from competitors by developing/launching EDGE (Expedited Data Gathering Environment), a high-performance offering credited with enabling important customer acquisitions and opening potential for unlimited revenue.

Key Engagements & Relationships

- Personally targeted and secured 70% of firm's clients. Built and managed relationships with client roster of world-class players (10+ Fortune 500 corporations) in the technology and telecom industry including Lucent, Telcordia, IBM, Sprint PCS, Motorola, Comverse, SBC (Ameritech and PacTel), and Qwest (US West).

- Determined market opportunity, go-to-market strategy, and development priorities for voice-based portal service targeting consumers and business customers. Realigned focus of marketing and development plans to maximize perceived value/willingness-to-pay and increase projected market penetration.

- Determined five-year view of user requirements for a provider of wireless handsets and infrastructure. Derived needs-based segmentation designed to reduce costs by enabling common solutions across industries with fewer products that more closely meet customers' needs.

GRAVES Corporation, West Holmes, OH   1993 to 1997

COO (1995 to 1997)
VICE PRESIDENT – BUSINESS DEVELOPMENT (1994 to 1995)
PRINCIPAL CONSULTANT (1993 to 1994)

Promoted rapidly based on performance in consulting, business development, and operations management roles with this global professional services firm, a provider of customer-centric marketing consulting and research solutions to major clients in the high-tech sector.

Functional areas of accountability spanned team building and leadership, project and engagement management, margin and performance improvement, business development and sales, product and service development/rollout, IT strategy and solutions, quality improvement, and customer service/relationship management.

Business Leadership & Operations Management

- Contributed to enterprise-level vision, strategy, decision-making, and leadership. Improved operational efficiency and performance. Held P&L accountability for engagements.

- One of few VPs and the only executive promoted from outside "original" group of managers. With promotion, acquired staffing, employee training/development, and team building/management functions, concurrent with operations and engagement management.

New Business Development & Marketing

- Personally generated 25% of total fees firm-wide as a consistent top-ranking revenue performer. Conceived, implemented, and drove aggressive business development, marketing, and customer acquisition activities.

- Brought expertise in multi-channel distribution. Integrated channel research, modeling, planning workshops, and related consulting into a high-margin ($250,000 net profit with IBM alone) service offering.

- Generated $250,000+ in new annual revenue by creating and leading market planning, strategy, and positioning workshops and training seminars—20+ workshops at $20,000 to $50,000 each. Led two-day sessions (global channel strategies for HW/SW products) for IBM in US, Europe, Asia, and Latin America.

Key Engagements & Relationships

- Met/exceeded all milestones and objectives—deliverables, quality, time, margins—on complex, long-term engagements for major clients including firm's principal account with IBM (Networking Systems - 10% of business).

- Salvaged important client relationship with Telcordia, improving their revenue performance from $30,000 to $200,000. Established relationship with IBM Networking Systems and positioned company as the channel's consulting firm of choice.

- Achieved 100% repeat business ratio on personal clients and shifted business to higher-margin practice areas.

223

PROFESSIONAL EXPERIENCE, continued

DEBCOM Communications, Inc., Greenvale, PA   **1987 to 1989**

DIRECTOR – PRODUCT MANAGEMENT

Recruited by VP of Marketing & Sales to join this growing technology start-up company as it was gaining forefront position in the emerging wireless LAN solutions arena. Managed strategic planning, market positioning, and all aspects of product management—launch strategy, packaging, pricing, targeting, build-rate forecasting, beta testing, press tour, advertising, investor/analyst affairs, sales scripting/training, and direct/indirect channel support.

- Drove full-scale market rollout for premier product line, LAWN (Local Area Wireless Network).
- Planned next-generation product offering wireless telephone system (on-premises cellular system with roaming capabilities).
- Earned "Editor's Choice Award" in Wireless LAN category, *PC Magazine*, May 28, 1990.

GPC Communications, Inc., Huntsville, OH   **1984 to 1987**

PRODUCT LINE MANAGER – ISDN ADAPTORS

One of two product managers for venture-backed technology start-up specializing in ISDN equipment—a premier ISDN vendor with commercially strong portfolio of technologies, products, and customers. Conceived, developed, and managed feature/function design, packaging, pricing, and quality/standards adherence. Developed launch strategies, analyzed/prioritized market targets, wrote sales presentations, and trained sales force. Provided pre- and post-sale advisory and support services. Member of Quality Management Team.

- Key player in capturing $1.5+ million contract with major Regional Bell Operating Company (RBOC), the then-largest sale of ISDN customer premise equipment.
- Delivered 50% of company's pre-ISDN revenue by repositioning/repackaging ISDN switch products as an ISDN CO simulator.
- Managed national relationships with network of OEMs, ISVs, RBOCs, and local telephone companies.

CHYP Corporation—Integrated Systems Operations, Clayton, WA   **1981 to 1984**

SENIOR PRODUCT LINE MANAGER—Xenix / Unix Line (1986 to 1987)
ARCHITECTURE / SOFTWARE SPECIALIST (1984 to 1986)

Launched career in technical sales and marketing with this world-class technology enterprise. Promoted to manage Xenix / Unix products, applications, LAN software, host communications, and ISO protocols for PC LAN server. Developed forecasts, managed build schedule, provided sales training/support, and managed PR and media activities. Directed seven individual product managers (in Xenix/Unix line), ISV liaisons, and marketing/communications personnel in a matrixed organization.

- Managed competitively important product line representing $42+ million in annual sales and 65% divisional revenues. Led a team of eight in developing five-year product line strategy.
- Carved position in government sector. Won RFP listing for MultiSever product line on $300 million government contract. Instrumental in persuading Unisys to partner with Intel in bid to AFCAC (Air Force Computer Acquisition Center).
- Roadshow presenter in launch of Intel's 80386 processor.

EDUCATION, DEVELOPMENT, AND ASSOCIATIONS

KINGSTOWN UNIVERSITY— BSEE (Concentration in Computer Science), 1980

Development: Gary Kane Associates—Quality Improvement Process Management College, 1989
Development: National Marketing Association—seminars on online market research techniques and brand equity

Member: National Marketing Association—Member, Internet e-Commerce Marketing SIG (Special Interest Group)
Member: Management Marketing Networking Group (MMNG)

GEORGE POWELL

SENIOR EXECUTIVE ●STRATEGY ● MARKETING ● LEADERSHIP

2859 Albany Avenue, Littletown, PA 22222
Home: 812-483-2873 ● Cell: 519-322-9090
E-mail: GeorgePow@yahoo.com
Website: www.GPowell.info

RESUME ADDENDUM ● CRITICAL LEADERSHIP INITIATIVES

Instrumental in start-up's rise to become *"The* ISDN Company."
As Product Manager, GPC Communications Inc., challenged to deploy pioneering ISDN product set into a market limited with ISDN switch capability, an initiative critical to start-up's funding. To create market demand, convinced GPC executive management to create a simulator product sold to companies wishing to gain ISDN experience.

Results Simulators generated 50% of firm's revenue for first 18 months and opened opportunities with Apple, IBM, and others. These and further sales of related products helped GPC become known as "The ISDN Company."

Strengths *"I see where the true opportunities lie, both at present and in the future. With this information I make subtle course corrections that have a great impact on the bottom line."*

Repositioned non-competitive line and developed $40 million+ revenue stream.
As Senior Product Line Manager, Intel, charged with maintaining revenue and positioning division for future growth despite declining revenue, fading product set, and demoralized team. Repositioned product line/set and focused on new niche.

Results Repositioning resonated with customers, the press, consultants, resellers, and Intel systems sales force. New product set exceeded two-thirds of division's $62 million goal. Teams rallied and gained momentum. Several concepts went on to be successful in other divisions.

Strengths *"I evaluate the market, competitive environment, and company/product positioning to optimize current and future opportunities. I work across disciplines, garnering buy-in and building excitement."*

Refocused firm in profitable direction.
As Vice President, GRAVES, challenged to refocus company's drift towards becoming a value-added market research organization, a less profitable business. Pioneered workshop methodology based on historical data and team expertise. Took cross-functional teams through structured planning methodology that leveraged skills, data, and industry expertise.

Results Workshops led to more management-oriented consulting, flipping practice areas from 90% value-added MR to over 50% consulting and allowing GRAVES to compete profitably in an area that could tolerate higher fee rates. Allowed utilization of the firm's best consultants, increased satisfaction, and decreased turnover.

Strengths *"I drive an organization forward through action, creating new products and services, building skills, generating momentum, and selling value add that increases perceived value of products and services."*

Directly responsible for 70% of clients and 50% of revenue year on year.
As President and Managing Director, PAL Associates, Inc., challenged to build new consulting and research practice. Leveraged client contacts to gain access to new decision-making areas. Created scenario analysis offering, enhanced planning workshop methodology, created a study of local communications resale to gain early revenue and open doors, and handled intensive cold calling. Focused on superior performance for branding and credibility.

Results Secured three new client companies (now ten) within first year of operation, expanding within each company, effectively doubling clients. Gained a strong, branded reputation with 95% of clients agreeing to act as references. CAGR was 42% over first six years.

Strengths *"My frankness and integrity are much appreciated by clients and allow me to develop a level of trust."*

Secured largest contract in company's history.
As Product Manager, GPC Communications Inc., challenged to grow revenue and presence in a pre-ISDN market. Together with CEO, pursued and negotiated custom contract with Eastern Phone to make the GPC PC Terminal Adapter part of their offering. "Sold" product/GPC technical capabilities. Worked with engineering to design and cost out.

Results $1.5 million contract was largest in company's history and the largest ISDN customer premise equipment contract in the industry. Company gained further credibility with its investors, securing upfront commitments and cash to continue corporate development.

Strengths *"I am a sales hit-man. I can be dropped into situations and add instant credibility through my professionalism and my command of the market, products, and technologies."*

JONATHAN BUCHANAN

EXECUTIVE PROFILE

Twenty+ years' senior-level management and consulting experience with world-class, complex, large-scale, one-of-a-kind, mixed-use land and real estate development projects valued in the hundreds of millions of dollars.

Notable Projects Include:

- Town Centre at Aston, Aston, GA ($300 million)
- WELCO Arena and BCB Center Renovations, Flanders, VA ($275 million)
- The Bay View, Barstock, DE ($125 million proposed / $ 300 million planned)
- National Science Hall (NSH), Llanview, SC ($200 million proposed)
- The Gates Racecourse, Pacifica, WA ($150 million proposed)

Areas of Expertise Include:

Site Selection & Pre-Development	Strategic Planning	Marketing Methodology	Budgeting & Monitoring
Public & Private Partnerships	Integrated Project Development	Market Acquisition Strategies	Concept Strategies
Revitalization & Renovation	Acquisition Due Diligence	Public & Private Financing	Real Estate Investment
Economic Development	Financial Performance	Place-Making	Lifestyle & Entertainment Centers
Highest & Best Use Analysis	Development Advisory Services	Zoning & Entitlements	Networking & Sourcing

PERFORMANCE DRIVERS

- **Versatile Manager and Consultant**

Skilled in complex interactions and relations within multiple horizontal/vertical uses and mixed product types. Often retained to manage challenging projects. Guide projects from viability evaluation and concept development, through corporate/government approvals, entitlements, site plans, permits (from URPs to PUDs), public/private financing and partnerships, design, construction, and lease-up. Keen focus on simultaneously balancing supply and demand of multiple project components.

- **Quality and Profit-Driven Steward**

Grounded in the principles of real estate with a thorough understanding of risk/reward ratios. Committed to delivering high-value, profitable projects that meet goals *and* contribute lasting quality-of-life and environmental impact, creating healthier markets, productive business conditions, and solid community relations.

- **Resourceful Solutions Provider**

Look for solutions and opportunities in every challenge, and creative ideas from self, team members, and consultants. Adept at quantifying issues, scoping sources, and using extensive network to locate resources. Involved in cutting-edge projects that do not conform to norm and that require resourceful thinking and persistence. These range from unanchored specialty retail (Town Centre at Aston), to location-based entertainment (LBE) for a horse track's surplus real estate (The Gates Racecourse), to an international science museum (National Science Hall).

- **Strategic Planner and Thinker**

Implement project strategies required to manage short-term issues while pursuing long-term objectives. Used these skills to achieve zoning approval for Town Centre at Aston, to achieve a museum site for the National Science Hall, and to gain governmental approvals after PILOTs for IHE were rejected.

- **Efficient Self-Starter**

Accomplished in activities and order of attack for complex projects, usually hitting achievable deadlines for even the most complicated projects. Require limited supervision, getting a job done quietly and efficiently. Currently running multi-faceted Inner Harbor East project with nominal client interface. Typically manage two to three efforts concurrently. While managing BCB Center renovations and WELCO Arena development, oversaw The Gates concept development and NSH pre-development.

- **Egoless Mentor and Team Builder**

Lead through example, for results, not glory. Articulate objectives and work tirelessly to achieve them. Motivate participants (especially young talent) through consistency, persistence, and constant communication, an important skill for Town Centre at Aston, with its multi-function, inter-disciplinary team and a high-octane, performance-driven culture.

3056 Great Neck Road, Little Plains, GA 29803 ● cell: 989-808-1414 ● fax: 992-392-3321 ● jbuchanan@yahoo.net

SENIOR-LEVEL CONSULTING MANAGEMENT EXPERIENCE

BUCHANAN, INCORPORATED : GREAT ROCK, VA; SILVER LAKE, GA; DEVILLE, MA   **1990 to Present**
Consultant/Principal

Development advisory/management firm specializing in high-density, mixed-use commercial projects blending lifestyle, entertainment, retail, restaurants, and other uses. Clients include Struever Bros. Eccles & Rouse, Inc. (SBER), Simpson Sports & Entertainment Development, Benton Broadcasting System, National Science Hall, The Enterprise Development Corporation, Montgomery County, MD, The Gates Racecourse, and many others.

Major projects include:

The Bay View, Barstock, DE ($125 million developed to date / $ 300 million planned)   6/02 to Present

Master developing three city blocks and providing development management services on 900,000-sf mixed-use building. Developing optimum program and managing design to achieve construction cost objectives, integrating cost-saving opportunities, pre-leasing office/retail, pre-selling hotel, and obtaining public financing incentives and public approvals ranging from site plans to urban renewal plans to planned unit developments.

- Attained TIF and PILOT approvals by Barstock Development Corporation only five weeks after rejection. Total tax incentives equaled $57 million in potential tax savings—$22 million from PILOT and $35 million from TIF.

- Achieved site plan, URP, and PUD approvals. Increased building heights (180 feet to 300 feet) and densities (18%), allowing project to begin construction based on current design.

- Developed project schedule to meet accelerated construction start and tenant requirements. Drove design from constructability perspective allowing for accelerated construction schedule.

National Science Hall (NSH), Llanview, SC ($200 million proposed)   10/99 to 4/02

Acted as National Science Hall Real Estate Planning and Development Director for NSH, a museum-sponsored proposed state-of-the art international science and technology center originally programmed for 365,000 sf/$200 million. Through negotiations and interaction with public, program was phased, with first phase at 250,000 sf/$150 million.

- Facilitated positioning of Museum to have capacity for project, elevating NSH to become one of top five goals for Greater Chamber of Commerce, key to building public sector momentum.

- Planned, advised on restructuring and repositioning museum operations for political constituencies (to meet expansion from 53,000 sf to 250,000 sf), coordinated with Llanview Art Museum to develop/share "museum park" site and with city/county officials to obtain public funding, and facilitated private fundraising campaigns and marketing to international community.

The Gates Racecourse, Pacifica, WA ($150 million)   3/99 to 2/00

Reported to Chief Executive Officer of The Gates. Provided development advisory services to owners who had ceased racing because of declining gaming revenues. Project was used as stalking horse to change Illinois gaming laws in early 1999. Once laws changed, motivation for project shifted and operation was sold.

- Assembled team, produced pro forma demonstrating financial viability, and delivered plan to carve 100 acres from 340-acre horse track for LBE ($150 million value entertainment/retail center) to co-exist with horse operations.

- Orchestrated design charrette to accelerate planning process, identified and engaged horse track operations designers to coordinate retail/racing interface, and identified, interviewed, and evaluated various LBE providers for site compatibility.

WELCO Arena / BCB Center Renovations, Flanders, VA ($275 million)   5/96 to 03/00
● **Vice President of Development, Simpson Sports & Entertainment Development Corporation** 1/98 to 03/00
● **Consultant (through TRG)** 5/96 to 1/98

Reported to President, Simpson Sports & Entertainment Development (a Benton Broadcasting System, Inc. subsidiary). Provided development management services for WELCO Arena, a $250 million / 20,000-seat multi-purpose sports / entertainment project. Initially managed site selection, identifying/evaluating five sites and negotiating with formidable and resistant owners including Flanders Journal Constitution, State Bar of Virginia, Federal Reserve Bank of Virginia, and Norfolk Southern Railroad.

In 1998, retained as 75% part-time VP reporting to SSED President. Concurrently oversaw $25 million retail renovation of BCB Center and Omni hotel, to mesh visually and operationally with arena. Components included obtaining all approvals, and managing design, internal/external improvements, remerchandising retail (ultimately doubling rents), upgrading BCB Studio Tour, redesigning/tripling size of Simpson Store, and initiating concept development for new destination attraction (to be constructed) for BCB to complement other daytime uses. Completed without disruption to 24/7 broadcasting.

CONSULTING EXPERIENCE, BUCHANAN, INCORPORATED / WELCO ARENA & BCB, CONTINUED

- Achieved senior management project approval, an important step as renovations increased BCB's visibility, improved public's perception, and doubled retail rents by moving retail environment from business to tourist. Completed on time/on budget.

- Oversaw arena's food service set-up ($15+ million revenues). Orchestrated food concessionaire selection process for premium and general concessions vendors. This was one of the first times general concessions operations functioned as a food court during non-event times. Creative food service enabled arena to achieve among the highest per-unit-suite sales in the country.

- Focused on branding opportunities and capitalized on media impressions of showcasing BCB/WBS brands. Managed all retail/entertainment including BCB Studio Tour renovation, Simpson Store expansion, and initial concept of Benton Experience, a second studio tour. Directed creation of arena's "Team Store" and Cartoon Network co-branded team store.

- Orchestrated/negotiated "high-impact" site selection, strategically accepting early losses to garner long-term gains. Facilitated public/private partnership, culminating in $65 million in public bonds sold prior to potential change in public financing laws and $130 million in private bonds backed by City of Flanders credit. Met extensive MBE/WBE goals (30%/6%).

- Co-managed team-building that successfully executed WELCO Arena from third-party perspective. Set up organization to manage BCB renovations.

Oasis Mall, Livingston County, DE ($600 million proposed)   10/96 to 4/97

Partnered with MRA International to provide market verification study of a proposed 2.0 million sf, $600 million mixed-use project in Duchess, DE (called the Oasis Mall), envisioned as a version of the Mall of the Americas.

- Evaluated potential and managed market verification study, developed essential conditions for success, and positioned County to pursue $150 million in public subsidies for project. Project ultimately died for lack of private financing.

SENIOR MANAGEMENT EXPERIENCE

LBK PARTNERS, CLAYTON, FL   1999 to 2000
● **Principal and Managing Partner**

LBK Partners invested in small-scale land development opportunities and provided development advisory services to major landowners and institutional investors for large mixed-use projects/developments and for acquisition portfolio due diligence analyses. In first year, generated annual fees up to $500,000 and serviced over $50 million in real estate property.

Oversaw Clayton Office and development director. Obtained entitlements, managed consulting teams and master planning, prepared pro formas, identified/pursued public financing opportunities, prepared private placement memorandum to raise project equity, marketed sites, and pursued new business opportunities/sourcing.

- Built office to $500,000 year-one fees from $0 by astute management of business procurement and client relationships.

- Provided master planning/development advisory services for 3 million sf mixed-use Clayton project and 280,000 sf Clayton telecommunications renovation. Successfully managed troubled 1,000-acre PUD's master planning/entitlement process. Supported Hartsburgh home office in master planning/entitlements of additional sites.

BRISTOL PROPERTIES, INC., A SUBSIDIARY TO BRISTOL, PLC, BALTIMORE, MD   1992 to 1994
● **President**

Bristol Properties, Inc. was a start-up subsidiary to Bristol, PLC, (at the time) the world's number-two construction materials firm. It has since been swallowed by hostile takeover.

Recruited to develop start-up business plan and manage North American entitlement, development, and disposition activities across 3,000 US and Canadian acres, with one asset in mix with a $5 billion value potential. Evaluated sales opportunities, site delivery costs, buyer pursuit/identification, and real estate opportunities as part of hostile takeover of another company. Participated in core business management activities. Reported to President of Bristol Properties, UK.

- Developed firm's start-up business plan. Assessed site marketability and entitlement/capital development needs. Created implementation business plan, a roadmap for placing real estate in play as market recovered.

- Provided reality check by auditing real estate holdings. When recruited, was told that company's real estate portfolio was valued at $200 million and was readily marketable with no required improvements. Put audit in play that indicated $60 million actual value, requiring annual $3 million to $4 million, five-year effort to create a solid revenue stream.

- Delivered risk/reward assessment of a limestone quarry to landfill conversion, an important factor in valuing Steetley's hostile takeover attempt.

SENIOR MANAGEMENT EXPERIENCE, CONTINUED

LATHAM / CLARKE FRANCES, ASTON, GA   **1985 to 1989**
● **Senior Development Director, TOWN CENTRE AT ASTON**

Firm developed Town Centre at Aston, one of the nation's premier suburban mixed-use, unanchored specialty centers. Co-managed daily project activities to design, construct, and lease $1.2 million sf mixed-use project—514 key Hyatt Regency Hotel—550,000 sf/office and 240,000 sf/retail ($300 million total project cost).

Managed (as number-two project lead) day-to-day development team and activities including building and managing all development, consulting, and office leasing teams, and directing all marketing/PR/event management planning/execution. Concurrent with project, periodically evaluated acquisition of alternative development properties in other parts of East Coast.

- Created Town Centre at Aston, an industry leader in entertainment-enhanced, mixed-use development. Participated in team's assemblage and managed follow-through/implementation details. Outstanding long-term results included new demand, new community lifestyle, office rents (at stabilization) of $4/sf above market, and a market-leading hotel.

- Directed all marketing/PR (print and media) and event planning for multi-event, three-month grand opening to put project on map. Crafted destination appeal and seasonal events, creating traffic and building property's perception as an "event" location. Repeat traffic translated into retail sales and events gave aura of Town Centre as "the place to be."

- Created foundation for new uses. Conceived idea of ice rink for events (with portability to test market demand). Rink was so successful that it was converted to a permanent rink and entertainment pavilion.

ASTON LAND CORPORATION (HANNIFORD LAND DEVELOPMENT CORP. SUBSIDIARY), ASTON, GA   **1984 to 1989**
● **Vice President Commercial Marketing and Development**

Firm managed disposition, marketing, and promotion of all real estate in Aston (including Aston Town Centre).

Directed sales strategies, purchaser identification, pursuit, and land sale negotiations. Managed master planning for Aston Town Centre. Oversaw development and master planning of six-building, 360,000-sf Cameron Pond Office Park.

- Constructed RTC Phase I business deal, attracting and attaining corporate approval for joint venture between Hanniford (their first 50-50 real estate JV and three years in the making) and Latham/Clarke Frances. Venture put wheels in motion for Aston Town Centre development while allowing significant owner control.

- Master-planned Aston Town Centre; assembled/managed planning team and internal master-planning "task force." Created flexible, evolving, market-driven, economically feasible project plan still being implemented today.

- Entitled last significant track of land in Aston—RTC 500-acre study area for 8.5 million-sf development. Crafted and negotiated flexible entitlements (in tough political environment), and managed community participation process.

- Sold $80+ million in commercial land in '80s. Negotiated/closed many land sales with developers and corporations. Oversaw increase in values ($1.50 to $2.00/sf to final sale at $20/sf), providing core development/sale income to owner.

- Managed significant commercial marketing of Aston including Aston Expressway campaign that enabled hitting 150% of projections in six months and driving awareness of Aston's accessibility and heightening interest in land holdings.

EDUCATION & PROFESSIONAL DEVELOPMENT

Georgia School of Technology and State University, Dawson, GA
- **MBA–concentration in Finance, 1974**
- **BS–Business Administration, Public Administration, 1971**

Memberships: Urban Land Institute, International Council of Shopping Centers, National Association of Office & Industrial Parks.

Professional Activities: Founding member of ULI's Entertainment Development Council, serving since 1995 formation and currently functioning as Vice Chair at Large. Served on ULI's Small Scale Development Council. Charter member, Northern Virginia NAIOP Chapter.

Attendee and speaker/panelist at conferences: Annual/semi-annual Urban Land Institute (ULI) and International Council of Shopping Centers conferences/conventions (since 1983). Periodic special purpose conferences on Developing Entertainment Destinations and other topics. ULI Entertainment Development Conference (eight since 1995). ICSC Annual Convention (since 1998).

Awards: Aston Town Centre received Northern Georgia NAIOP award for "Best Large-Scale Mixed-Use Project" in 1992 and was selected as a Finalist for 1995 ULI Awards for Excellence.

Gerald F. Hewlitt

Sales + Marketing + Owner Mentality + Technology + Daring Creativity = SUCCESS

Executive Profile

Over twenty years' experience in every facet of the hospitality industry in positions as general manager, consultant, and/or owner with a solid background in successful traditional and entrepreneurial venues. Use a real-world approach to problem solving and a deep well of experience to meet the challenges of this fast-paced, high-turnover industry.

- Have operated multiple restaurants accommodating 900+ patrons and managed events for up to 2,000 attendees while partnering with diverse management, overseeing a multitude of activities, and managing half-million-dollar budgets/P&Ls.

- Proven team-forming and motivational skills have delivered unmatched loyalty and a nearly unheard of staff turnover rate of less than 25%, far below the 61% industry standard. Consistently develop cost-cutting and profit-building initiatives.

- Honed and demonstrated project planning and management skills in supremely high-stress scenarios where failure was not an option and the wrong decision could end a career and/or deliver substantial personal loss.

- Skilled at simultaneously supervising several restaurants and projects. Directed management of two separate restaurants, 20 miles apart for five years. Worked 18+ hours concurrently managing early-morning renovations and late-night operations.

- Use life-long interest in computers/IT to enhance every business opportunity and activity from marketing to inventory control, to menu preparation, to catering scheduling, etc. Hold Certificate in Computer Science from Adelphi University (2001).

- Strategic business sense, uncompromising work ethic, and natural sincerity have helped create consistent profits and have won loyal support and motivation of customers, employees, partners, managers, community leaders, suppliers, and local officials.

Summary of Qualifications

- multi-unit operation management
- multimillion-dollar P&L management
- facility management
- event management & promotion
- troubleshooting & change management

- project planning & systems development
- advanced IT knowledge
- risk management & inventory control
- purchasing & negotiation
- vendor sourcing & negotiating

- sales / product / market analysis
- food / labor / marketing cost controls
- customer relations & satisfaction
- human resources management
- team building & staff retention programs

Career Development

PRESTIGE FOOD AND SPORTS ENTERPRISE, INC. (PFS), OYSTER BAY, NY
1988 to present

President and COO
Partner/Manager

PFS operated two consecutive successful theme restaurants on Long Island. Original concept, Charlie's Big City Grill, opened in 1989 as an 800-patron sports bar restaurant much like The ESPN Zone restaurants.

- In FY 1990, Charlie's grossed over $2 million, and $2.4 million in FY 1992 and 1993. Well-trained staff (only 25% turnover rate), value menu, and "almost as good as being at the game" mentality built a loyal customer base of young professionals, over-30 single clientele, families, and out-of-town guests.

- Restaurant was featured in numerous publications as a top sports bar/café and was one of the first sites in metro New York to feature complete sports broadcast from satellite transmission, with Sunday NFL football afternoons attracting over 1,500 guests.

In proactive response to increased competition from satellite dishes and sports bar market saturation, renovated site and in 1995 transitioned Charlie's to the New Orleans Roadhouse, a Cajun menu "House of Blues" style restaurant

- Took only four months to plan and develop this restaurant/entertainment concept entirely new to metro New York. Handled politicking/project planning necessary to get permits, plans, contractors, and equipment in place for summer renovation (slow season.) Opened on Labor Day weekend 1995, two weeks ahead of schedule and below $750,000 budget.

- Negotiated with property management company for an additional 10 years on lease and lower rent (both valuable assets for future sale). Fine-tuned, upgraded, and enhanced facility including handicap access, risk management, and venue flexibility. Planned menu, hired kitchen staff, developed company's first employee manual, created marketing plans, and booked live entertainment.

- Now a top rhythm and blues showcase and popular Cajun/Creole dining destination, the Grill was recently sold for a profit.

---

25 Bay Drive, Amityville, NY 11701
phone: 631-237-8909 ■ fax: 631-989-2837 ■ cell: 516-555-2837 ■ e-mail: GH.PFS@email.com

230

Career Development, continued

Key Leadership Initiatives at Prestige Food and Sports Enterprise:

Developed Successful Theme Restaurant in Highly Competitive Area

Developed and operated a major theme restaurant in Nassau County, NY. Created concept from emerging sports bar trend, incorporating local venue elements into large-scale restaurant. Composed business plan and sought financing from US Small Business Administration. Took possession of 10-year lease, construction, and physical development in less than four months. Driven by desire to succeed, took Charlie's Big City Grill from concept to creation in under a year.

Key Results:

- First year's gross sales exceeded $2 million, with sales growing by more than 20% in next four years.

Reduced Staff Turnover in High Turnover Industry

Challenged with creating a strong team environment to reduce turnover of staff. Trained managers in "team management" principles, focusing on workplace pride. Compiled PC-based employee guidebook. Shared company's success with employees through annual bonuses, social gatherings, and benefit options.

Key Results:

- Delivered industry-low, 25% turnover rate, even keeping 25% rate during renovation closure.
- Retaining competent and recognizable employees increased sales by building repeat customer/staff bond.
- Increased service quality and customer loyalty through better, more knowledgeable employees.

Managed Redevelopment and Construction of Successful Theme Restaurant

Challenged to co-develop and implement a new, next-generation theme-restaurant concept; to outperform, within five years, previous years' flat growth; to implement changes within a 90-day window; and to retain core customer base, as well as staff crucial to immediate success and profitability.

Identified key areas of planning and attention, set calendar, and assigned management/partner responsibilities. Researched themes/concepts. Established $750,000 budget, developed project plan, and scheduled major construction for traditionally low-performing period. Renegotiated a lengthened lease, concessions for capital improvements, and lower rent. Established cooperative dialogue with town and county officials to expedite necessary permits and approvals.

Key Results:

- Completed construction of The New Orleans Roadhouse below budget and two weeks ahead of schedule.
- After renovation, year-one gross revenue rose to $2.6 million from $2.3 million.
- Reduced maintenance costs by 18% and energy consumption by 8%+, by updating infrastructure, HVAC, and layout.
- Achieved reduced insurance risk through facility changes that allowed full handicap accessibility.
- Retained market share, provided exposure to different market areas, and positioned firm for strong short-term growth.
- Booked live performances by top entertainers and expanded catering capacity.

Rebranded Local Restaurant to Attract New Customers

Challenged with marketing New Orleans Roadhouse without conveying rural image. Recognized traditional radio spots did not take advantage of new theme, so explored and implemented 30- and 60-second local television spots with a major metro NY cable television provider.

Key Results:

- Quarterly sales increased 21%. Ads generated qualified first-time customers and helped in rebranding.

Reduced Marketing Costs While Increasing Market Visibility to Targeted Customers

Challenged to develop effective, low-cost method of advertising to main customer base. Researched and implemented customer databases for direct mail and target marketing strategies, integrated direct mail software for in-house mail sorting, and added POSTNET bar coding to meet USPS regulations. Appended 80,000-member database with phone numbers leading to telemarketing efforts. Eliminated manual removal of outdated customer information from database by using USPS National Change of Address files to automate process.

Key Results:

- Slashed direct mail costs to 33% from $63,000 to $42,000. Reduced marketing budget to 15%.
- Realized 3% to 7% annual postage and labor cost savings by updating database with USPS.

25 Bay Drive, Amityville, NY 11701
phone: 631-237-8909 ■ fax: 631-989-2837 ■ cell: 516-555-2837 ■ e-mail: GH.PFS@email.com

231

Career Development, continued

THE LINDEN TREE CAFÉ, BABYLON, NY   **General Manager and Principal**
1999 to 2000 and 1982 to 1995

The Linden Tree Café is a well-established neighborhood café located in a historical building in one of Long Island's largest downtowns, Babylon, an urban /suburban town attempting revitalization from ongoing effects of "mall creep."

Early Successes

- In 1982, identified closed cafe as a good prospect—surrounding area's demographics were upscale, community revitalization efforts were strong, and circa 1880 building matched current trend for historic charm. Successfully negotiated 10-year lease with option to purchase building within five years at 1982 value, with half of paid rent credited towards purchase price.

- Working with Town of Babylon officials, the Babylon Historical Society, and the Chamber of Commerce, renovated building's façade to circa 1880, funding 70% of work through state and federal historic preservation funds.

- Opened in November of 1982 and quickly established a loyal clientele. Café steadily grossed over $700,000 annually in early '80s. Although maintaining an historic building with apartments was an ongoing challenge, in 1986, purchased building at 1982 negotiated price of $110,000 rather than appraised price of $225,000.

Midstream Challenges

- Restaurant's revenues began to falter in the late '80s as national recession reached Long Island, mall creep continued to deflect downtown business, town's road and sidewalk repairs limited access for months, and the large summer beach crowd started to gather at bay-front restaurants close to the ferries, rather than in the downtown area.

- In 1990, planned complete building renovation including infrastructure. To reduce effect on business, completed entire renovation in under four months. Kept core customer base informed of upcoming grand re-opening with a 20,000+ newsletter mailing and invited best customers and community leaders to menu tastings and mock service dining shortly before re-opening.

- Renovation and new menu generated results above initial projection, but with unsteady growth. Decided to sell when a generous offer was received in 1994. Completed sale in 1995. Kept possession of building and separate real estate company; transitioned professional activities into new investment areas.

- New owners' establishment closed after only four years through owners' series of business-devastating decisions.

Turnaround and Sale

- Determined to personally rebuild and reestablish business and then sell to a buyer or team who could maintain and enhance it. Repossessed property in winter of 1998, facing enormous challenges as landlord of a building in need of a tenant and as a member of a community that wanted to see/solicit a fine establishment in the area.

- Achieved this goal in less than 18 months with under $100,000 investment after reestablishing cordial community and business working relationships. Reopened in spring 1999 with Chamber of Commerce celebrating the event with a party at the establishment in June 1999. In August 2000, business was sold for a profit and continues to develop.

Education and Certification

Bachelor of Science in Management, Adelphi University, Garden City, New York

Adelphi University, Garden City, New York
Certificate, 320 hours, Computer Science, 2001
Earned while running two businesses.

Comp USA
MS Excel (2 days)
Advanced use of Corel Draw software (2 days)

National Restaurant Association
Preventing Sexual Harassment in the Workplace
Restaurant Catering
Trends in Restaurant Design

New York Restaurant Association
Writing an Operation Manual (2 days)

Hospitality Certifications
Food Service Managers Certificate, No. 92122, County of Suffolk Department of Health Services
Food Service Managers Certificate, Nassau County Department of Health

25 Bay Drive, Amityville, NY 11701
phone: 631-237-8909 ▪ fax: 631-989-2837 ▪ cell: 516-555-2837 ▪ e-mail: GH.PFS@email.com

232

CHAPTER 13

Best Resumes for Transitioning From Military to Civilian Careers

Building the Foundation

Transferability of skills is the foundation upon which every effective career transition resume is written. Your challenge, therefore, is to identify the skills, qualifications, experiences, and competencies you have that will be of value in your new job, career, or industry. Those skills then become the key points in your resume around which everything else is written.

To help you get started with identifying your transferable skills, review the brief listing below of *some* of the skills, qualifications, and competencies that companies and recruiters look for in candidates transitioning from military to civilian careers. *(Note that this is only a partial listing of the scores of different skills that companies look for in qualified candidates.)* The single most critical item that is you use "civilian" language when writing and not military "lingo" that the corporate world will not be familiar with.

Carefully review the keywords and keyword phrases to identify those that accurately reflect skills you possess and which are transferable into your new position. Then, be sure to incorporate those words into your resume, your cover letters, and any other career marketing documents that you create. They will capture a prospective employer's interest and open the door to interviews and opportunities.

Benchmarking	Personnel Development & Leadership
Budgeting & Cost Control	Policies & Procedures
Contract Negotiation & Administration	Process Optimization
Executive-Level Presentations	Public Relations
Global Affairs	Quality Improvement
Human Capital	Resource Management & Allocation
Intelligence & Security	Strategic Planning
Logistics Management	Supply Chain Management
Marketing & Business Development	Team Building & Camaraderie
Organizational Leadership	Workflow Optimization

Sample Career Transition Resumes

Following are six sample resumes for individuals transitioning from military into civilian careers. Each of these resumes was written by a professional resume writer with extensive experience working with, writing for, and positioning individuals in career transition. Full contact information for each of these writers is in the Appendix. To understand why these resumes were written and designed the way that they were, it is critical that you read the following information, which explains the specific objective of each of these job seekers and the particular strategy that was used to prepare their resume.

Resume:	Mac Kaminski (pages 236-237)
Writer:	Debra O'Reilly
Objective:	To transition from military career in purchasing and supply chain management into a similar position with city, state, or federal government.
Strategy:	Showcased Mac's expertise in three distinct areas: (1) intimate knowledge of suppliers' products; (2) comprehensive understanding of military purchasing protocol; and, (3) excellent relationship-building skills. Unlike many military-to-civilian career transitions, the technical/military jargon was not de-emphasized since it is directly relevant.

Resume:	Charles Milverton (pages 238-239)
Writer:	Don Orlando
Objective:	To transition from military technology career into civilian technology career.
Strategy:	To optimize transferability of skills, used "real" corresponding civilian job titles for his military positions and indicated how often he was recognized for his contributions, not by military awards but by promotion, a concept that the private sector clearly understands. Bold print used to draw visual attention to key achievements, concepts, results, and skill sets.

Resume:	Gregory T. Jones (pages 240-241)
Writer:	Diane Burns
Objective:	To transition out of military career in logistics operations into a position in arms treaty control and force protection in the private sector, most likely with a government contractor.
Strategy:	Focused resume on relevant military background and highlighted activities of international interest. Heavy emphasis on related skills in international/ foreign military training and customs, operations management, arms control management, and international liaison affairs.

Resume:	Helen Redman (pages 242-243)
Writer:	Debra O'Reilly
Objective:	To transition from military training career into private sector human resources career.

Strategy: Started with headline to clearly communicate her career objectives and then followed with core qualifications and accomplishments as they relate to HR, training, leadership, communications, and personnel. Dedicated page two to a very brief summary of military career, with emphasis on rapid promotion to positions of increasingly important HR and training responsibilities.

NOTE: *The following two resumes were prepared for the same candidate – John S. Ramirez – who was transitioning from a military to civilian career. These two resumes are excellent examples of how you can "paint the picture" that you want your reader to see by re-weighting all of the information in a resume and emphasizing an entirely different set of skills and qualifications.*

Resume: John S. Ramirez-1 (pages 244-245)
Writer: Marcy Johnson
Objective: To transition from distinguished military career in logistics management into new career track in college/university admissions and student counseling.
Strategy: Created a resume that effectively communicated he was a talented leader of admissions, counseling, and related academic programs. Extensive career summary section used to highlight relevant skills, competencies, and accomplishments. Current job description focused heavily on education administration; other job descriptions focused on related skills whenever possible and on notable career achievements.

Resume: John S. Ramirez-2 (pages 246-247)
Writer: Marcy Johnson
Objective: To transition back into his earlier military career specialty in logistics and capture a mid- to senior-level management position in logistics in the private sector.
Strategy: Used headline format to communicate his positioning and devoted all of page one to his expert performance in logistics, cost savings, process improvements, team building, and more. Included prominent display of MBA in logistics degree to further substantiate qualifications. Used page two to summarize military career with an emphasis on promotion and achievement.

Mac Kaminski

Developing rapport through integrity, openness and trust

4232 Private Terrace
Lynn, MA 01711   mac.kam@edress.com   Home: 708-588-1235
                                                                                 Cell: 708-622-5511

GOVERNMENT PURCHASING & SUPPLY CHAIN MANAGEMENT

Qualifications:
- Twenty-two year U.S. military career, successfully managing personnel, tools and equipment.
- Authorized high-volume equipment purchaser for the past ten years.
- Exceptional interpersonal and training skills, in combination with a strong customer-service focus, to ensure high customer satisfaction and quality assurance.
- Currently hold **Secret** clearance; **Top-Secret**-cleared at past assignments.

PROFESSIONAL EXPERIENCE

U.S. MILITARY   1983-Present

Assistant Support Section Chief / Program Manager, Military Base, Eastern US (2000-Present)
Full operational support for aircraft maintenance unit, with additional program management responsibility for specialized equipment procurement and inspection programs. Manage training, development, scheduling and periodic evaluations for 12 direct reports. Track all technical data and tools in support of flight line (26 high-performance aircraft). Facilitate continuous improvement; maintain diagnostic & testing equipment. Oversee $12 million equipment inventory, using customized military equipment tracking system. Conduct product research and place orders.

- Hand-picked by Base Commander to authorize high-dollar purchases. Research vendors; negotiate contracts; provide follow-up to ensure timely delivery. Verify expenses and validate payments monthly.
- Department has achieved excellent annual audits for seven of the last 10 years, with zero discrepancies for the past two years.
- Key player in development and testing of partnership program with major tool manufacturer to facilitate ordering, inventory and product pricing. This program has achieved a 50% improvement in production time to date, with a projected 90%+ reduction in labor hours.

Weapons Load Crew Chief / Trainer, Military Base, Korea (1999-2000)
Managed staff of three. Responsible for evaluation, certification and re-certification of 25 weapons load crews (75 total). Additionally, served as Hazardous Waste Monitor.

- Constructed receptacles / implemented onsite disposal procedures that reduced processing time by 80%.
- Conducted accelerated training program, successfully increasing productivity by 50% in just four months.

Assistant Support Section Chief / Program Manager, Military Base, Western US (1993-1999)
Supported unit of 28-30 high-performance aircraft. Managed equipment assets of $4 million. Directed all equipment procurement and tracking programs.

- Served as chief architect of hazardous material management program, earning outstanding evaluations for effectiveness of process. Resulted in unique 2-time unit recognition for environmental compliance. Hazardous material management process was subsequently adopted as a template to develop division-wide standardized procedures.
- Earned citation for key role in processing / movement of 120 tons of equipment, within a 14-hour window, to support a major overseas deployment effort.

Developing rapport through integrity, openness and trust

Weapons Load Crew member, Military Base, Western US (1991–1993)
Member of base closure team.

Weapons Load Crew member, Military Base, Europe (1989–1991)
Loaded/ unloaded unit–committed munitions. Performed functional checks and installed equipment.

Weapons Loader / Trainer, Military Base, Eastern US (1983–1989)
Recommended by supervisor to interview for training position. Success led to expansion of training duties to instruct 75 crews.

EDUCATION / CERTIFICATION

Community College of the Military
Numerous credit and non–credit courses in categories including hazardous material management, customer service, leadership, employee relations, quality assurance, environmental awareness, train–the–trainer, security, logistics and safety.

Certifications: Certified Equipment Manager; Hazardous Waste Management

COMMUNITY INVOLVEMENT

Volunteer, Habitat for Humanity
Volunteer, Solo (an outreach program in Korea at Assisted Living Facilities)

Available for relocation

CHARLES MILVERTON

1500 Felder Avenue

Montgomery, AL 36100   charles.milverton@gunter.af.mil

334.299.3892 (Direct office line)

334.296.3999 (Home)

WHAT I OFFER THE REVERE GROUP AS YOUR NEWEST SENIOR IT CONSULTING PRACTICE MANAGER:

Customer focus that lets clients think my solutions are their own good ideas,

Communication skills that help people break down barriers to productivity, and

Experience to transform groups of strangers into smoothly running teams.

RECENT EMPLOYMENT HISTORY WITH SELECTED CONTRIBUTIONS TO PRODUCTIVITY:

More than 18 years of increasingly responsible managerial positions as a commissioned Air Force officer, including these most recent assignments:

Promoted to Chief of **Client Support** *and* Director of **IT Operations Planning**
(VICE PRESIDENTIAL POSITIONS), Standard Systems Group, Gunter Air Force Base,
Montgomery, AL   Jun 00 – Jun 05

*The Standard Systems Group is the **Air Force's largest, central IT systems design center**. The Group develops, validates, tests, installs, maintains, and upgrades complete networking and IT-based solutions for thousands of users around the world. Manages $10B in software.*

Supervise four senior and mid-level managers directly and 200 mid-level executives and specialists indirectly. Build and defend a growing budget (currently $11M) annually.

Transformed a corporate vision of improved customer service into a responsive help desk that serves more than 8,000 diverse users. Guided employees to change their outlook from "turf protection" to team building. *Payoffs:* **Productivity rose** and stayed high across the board. Expensive specialists freed to make **maximum contributions** to our mission.

Guided a **major technology changeover**. Designed, advocated, and tested new ways to help hundreds of people work much more collaboratively. *Payoffs:* New tools made us focus on solving problems, not react to symptoms. **Costs reduced 60%** in only eight months. Our work became the **corporate standard worldwide**.

Chosen to "bullet proof" the Air Force's Y2K plans—six months before the deadline. Led 130 customers to build solutions they could own. Then **made the tough sell** that persuaded **20 CEO-equivalents** (and their CIOs) to relinquish some control of their proprietary data for the greater good. *Payoff:* **Y2K** transition **trouble-free** at over 300 locations around the globe.

Converted part of a 40-year-old building into one of most advanced communications and business innovation centers in the world—in six months. Worked with customers to produce pioneering software in 15 days. *Payoffs:* Our center featured in <u>Internet World</u>. Our software now **the standard for** Air Force **network status reporting**.

Found an incipient problem: the need for new expertise to push our R&D forward. Drew on experience to find just the right contractor. Then used my **ROI analysis** to persuade management to fund them. *Payoff:* **Captured a multi-million dollar "account"** with the fresh insights we gained.

Promoted to **Chief of Analysis** *promoted to* Deputy **Chief Information Officer** (ASSISTANT VICE-PRESIDENTIAL POSITIONS), National Guard Bureau, Washington, D.C.   Aug 97 – Jun 00

More indicators of performance to support The Revere Group's mission

Applied **technology** in **completely new ways**: helped change how a 50-year-old corporate culture valued diversity. Led **large group interventions** (up to 250 people) to produce everything from strategies to metrics to tools. *Payoffs:* Employers, diversity leaders, managers, and entry-level workers came together as a team. Worldwide implementation, ownership, and QA **all Internet based**.

Realigned corporate and production **goals** that had drifted us into conflict. Got team members recommitted to our mission. *Payoff:* **108,000 people** focused on just 14 goals and 22 objectives.

In-Residence Student, U.S. Naval War College, Newport, RI   Aug 95 – Aug 97

Chosen among the top 2% of senior executives to attend this 10-month school. Showed senior leadership the benefits of electronic brainstorming. **Pulled together 25** of the **best minds** from academia and the private sector to validate and improve my work. *Payoff:* CEOs built facilities still dedicated to this method.

Promoted to **Chief of Analysis** *promoted to* Director, Air **Operations** and **Contingency Support** Centers *promoted to* Manager of **Business Process and Data Modeling** (ASSISTANT VICE-PRESIDENTIAL POSITIONS), Andrews Air Force Base, MD   Jul 89 – Aug 95

Overhauled the inefficient way we served our customers' most pressing needs. **Defined** the **best practices**. Designed a tailor-made facility to exploit the right worker competencies. *Payoff:* New **single point of service** got users information they needed: fast and right.

COMPUTER SKILLS:

Proficient in Remedy (a software suite than manages **trouble-ticketing, assessment,** and **customer relationships**), BusinessObjects (**business intelligence software** that provides **on-line, analytical processing**), System Dynamics business modeling and simulation software. Word, Excel, Outlook, PowerPoint, Access, MS Project, Internet search protocols, and Palm OS.

Working knowledge of SQL, VMS, UNIX, Mac OS, HP OpenView, Axent Enterprise **Security Manager**, Sidewinder (**firewall**), Tivoli, group facilitation software, and CA Unicenter (both software suites **manage large enterprises** from one location).

RELEVANT PROFESSIONAL DEVELOPMENT:

MBA, Kenan-Flager Business School, University of North Carolina, Chapel Hill, NC, 88

BS, U.S. Air Force Academy, Colorado Springs, CO, 77 *Dean's List five out of eight semesters. Commandant's List (of top 25% of students).*

Certificate in **Advanced Studies in Systems Dynamics**, Massachusetts Institute of Technology, Cambridge, MA; expect award in Dec 2005.

"Managerial Statistics," National Guard Bureau, three days, 01

"Process and Data Modeling," Dacom, one week, 00

"Quality Management for Managers," United States Air Force, two weeks, 99 *Chosen by senior management as* **one of 16** *(from 2,000 eligibles) to build our first quality team.*

Regular, recurring training in combating sexual harassment and drugs in the workplace, **ethical contracting, leading diverse workforces,** and **computer security**.

Page two

GREGORY T. JONES

Permanent: 2874 Lemon Drop Path * Columbia, MD 21045
410-555-9837 * gregtjone@aol.com

CAREER FOCUS

ARMS TREATY CONTROL SPECIALIST ▪ **FORCE PROTECTION**

PROFESSIONAL AND PERSONAL VALUE OFFERED

▪ *Twenty years' professional experience as an Operations Manager with specific expertise in large-scale transportation and supply management operations as well as **Arms/Range** operations for the U.S. Army and private firms. Knowledge of treaties and regulations governing arms control and property book control.*

▪ *Draft and implement policies and procedures. Manage logistical and administrative requirements for hundreds of personnel supporting thousands of customers in multiple countries.*

▪ *Apply superior technical and interpersonal communications. Conduct liaison with officials from numerous countries.*

▪ *Quickly assess operations and initiate improvements in staffing, organization, and procedures. Manage multiple, simultaneous, and complex projects and programs in international venues.*

▪ *Assemble, motivate, train, and inspire talented working teams/staffs. Consistently produce quality-oriented departments.*

PROFESSIONAL EMPLOYMENT AND SELECTED EXAMPLES OF QUALIFICATIONS IN ACTION

INTERNATIONAL RANGE CONTROL and SAFETY OFFICER   03/2004 — present
Iraq Defense Office, Iraq

- Manage administration, planning, safety coordination, and operations for the International Range Complex which serves 18 separate **international organizations** and the entire local National Guard (approximately 17,000 soldiers). Create schedules and communicate with customers for military training exercises and scheduling requirements.
- Serve as a consultant and advisor to the International Range Control Director regarding safety, operations, and specific issues. Communicate often with the Range Control Director, coordinate Range Control Training with organizations/customers, and ensure compliance with safety measures and procedures.
- Formulate safety guidelines and policies for all range operations and brief organizational personnel. Provide operational guidance regarding the complex in an **international** environment. Monitor that all customers adhere to safety policies; train training units on range safety and operations, including combat equipment.
- Analyze organizational requirements to meet qualifications using regulations, policies, and guidelines for an **international** system. Coordinate with **customs officials** as required. Write reports and submit documentation.

OPERATIONS MANAGER   01/2003 — 03/2004
ACCOUNT MANAGER   01/2001 — 04/2003
Titan Corporation, Germany

- Supervised warehouse operations and 55 personnel including 8 administrative staff, 4 subcontractors, 35 warehouse personnel, and 8 contract security personnel responsible for warehousing and storage of $35 million of perishable and non-perishable products in an international environment. Worked with customs officials and monitored Status of Forces Agreements (SOFA) regulations.
- Coordinated incoming shipments with shipping contractors (military and civilian), managed the workload, monitored manpower requirements, and processed special orders and critical deliveries. Tracked shipments. Prepared various reports and monitored accounting procedures.

Operations Management Continued...

- Managed customer service, ensuring customer satisfaction. Developed SOP to track shipments.
- Managed, coordinated, and processed requests for Tool Kits. Acted as consultant to area managers to prepare quotes, monitor shipments, and coordinate deliveries within Europe and Eastern Asia. Provided guidance to management staff regarding daily distributions, cargo-pickup, and direct delivery to customers.
- Supply Center Program – Europe Account Manager: Managed requisition and supply accounts. Coordinated resources with local vendors for purchases up to $14 million. Negotiated prices and developed quotes.

U.S. Army (Senior Noncommissioned Officer) (Overview - 1981 – 2001)
SENIOR ADMINISTRATOR, First Infantry Division   03/1996 – 01/2001

- Directed logistical operations for 31 sub-divisional units including field deployments, division gunneries, and maneuver densities. Managed hand receipts for $600,000 worth of equipment. Oversight direction for administration and coordination of training support, safety control and supply requirements during deployment/redeployment and contingency training in a split operation (Bosnia and Germany).
- Selected to provide logistical training support and **foreign military training** in the Ukraine. Coordinated logistical requirements for units from 14 NATO countries (approximately 4,200 personnel) and trained individual delegations on logistical support from setting up a command to managing a supply channel (planning, operations, administration, tactical skills, and automated simulation combat training including food supplies, service, and procurement activities for large-scale field operations).
- As a consultant, provided logistical support and training in distribution and inventory procedures, procurements, and requisitions for **Allied Training Programs** (**Partnership for Peace**).
- Accounted for $23 million worth of equipment and managed an annual budget of $190,000. Wrote SOPs, internal policies, and guidelines.
- Trained personnel in security and safety for transportation and distribution of hazardous materials.

OPERATIONS SUPERVISOR, Germany   12/1992 – 03/1996

- Coordinated and directed **maneuvers**, supply operations, inventories, hand-receipts, special procurements, and other logistical requirements for 45 sub-divisional organizations including inspections and evaluations.
- Managed training cycles. Organized and managed logistical support and supply requirements including equipment for training using the Defense Property Accountability System, Standard Army Retail Supply System, and Single Army Logistics Enterprise (SALE). Managed financial accounts and budgets.
- Supervised **range control** procedures and training. Directed logistical requirements including supply, purchasing/ordering, receipt, storage, shipment, equipment records and parts, material control, and accounting/property book requirements for subsistence supply and all classes of equipment.
- Implemented emergency, disaster, and combat feeding plans (computed supply usage factors). Developed and initiated standard operating procedures for safety, energy, security, and fire prevention programs.

EDUCATION

- Master of Business Administration, Phoenix University, Overseas Campus, 1999
- Bachelor of Science in Political Science (Minor in Economics), University of Maryland, Baltimore, MD, 1987

TRAINING AND AWARDS

- International Merchant, Purchase Authorization Card
- Requisition and Local Procurement Management Training (International Requirements)
- Range Control and Safety Training
- Senior Advisor and Management Course
- Advanced Noncommissioned Officer Course (Leadership and Management)
- Meritorious Service Medal ▪ Army Achievement Medal x 4 ▪ National Defense Service Medal ▪ Marksmanship Badge ▪ Army Commendation Medal x 2

HELEN REDMAN

16 Villa Avenida, Bristillo, AZ 85000
602.444.9365
redman.hr@emailaddress.com

HUMAN RESOURCES EXECUTIVE

Accomplished and energetic senior HR professional with extensive leadership qualifications in all aspects of global human resources initiatives and programs. Trusted confidant to Senior Management. Strategic planner, providing vision and expertise in organizational leadership, HR policies and procedures, human capital, HRIS, benefits/compensation administration, and leadership development.

CORE QUALIFICATIONS

HR Management/Employee and Labor Relations: Managed multi-million-dollar annual operational budgets. Confidential advisor to senior-level management. Served as Human Relations/Equal Opportunity Representative, Safety Manager, Family Support Officer, and Internal Control Officer. Prepared/conducted risk-management assessments.

Organizational Development/Leadership / Training: Implemented HRIS training programs, seminars, and workshops. Developed skills-related assessment tools to build a solid team capable of maintaining safety and security in a highly sensitive environment. Streamlined infrastructure to consolidate recruitment, training, and assignment functions.

Staffing and Recruitment/Diversity: Recruited, interviewed, and hired individuals with exceptional integrity, commitment and ability to handle highly sensitive material. Advised employees on retention, assignments, development, retirement plans, and benefits. Facilitated quarterly sexual harassment and diversity training.

Compensation and Benefits: Defined retention and retirement compensation benefits. Counseled employees on implications and benefits of HIPAA and FMLA.

SELECTED ACCOMPLISHMENTS

- Successfully executed dual challenges of organizational turnaround and the launch of a complete information management system for a newly incorporated high-tech venture.
- Redesigned infrastructure to facilitate recruitment, training, and staff assignments.
- Increased efficiency of evaluation screening process by 50% within first six months of operation.
- Orchestrated complete redesign of management information system; exceeded initial production objectives by nearly 50%.
- Key member of team that expedited lengthy, bureaucratic advancement process. Wrote recommendation to simplify/localize process. Reduced process from two-month to two-day turnaround.
- Negotiated contracts for office equipment and supplies totaling $250K, reducing costs by 15-20%. Solicited/approved bids for service and maintenance contracts.
- Reduced injury-related absences by 40%.
- Key player in reengineering of HR system globally for performance evaluations. Analyzed personnel evaluation reporting process to increase completion and accuracy rates. Provided additional training for raters and created tracking system. Results: Completion rate increased 35%; eliminated 3-year backlog.

HELEN REDMAN

PROFESSIONAL EXPERIENCE

U. S. ARMY

Advanced on a fast track through increasingly responsible, high-profile management positions, culminating with coordination of a major military healthcare program. Successfully promoted on merit from Enlisted to Officer rank.

Operations and Training Management, Regional Readiness Command, Southwestern US
Human Resources Coordinator, specialized healthcare program (2002–2004)
Administration/Training Management, Regional Readiness Command, Southwestern US
Senior HR Manager (2000–2002)
Operations and Training Management, Human Resources Command, Midwestern US
HR Manager/Director of Evaluations Support (1998–2000)
HR Counselor/Coordinator for employee career-track progression (1996–1998)
Administration and Training Management , Finance Group, Western US
HR Manager (1994–1996)
Early enlisted assignments in clerical and administrative positions.

EDUCATION AND PROFESSIONAL DEVELOPMENT

Master of Arts, Management, Masters University, St. Louis, MO (GPA 3.8)
Bachelor of Science, Business Administration, State University of Maryland
Associate in Arts, Arnold City College

Ongoing education in the areas of leadership, organizational management, regulatory compliance, safety, record-keeping, labor relations, and logistics management.

HIGHLIGHTS OF HONORS

- Received numerous awards for outstanding Human Resources performance.
- Employee of the Quarter (chosen from 1,100 employees).
- Commended for "superbly conduct(ing) HR pre-inspections of regional structure EEO, FMLA, HIPAA, AAP, ERISA, COBRA, ADA, employee benefits, and new hire reporting, ensuring the … effectiveness of human resources accountability."

PROFESSIONAL AFFILIATIONS

Society for Human Resource Management
Warrant Officer Association

Adjutant General Association
Reserve Officers Association

ETC.

Volunteer mentor, tutoring/supporting students at a local elementary school.
Computer knowledge: MS Office (Word, Excel, PowerPoint, Outlook); company-specific HR systems.

John S. Ramirez

450 W. Jackson #30
Chicago, Illinois 60661

johnsramirez@earthlink.com

(h) 312-942-8843
(c) 312-876-1212

Career Focus: Career Development • Educational Counseling • Admissions

Proactive, highly organized administrative professional with over two years of experience providing academic advising, recruitment, assessment, mentoring, retention, and orientation activities to naval science students at a major Big Ten university. A diplomatic, people-oriented advisor who builds rapport, extracts maximum effort, and enables students to succeed. Background working closely with other academic advisors to provide timely information on courses, options, and policy. Accomplished written and oral communicator with training in media relations.

Notable:

▸ Guided students through academic cycle, achieving 100% success rate during first formal schooling assignments.

▸ Actively interpreted requirements, counseled, and supported almost 200 future leaders through the academic process.

▸ Assimilated college freshmen quickly by reinstituting freshman orientation, a mentoring program, and team activities.

▸ Designed curriculum and initiated senior-level professional development class offering "real-life" applications.

▸ Developed positive, educated, and well-rounded students and citizens with a strong commitment to community.

▸ Used solid analysis and problem-solving skills to elicit high levels of productivity and success from groups up to 1,000.

Competencies:

Academic Advising... Recruitment... Orientation... Educational Planning... Transfer Credits and Requirements... Application Procedures... Counseling... Graduation Requirements... Academic Skills... Career Planning... Career and Interest Assessments... Budgeting ... Event Planning... Goal Setting

---

CAREER HISTORY

UNITED STATES MARINE CORPS, 1976–Present

Career in increasingly responsible positions as a Commissioned Marine Corps Officer, including these recent assignments:

Department Head, Naval Science Department, Chicago, Illinois   **2001 to Present**

Professor of Naval Science leading nine-member department advising, assessing, and training 65 junior executives for positions with joint, multinational, and high-level service organizations. Forecast, track, analyze, and manage university, federal, and alumni budgets simultaneously, balancing dynamic organizational mission with small operating budget. Develop and modify curriculum to meet high standards of leadership development and succession planning.

• Developed and implemented dynamic professional development class focused on real-life applications. Lent an active hand guiding next generation of leaders through training cycle, achieving 100% success rate during first formal schooling assignments.

• Conducted complete assessment of existing Naval Science Department program, changing process from inventory-based model to information-based model with goal of reducing inventory by $100,000.

Director, Force Protection Development, U.S. Second Fleet, Norfolk, Virginia   **2000 to 2001**

Assembled a team of cross-functional experts to conduct a market survey, analyze information, and initiate actions to develop effective measures, tactics, techniques, doctrine, and exercises that changed the framework of U.S. Navy security after the USS Cole disaster. Served as member of senior management team and liaison to help plan and execute three joint and NATO combined initiatives, earning Legion of Merit Award.

• Developed multinational logistics program and helped lead organization through its most significant logistics restructuring in 50 years.

(continued)

CAREER HISTORY

- Noted as one of the single most important players in a dramatic shift and improvement plan for the U.S. Second Fleet. Created a detailed system for review and personally assembled an expert team to revise plans.

- Ensured solid working relationships and served as liaison to procure equipment and develop standard operating procedures that enhanced ability to defend U.S. Second Fleet against threats after USS Cole incident.

- Took lead role in transformation of traditional logistics exercise into premier NATO joint venture. Coordinated 96 NATO and U.S. senior officers from 21 nations in first-ever combined exercise conducted in the Ukraine.

Director, Logistics, Plans & Exercises, Norfolk, Virginia   **1998 to 2000**

Developed budget and initiated multinational planning and coordination for expansion of NATO exercise, including joint logistics for cross-functional teams. Coordinated initial development of standard operating procedures (SOP) and reprogrammed logistics training objectives. Participated in development of first agreement between United States Joint Forces and NATO forces exercising on U.S. soil. Served as Logistics Division representative to review board and executive team. Chaired NATO Logistics Syndicate and co-chaired Western European Union Logistics Syndicate for logistics exercise.

- Made significant contributions to logistics system and tactical vehicle readiness of fleet valued at more than $302 million, saving nearly $1.5 million.

Commanding Officer, 7th Motor Transport Battalion, Camp Pendleton, California   **1995 to 1997**
(Position equivalent to Chief Operating Officer)

Administered $265 million budget and directed 1,000-member team while managing life cycle of complex logistics system, including long-term planning, funding, testing, quality control, contract administration, and logistics support.

- Reduced vehicle repair cycle by 60% initially, continuing to implement process improvements for 70% total reduction. Won National Defense Transportation Association Award; recognized as top transportation unit.

Early career: Senior Management Positions in Procurement and Logistics

Fielded a 945-vehicle fleet valued in excess of $302 million, saving $1.49 million by negotiating an innovative lift program from the United States to Okinawa on a space-available basis instead of reserving exclusive transportation. Carried out benchmarking truck acquisition project from cradle-to-grave, creating a 20-year plan for rebuilding and use of fleet. Integrated logistics support and operational requirements saving thousands of dollars on multi-year contract worth over $300 million.

EDUCATION AND TRAINING

MA – National Security and Strategic Studies, College of Naval Warfare, Newport, RI 1998
MBA – Logistics, Florida Institute of Technology, Melbourne, FL 1988
BA – Business Management, University of Northern Iowa, Cedar Falls, IA 1976

Additional Training: Numerous leadership, business management, media training, and strategic planning courses
Computer Skills: Microsoft Word, Excel, PowerPoint

HONORS AND AWARDS

Legion of Merit, the Defense Meritorious Service Medal, the Meritorious Service Medal (with Gold Star), the Navy Commendation Medal, the Navy Achievement Medal, and numerous unit awards.

John S. Ramirez

450 W. Jackson #30 • Chicago, Illinois 60661
(h) 312-942-8843 • (c) 312-876-1212 • johnsrameriz@earthlink.com

LOGISTICS/TRANSPORTATION EXECUTIVE
Supply Chain Management • Integrated Logistics Management • Leadership Development

Strategic leader combining initiative and integrity with international experience directing expansive logistics and transportation systems. Big-picture thinker readily assimilating into new environments, ensuring process improvements, and delivering cost reductions of $3+ million. Motivational team builder eliciting high levels of productivity, loyalty, and success from cross-functional teams of 9 to 1,000. Liaison between government executives, manufacturers, and operators. Accomplished written and oral communicator trained in media relations.

Demonstrated success in:
STRATEGIC PLANNING • PROCESS IMPROVEMENTS • STAFF DEVELOPMENT
ASSET MANAGEMENT • FLEET MANAGEMENT • LOGISTICS MANAGEMENT

Cradle-to-Grave Procurement… Carriage/Fleet Management… Inventory Optimization/Inventory Planning… Asset Management… Vendor Alliances… Cost Savings and Reductions… Precision Logistics… Acquisition Management… Contract Transportation Services… Regulatory Compliance… Safety Management… Workflow Optimization

MBA in Logistics, Florida Institute of Technology

CAREER HIGHLIGHTS

Cost Reductions and Savings

- Saved $1.49 million by negotiating an innovative vehicle lift program from the United States to Okinawa. Managed life cycle of complex logistics system and fielded a 945-vehicle fleet valued in excess of $302 million.

- Made significant contributions to logistics system and tactical vehicle readiness of fleet valued at more than $302 million, saving nearly $1.5 million.

Process and Inventory Improvements

- Reduced vehicle repair cycle 60%, continuing to drive process improvements for 70% total reduction. Won National Transportation Association Award and recognized as top transportation unit in U.S. Marine Corps.

- Developed multinational logistics program and helped lead organization through its most significant logistics restructuring in 50 years.

- Created a detailed system for fleet-level review of every ship's force protection plan. Noted as one of the single most important players in a dramatic shift and improvement in force protection for the U.S. Second Fleet.

- Conducted complete assessment of existing Naval Science Department program, changing process from inventory-based model to information-based model with goal of reducing inventory by $100,000.

Team Building and Training

- Ensured solid working relationships at all levels, procured equipment, and developed standard operating procedures to enhance ability to defend U.S. Second Fleet against asymmetrical threat after USS Cole incident.

- Took lead role in transformation of traditional logistics exercise into premier NATO joint venture. Successfully coordinated participation of 96 NATO and U.S. senior officers from 21 nations in first-ever combined exercise.

- Re-established mentoring program, lending an active hand guiding next generation of leaders through training cycle. Achieved 100% success rate during first formal schooling assignments in multinational environments.

Endorsement: "Through [John's] positive leadership, the department has been a "can-do" organization…People orientation, sincerity, and rapport enables him to extract maximum efforts while maintaining a high state of morale."
S.B. Johnson, Chief Operating Officer

CAREER PROGRESSION

UNITED STATES MARINE CORPS, 1976–Present

Career in increasingly responsible positions as a Commissioned Marine Corps Officer, including these recent assignments:

Department Head, Naval Science Department, Chicago, Illinois   **2001–Present**

Professor of Naval Science leading nine-member department training 65 junior executives for positions with joint, multinational, and high-level service organizations. Forecast, track, analyze, and manage university, federal, and alumni budgets simultaneously, balancing dynamic organizational mission with small operating budget. Develop curriculums to meet high standards of leadership development and succession planning.

Director, Force Protection Development, U.S. Second Fleet, Norfolk, VA   **2000–2001**

Assembled a team of cross-functional experts to conduct a market survey, analyze information, and initiate actions to develop effective measures, tactics, techniques, doctrine, and exercises that changed the framework of U.S. Navy security after the USS Cole disaster. Served as member of senior management team and liaison to help plan and execute three joint and NATO combined initiatives, earning Legion of Merit Award.

Director, Logistics, Plans, & Exercises, Norfolk, VA   **1998–2000**

Developed multimillion-dollar budget and initiated multinational planning and coordination for expansion of NATO exercise, including joint logistics for cross-functional teams. Participated in development of first agreement between United States Joint Forces and NATO forces exercising on U.S. soil. Served as Logistics Division representative to review board and executive team. Chaired NATO Logistics Syndicate and co-chaired Western European Union Logistics Syndicate for logistics exercise.

Commanding Officer, 7th Motor Transport Battalion, Camp Pendleton, CA   **1995–1997**
(Position equivalent to Chief Operating Officer)

Administered $265 million budget and directed 1,000-member team while managing life cycle of complex logistics system, including funding, testing, quality control, contract administration, and logistics support.

Early career: Senior Management Positions in Procurement and Logistics

Fielded a 945-vehicle fleet valued in excess of $302 million, saving $1.49 million by negotiating an innovative lift program from the U.S. to Okinawa on a space-available basis instead of reserving exclusive transportation. Benchmarked truck acquisition project from cradle-to-grave, creating a 20-year plan for rebuilding and use of fleet. Integrated logistics support and operational requirements, saving thousands of dollars on multi-year contract worth over $300M. Ensured a high state of motor transport readiness and reorganized five-ton truck fleet.

EDUCATION AND TRAINING

MA — National Security and Strategic Studies, College of Naval Warfare, Newport, RI 1998
MBA — Logistics, Florida Institute of Technology, Melbourne, FL 1988
BA — Business Management, Northwestern University, Chicago, Illinois 1976

Computer Skills:
Microsoft Word, Excel, PowerPoint

Additional Training:
Leadership/Business Management • Motor Transport Maintenance • Supply Chain Management
Advanced Logistics • Executive Media Relations • Management/Strategic Planning

---

Endorsement: "Intelligent, Aggressive. Considerate. [John] has distinguished himself in all areas with exceptionally sound performance and absolute integrity. He has demonstrated unusual sensitivity and rare people skills.
Richard G. Barkema, Director, Logistic Plans and Readiness

APPENDIX

List of Contributors

Following is a detailed listing of the 19 professional resume writers who have contributed their work and knowledge to this book. Each has earned at least one, if not several, notable certifications or credentials for their expertise in resume writing and design. What's more, each of these writers is a member in good standing of the Career Masters Institute (www.cminstitute. com), a prestigious professional association supporting the top resume writers, career coaches, career counselors, outplacement consultants, and other career professionals in the U.S., Canada, and abroad.

Certifications & Credentials

CCM	Credentialed Career Master
CCMC	Certified Career Management Coach Master Coach (Harvey)
CECC	Certified Electronic Career Coach
CEIP	Certified Employment Interview Professional
CMP	Certified Management Professional
CPBS	Certified Personal Brand Strategist
CPRC	Certified Professional Retirement Coach
CPRW	Certified Professional Resume Writer
CRW	Certified Resume Writer
CWPP	Certified Web Portfolio Practitioner
FJST	Federal Job Search Trainer & Counselor
FRWC	Federal Resume Writer & Coach
JCTC	Job & Career Transition Coach
JST	Job Search Trainer
LPC	Licensed Professional Coach
MCC	Master Career Counselor
MCDP	Master Career Development Professional
MRW	Master Resume Writer
NCC	Nationally Certified Coach
NCCC	Nationally Certified Career Counselor
NCRW	Nationally Certified Resume Writer

Janet Beckstrom, CPRW
Word Crafter
1717 Montclair Avenue
Flint, MI 48503
Phone: 800-351-9818
Email: wordcrafter@voyager.net

As Principal/Owner of Word Crafter, Janet Beckstrom has served a wide range of clients from entry-level production workers to experienced educators, human service professionals, and business leaders since 1991. Janet has been published in more than 22 resume-writing books and is a charter member of the Career Masters Institute. She is also a member of the Professional Association of Resume Writers.

Diane Burns, CCMC, CPRW, CCM, FJST, CPCC, CEIP, JCTC
Career Marketing Techniques
Am Birkenweg #1
97258 Geisslingen/Oberickelsheim, Germany
Phone: 011-49-9335-997648
diane@polishedresumes.com
www.polishedresumes.com

Diane Burns is an award-winning resume writer and career coach. She is quoted as a career expert in national newspapers, is a nationally published author, and speaks at international conferences around the globe. She is also a respected authority on military transitions and federal resumes. Diane is a Career Change Coach/Trainer/Agent providing clients with successful results for career transition and position placement. As a former recruiter for a major aerospace corporation she has the inside scoop on managing a successful career search campaign.

Annemarie Cross, CPRW, CRW, CEIP, CCM, CECC, CWPP
Advanced Employment Concepts/AEC Office Services
PO Box 91
Hallam, Victoria, Australia 3803
Email: success@aresumewriter.net
www.aresumewriter.net

Annemarie Cross is a multiple award-winning Professional Resume Writer, Career and Workplace Counselor, and Interview Coach, holding dual certifications in resume writing, and in employment interviewing, human resources, training, and career and workplace counseling. She has worked with senior-level executives from diverse backgrounds and industries and has crafted resumes and cover letters that have propelled the careers of many clients spanning the globe.

Jean Cummings, MA, CPRW, CEIP, CPBS
A Resume For Today
123 Minot Road
Concord, MA   01742
Phone: 978-371-9266
Email: jc@aresumefortoday.com
www.aresumefortoday.com

Jean Cummings distills each executive's complex career into its unique essence. She works with leaders across all functions in the innovation-driven technology sector to create resumes that clarify their authentic personal brands. With a cut-to-the-chase writing style, Jean is uniquely positioned to develop the value equations that make an immediate impact and pave the way for high-value job offers. She holds a master's degree from Harvard University. She is Resume Expert/Career Strategist for ITHotJobs.com and author of "Turbocharged Networking for $100K+ Jobs." She offers value-added services throughout the job search life cycle in support of her message: Work where you want™.

Kirsten Dixson, CPBS, JCTC, CPRW, CEIP
Brandego LLC
PO Box 963
Exeter, NH 03833
Phone: 603-418-0023
Email: kirsten@brandego.com
www.brandego.com

Kirsten Dixson is the Career and Personal Branding Strategist who is passionate about employing leading-edge technology solutions to help entrepreneurs and intrapreneurs take control of their own career and business growth. Utilizing a powerful mix of personal branding, career planning methodology, and her caring, consultative style, Kirsten guides her clients through the process of defining and expressing their unique value and creating a niche in which they can be outstanding. Her career-related Internet ventures include Brandego, the leading provider of web portfolios for executives and solopreneurs, and the Reach Branding Club, a fun and innovative e-learning environment for personal branding. She also serves as Technology Master for the Career Masters Institute, serving as a thought leader for career service providers. Kirsten is a contributor to 14 national career books.

Joyce Fortier, MBA, CCM, CPRW, CCMC
Create Your Career
23871 W. Lebost
Novi, MI 48375
Phone: 248-478-5662
careerist@aol.com
www.careerist.com

With over 15 years' experience working with people in career transition, Joyce Fortier provides a full range of services that bring peace of mind and personal security to her executive clients. She effectively supplies them with the knowledge and tools necessary to successfully market themselves to potential employers. Consequently, her clients learn how to convey their full value, and they get a realistic perspective of what to expect during their job search. Recently, Joyce has added tele-classes to the services she offers. These classes, given over the phone, cover such subjects as "How to Work With Recruiters," "Effective Job Search Strategies," "Acing the Interview," and other topics of relevance to job seekers. She is known for her true desire to help people recognize their full potential, and for her capability to match people's skills to specific employer requirements. Joyce belongs to several professional associations, and examples of her work are included in 12 career books.

Roberta Gamza, CEIP, JCTC, JST
Career Ink
Louisville, CO 80027
Phone: 303-955-3065 or 877-581-6063
roberta@careerink.com
www.careerink.com

Roberta Gamza is a marketing communication strategist and the founder of Career Ink, offering career marketing and communication strategies and tools. Before starting Career Ink, she enjoyed a distinguished 15-year marketing career at Hewlett-Packard. She effectively crafted and executed marketing and communications strategies that earned her outstanding recognition four times and five promotions. Her core competencies include informational design, organizational structuring, finely honed writing skills, and keen marketing insight. Possessing both liberal arts and technical degrees, Roberta is an active member of four professional career and resume writing associations.

Louise Garver, MA, CPRW, JCTC, CMP, CEIP, MCDP
Career Directions, LLC
115 Elm Street
Enfield, CT 06082
Phone: 860-623-9476
Email: TheCareerPro@aol.com
Website: www.resumeimpact.com

An award-winning, certified career coach and professional resume writer, Louise Garver provides the strategies and tools that successfully guide executives and management professionals worldwide to their next career move. With more than 18 years of experience, her expertise includes strategic job search coaching, resume development, interview and negotiations training, in career-change management, outplacement, and corporate recruitment. She is featured as an expert on career sites online and has written numerous career- and resume-related articles; samples of her compelling documents appear in multiple resume and cover letter books. Louise is active in several professional career-related associations.

Susan Guarneri, MS, NCC, NCCC, LPC, MCC, CCMC, CPRW, JCTC, CWPP
Susan Guarneri Associates/CareerMagicCoach
6670 Crystal Lake Road
Three Lakes, WI 54562
Phone: 866-881-4055
Email: Resumagic@aol.com
Website: www.Resume-magic.com

SusanGuarneri's unique combination of credentials represents the "cream-of-the-crop" for the careers industry. She has 20 years' experience in career counseling and consulting, resume writing and outplacement for individuals as well as Fortune 500 companies, colleges, and nonprofit agencies. Susan's articles, resumes, and cover letters have been published in The Princeton Business Journal, careerjournal.com, and the Career Planning and Adult Development Journal, as well as many resume books.

Michele Haffner, CPRW, JCTC
Advanced Resume Services
1314 W. Paradise Court
Glendale, WI 53209
Phone: 414-247-1677
Email: michele@resumeservices.com
www.resumeservices.com

Since 1995, Michele Haffner has helped thousands of people in the U.S., Canada, and Europe successfully transition into their next job or career. Her specialty is mid- to senior-level managers, professionals, and executives. Prior to forming Advanced Resume Services, Michele worked in recruitment and staffing for manufacturing, financial service, and start-up technology firms. She holds a bachelor's degree in business administration from the University of Wisconsin in Milwaukee, and is a Certified Professional Resume Writer and an internationally certified Job and Career Transition Coach.

Beverly Harvey, CPRW, JCTC, CCM, CCMC, MRW
Beverly Harvey Resume & Career Services
P.O. Box 750
Pierson, FL 32180
Phone: 386-749-3111 or 1-888-775-0916
Email: beverly@harveycareers.com
Website: www.harveycareers.com

Beverly Harvey has been coaching senior managers and C-level executives in career transition and career marketing strategies for 14 years. Endorsed as a preferred provider and resume expert by many executive recruiters, she consults with clients worldwide to develop the best career transition programs. She personally writes each resume and portfolio of accompanying materials, develops a comprehensive job search plan, and coaches clients in all aspects of career transition. Beverly is also a member of the Board of Directors of Career Masters Institute.

Marcy Johnson, NCRW, CPRW, CEIP
First Impression Resume & Job Readiness
11805 US Hwy. 69
Story City, IA 50248
Phone: 515-733-4998 or 877-215-6009
Email: success@resume-job-readiness.com
Website: www.resume-job-readiness.com

Marcy Johnson directs an elite career transition company providing services to executives and other professionals. She serves on the National Resume Writers' Association certification team and recently completed a two-year post as secretary on the board of directors. As a cutting-edge job search strategist, she moves quickly to provide more than a service but a valued experience positioning clients at the top of those competing in today's highly competitive job market. Her work is featured in 12 career-related books.

Bill Kinser, MRW, CCM, CPRW, CEIP, JCTC
To The Point Resumes
P.O. Box 135
Fairfax, VA 22038-0135
Phone: 703-352-8969 or 1-866-RESUME-1
Email: bkinser@tothepointresumes.com
Website: www.tothepointresumes.com

Bill Kinser holds five globally recognized careers industry certifications. Most notably, he is currently one of only a few certified Master Resume Writers (MRWs) in the world. The MRW is awarded only to those select individuals who have truly reached the top tier in the resume writing industry. In 2001, Bill received three national resume writing awards from the Professional Association of Resume Writers (PARW). Since 2002, samples of his dynamic resumes and cover letters have been published in 11 books.

Cindy Kraft, CCMC, CCM, CPRW, JCTC
Executive Essentials
PO Box 336
Valrico, FL 33595
Phone: 813-655-0658
Email: cindy@career-management-coach.com
Website: www.career-management-coach.com

Cindy Kraft has 10 years of experience in resume writing and career coaching. She works with financial, operations, and sales and marketing professionals and executives, preparing them to outperform the competition with top-notch marketing documents and a focused branding strategy. Her job search strategizing sessions pave the way for the creation of a multi-faceted, effective, and executable job search plan.

Lorie Lebert, CPRW, JCTC, CCMC
The LORIEL GROUP/Resumes For Results
PO Box 267
Novi, MI 48376
Phone: 800-870-9059
Email: Lorie@DoMyResume.com
Website: www.CoachingROI.com

Lorie Lebert offers individualized coaching to help and encourage professionals to advance into a more satisfying job, career, or position. Through identifying strengths, skills, values, and interests, Lorie and her client formulate realistic choices that meet and exceed both the requirements of the client and the highest industry standards. She has been an independent business owner since 1991, with satisfied clients in all professions. As a dedicated professional coach and resume design expert, she provides a full range of practical career management and employment coaching, career transition, salary negotiation, job-search strategies, networking, online initiatives, resume and cover letter writing – vital for success in today's unpredictable and ever-changing business climate. Lorie is nationally recognized, with many of her resumes and cover letters featured in numerous professional publications. In a national writing contest, she was selected from among professional writers worldwide as representing the "Best of the Best."

Debra O'Reilly, CPRW, CEIP, JCTC, FRWC
A First Impression Resume Service/ResumeWriter.com
16 Terryville Avenue
Bristol, CT 06010
Phone: 860-583-7500
Email: debra@resumewriter.com
Website: www.resumewriter.com

Debra O'Reilly supplies the tools to jump-start your job search or career transition. Published author, award-winning writer, and successful motivator, she coaches job seekers and career changers to better positions and greater satisfaction. Debra is a ghostwriter by trade, although not in the traditional sense. She produces "abbreviated biographies" in the form of resumes, cover letters, and professional profiles, relating her clients' stories by focusing their energies and expressing their own uniqueness in print. Debra has also ghostwritten a memoir, " If You Have Confidence, You Have Everything."

Don Orlando, MBA, CPRW, JCTC, CCM, CCMC (OK)
The McLean Group
640 South McDonough Street
Montgomery, AL 36104
Phone: 334-264-2020
Email: yourcareercoach@aol.com

> *As one of America's first personal career coaches, Don Orlando helps people win the careers they've always deserved. He serves senior and very senior leaders in nearly every profession, all across the country and overseas. In addition, he is a mentor to other career coaches and resume writers. Don writes, researches, and teaches actively in the field. His work was chosen to be in 34 nationally published collections of the best resumes and cover letters in America. His articles are seen regularly in trade magazines, and he's been quoted in The Wall Street Journal. As a founding member of Career Masters Institute, Don wrote the Code of Ethics for that organization. In addition, he was the developer of the exam that the Professional Association of Resume Writers uses to grant their resume-writing certification.*

Vivian VanLier, CPRW, JCTC, CEIP, CCMC, CPRC
Advantage Resume & Career Services
6701 Murietta Ave.
Los Angeles, CA 91405
Phone: 818-994-6655
Email: Vivian@CuttingEdgeResumes.com
Website: www.CuttingEdgeResumes.com

> *Vivian VanLier is a certified career and retirement coach who partners with clients throughout the U.S. and internationally in re-examining, re-vitalizing, and re-inventing their careers. She is a frequent speaker and facilitator at career conferences, organizations and public events; has been a contributor to more than 25 books; and has been quoted as a career expert in over 100 newspapers and publications. Her practice focuses on baby boomers and — believing that it's never too late to pursue your dreams — she guides her executive and professional clients through an exciting process of uncovering their innate talents, values, passions, and purpose.*

Deborah Wile Dib, CPBS, CCM, CCMC, NCRW, CPRW, CEIP, JCTC
Advantage Resumes of NY/Executive Power Coach
77 Buffalo Avenue
Medford, NY 11763
Phone: 631-475-8513
Email: deborah.dib@advantagesresumes.com
www.advantageresumes.com

> *Deb Dib, America's Executive Power Coach, helps very senior executives stand out, get to the top, and stay at the top! Using powerful executive branding and career advancement strategies developed over 16 years in the careers industry, Deb partners with C-*

suite and senior executives in all areas of career management — from personal branding to resumes, to success coaching. Deb has earned seven certifications in personal branding, coaching, and resume writing and has been featured in 25 career books. One of the world's first certified personal brand strategists, she serves on the Career Masters Institute Board of Directors, is a co-developer of the Resume Writers Academy, is a founding member of the National Resume Writers' Association, and frequently presents at national career conferences.

Career Resources

The following career resource are available directly from Impact Publications. Complete the following form or list the titles, include postage (see formula at the end), enclose payment, and send to:

IMPACT PUBLICATIONS
9104 Manassas Drive, Suite N
Manassas Park, VA 20111-5211
1-800-361-1055 (orders only)
Tel. 703-361-7300 or Fax 703-335-9486
Email address: info@impactpublications.com
Quick and easy online ordering: www.impactpublications.com

Orders from individuals must be prepaid by check, money order, Visa, MasterCard, or American Express. We accept telephone and fax orders.

Qty.	Titles	Price	TOTAL

RESUMES AND LETTERS

Qty.	Titles	Price	TOTAL
_____	101 Quick Tips for a Dynamite Resume	$21.95	_____
_____	201 Dynamite Job Search Letters (4th Edition)	$19.95	_____
_____	Best Cover Letters for $100,000+ Jobs	$24.95	_____
_____	Best KeyWords for Resumes, Cover Letters, and Interviews	$17.95	_____
_____	Best Resumes and CVs for International Jobs	$24.95	_____
_____	Best Resumes for $100,000+ Jobs	$24.95	_____
_____	Best Resumes for People Without a Four-Year Degree	$19.95	_____
_____	Cover Letters for Dummies	$16.99	_____
_____	Dynamite Cover Letters (4th Edition)	$14.95	_____
_____	Dynamite Resumes (4th Edition)	$14.95	_____
_____	e-Resumes	$11.95	_____
_____	Expert Resumes for People Returning to Work	$16.95	_____
_____	Haldane's Best Cover Letters for Professionals	$15.95	_____
_____	Haldane's Best Resumes for Professionals	$15.95	_____
_____	High Impact Resumes and Letters (8th Edition)	$19.95	_____
_____	Resumes for Dummies (2nd Edition)	$16.99	_____
_____	Resumes in Cyberspace	$14.95	_____
_____	Resumes That Knock 'Em Dead	$12.95	_____

_____	Savvy Resume Writer	$10.95	_____
_____	Sure-Hire Resumes	$14.95	_____

CAREER EXPLORATION, EMPLOYERS, AND RECRUITERS

_____	25 Jobs That Have It All	$12.95	_____
_____	50 Cutting Edge Jobs	$15.95	_____
_____	300 Best Jobs Without a Four-Year Degree	$16.95	_____
_____	Almanac of American Employers	$199.95	_____
_____	America's Top 100 Jobs for People Without a Four-Year Degree	$19.95	_____
_____	Directory of Executive Recruiters	$49.95	_____
_____	Occupational Outlook Handbook	$18.95	_____
_____	The O*NET Guide	$38.95	_____
_____	Quick Guide to Career Training in Two Years or Less	$18.95	_____
_____	Quick Prep Careers	$18.95	_____

JOB SEARCH STRATEGIES AND TACTICS

_____	95 Mistakes Job Seekers Make and How to Avoid Them	$13.95	_____
_____	America's Top Internet Job Sites	$19.95	_____
_____	CareerXroads	$26.95	_____
_____	Change Your Job, Change Your Life (8th Edition)	$17.95	_____
_____	Guide to Internet Job Searching	$14.95	_____
_____	The Job Hunting Guide	$14.95	_____
_____	Job Search: Marketing Your Military Experience	$16.95	_____
_____	Jobs and the Military Spouse (2nd Edition)	$17.95	_____
_____	No One Will Hire Me!	$13.95	_____
_____	Quit Your Job and Grow Some Hair	$15.95	_____
_____	What Color Is Your Parachute?	$17.95	_____

ASSESSMENT AND INSPIRATION

_____	Career Tests	$12.95	_____
_____	Discover the Best Jobs for You (4th Edition)	$15.95	_____
_____	Discover What You're Best At	$14.00	_____
_____	Do What You Are	$18.95	_____
_____	I Don't Know What I Want, But I Know It's Not This	$14.00	_____
_____	Pathfinder	$14.00	_____
_____	Seven Habits of Highly Effective People	$14.00	_____
_____	What Should I Do With My Life?	$24.95	_____
_____	What Type Am I?	$14.95	_____
_____	What's Your Type of Career?	$18.95	_____
_____	Who Moved My Cheese?	$19.95	_____

DRESS AND IMAGE

_____	300 Best Jobs Without a Four-Year Degree	$16.95 _____
_____	300 Best Jobs Without a Four-Year Degree	$16.95 _____

INTERVIEWS, NETWORKING, SALARY NEGOTIATIONS

_____	101 Dynamite Questions to Ask At Your Job Interview (2nd Edition)	$13.95 _____
_____	Dynamite Salary Negotiations (4th Edition)	$15.95 _____
_____	A Foot in the Door	$14.95 _____
_____	Haldane's Best Answers to Tough Interview Questions	$15.95 _____
_____	Interview for Success (8th Edition)	$15.95 _____
_____	Job Interview Tips for People With Not-So-Hot Backgrounds	$13.95 _____
_____	Job Interviews for Dummies	$16.99 _____
_____	KeyWords to Nail Your Job Interview	$17.95 _____
_____	Nail the Job Interview	$13.95 _____
_____	Savvy Interviewer	$10.95 _____
_____	The Savvy Networker	$14.95 _____

GOVERNMENT, INTERNATIONAL, AND NONPROFIT

_____	Book of U.S. Government Jobs	$21.95 _____
_____	Directory of Websites for International Jobs	$19.95 _____
_____	Electronic Federal Resume Guidebook, with CD-ROM	$44.95 _____
_____	Federal Applications That Get Results	$23.95 _____
_____	Federal Resume Guidebook (3rd Edition)	$21.95 _____
_____	FBI Careers	$18.95 _____
_____	Find a Federal Job Fast!	$15.95 _____
_____	Global Citizen	$16.95 _____
_____	Going Global Career Guide	$199.95 _____
_____	Inside Secrets to Finding a Job in Travel	$14.95 _____
_____	International Job Finder	$19.95 _____
_____	International Jobs	$18.00 _____
_____	Jobs and Careers With Nonprofit Organizations	$17.95 _____
_____	Jobs for Travel Lovers	$19.95 _____
_____	Post Office Jobs	$17.95 _____
_____	Ten Steps to a Federal Job	$39.95 _____

SUBTOTAL _____
Virginia residents add 5% sales tax _____

POSTAGE/HANDLING ($5 for first product
and 8% of SUBTOTAL over $30) _____

8% of SUBTOTAL . . . . _____

TOTAL ENCLOSED . . . . _____

Name _____

Address _____

_____

_____

❏ I enclose check/money order for $_____ made payable to IMPACT PUBLICATIONS.

❏ Please charge $_____ to my credit card:

  ❏ Visa   ❏ MasterCard   ❏ American Express   ❏ Discover

Card # _____ Expiration Date _____/_____

Signature _____